ARGENTINA

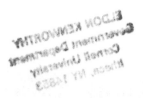

ARGENTINA

ILLUSIONS
and
REALITIES

Gary W. Wynia

 Holmes & Meier   New York · London

First published in the United States of America 1986 by
Holmes & Meier Publishers, Inc.
30 Irving Place
New York, N.Y. 10003

Great Britain:
Holmes & Meier Ltd.
Pindar Road
Hoddesdon, Hertfordshire
EN11 0HF

Library of Congress Cataloging-in-Publication Data

Wynia, Gary W., 1942-
  Argentina: illusions and realities.

  1. Argentina—Politics and government—1983-
I. Title.
F2849.2.W95 1986   982'.064   86-9839
ISBN 0-8419-0956-3
ISBN 0-8419-0957-1 (pbk.)

Book design by Gloria Tso

Manufactured in the United States of America

To: Daniel
        Gladys
        David
        Martin
        and Johnny

CONTENTS

Preface

A decade that began with Juan Perón's death ended with Raul Alfonsín's election in 1983. The burial of one president and the selection of another are not unusual events in most places, but seldom are they separated by seven years of military repression and soldiers killing nearly 9,000 citizens as they were in Argentina. Nor have many countries lost a war with Great Britain recently as Argentina did in 1982. No matter how one looks at it, it was an unhappy time for this troubled nation.

Political volatility is not new to Argentina, of course. As far back as 1930 the military was deposing democratic governments. In the 1940s an officer named Juan Perón was elected president, but ten years later he too was evicted by military colleagues. No one managed to govern the country successfully during the next eighteen years, and Perón's return in 1973 ended with another coup three years later.

Economic life has not been much more comforting. Three decades of rapid growth and prosperity ended with the 1929 depression, and ever since Argentines have been riding an economic roller coaster that descended into deep recession and hyper-inflation in the 1980s. Self-sufficiency in petroleum, fertile prairies, hundreds of large industries, and a literate population are supposed to generate prosperity in this day and age, but they have not been enough in Argentina.

What went wrong? Many things, actually, nearly all of them related to one another. The nation's colonial origins and its disorganization after independence along with the narrow base of its economic development played a part. So has the way power was distributed in society and used for partisan advantage by those with the largest shares of it. Together they produced a politics known for its seemingly irresolvable conflicts. Modes of confrontation that most societies find dangerous and self-destructive became the way of life in Argentina. But while certain sectors in society thrived on it, the nation as a whole paid a high price for its political *modus vivendi*. That is why intense efforts to change old habits were begun in the 1980s despite dim prospects for success.

Interpreting Argentine behavior is challenging but never dull or disappointing. In preparing this volume I have learned a great deal from many prominent scholars, among them Guido Di Tella, Javier Villanueva, Roberto Alemann, Juan Carlos de Pablo, Guillermo O'Donnell,

Felix Luna, Robert Potash, James Scobie, and Alain Roquie. I have also benefited immensely from the scholarship of a new generation of Argentine historians, economists, and political scientists whose writings began to appear in 1983 after press freedom was restored. Marcelo Cavarozzi, Carlos Escude, Jorge Schvarzer, Marcelo Luis Acuña, and Ruben Perina are just a few. And finally, I am indebted to the William Kenan Foundation for financing my recent visit to Argentina, to Holmes and Meier editors for inviting me to write the book, and to colleagues and students at Carleton College for tolerating my obsession with the completion of this project.

My education in Argentina started in 1963 as an exchange student in provincial Corrientes. Nine months later I returned to spend a year in Córdoba and Buenos Aires, and I have been going back ever since. The past twenty years have been exciting as well as depressing times, but being in Argentina was never more refreshing than it was in 1983 and 1984 when I witnessed a long-repressed people resurrect themselves and try harder than ever to deal with the real rather than the illusory world confronting them. I hope that I have communicated something of their experience in this book.

ARGENTINA

1

A Curious War

He had not wanted war, General Leopoldo Galtieri would later testify. Argentina was a peaceful nation, neutral in World War I and during most of World War II, and it had proudly stood apart from other peoples' conflicts ever since. But war was what he achieved in 1982, and neither he nor his country has been quite the same since.

Argentine troops went ashore at Port Stanley on April 2, 1982, and easily overcame meager resistance, ending 150 years of uninterrupted British rule over the remote Falkland Islands located 300 miles off Argentina's southern shore.[1] In Buenos Aires the event was celebrated euphorically while the rest of the world watched in amazement, most people unaware that descendants of the British still lived there or that Argentines wanted the islands back badly enough to risk war to get them. The celebration would be brief, however, for a few weeks later the British replied with force, and after 937 lives were lost in combat (712 of them Argentine and 225 British), a humiliated Argentine army returned to the mainland defeated.

Responsibility for the tragedy belongs to neither country exclusively. Pedestrian British diplomacy and the insensitivity of successive governments to nationalist sentiments in Argentina, sentiments that deep English economic involvement in the country helped foster long ago, are partially to blame. For years the Argentines had been asking for a reasonable diplomatic solution to the dispute only to have been refused it time and again. It is also a product of Argentine politics, the temerity of the country's insecure but self-important military commanders, and its people's longing for a cause to celebrate. The time seemed right for the bold initiative, but as with so many other Argentine adventures, its initiators' view of reality turned out to be quite different from everyone else's.

Why the Falklands?

Like most perplexing conflicts, this one began long ago. No one knows for certain who discovered the islands. It might have been Amerigo

3

Vespucci when he passed through the area in 1504, but the first to record going ashore was an English mariner named John Strong, who was driven off course by violent winds in 1690. He named the islands after Viscount Falkland, treasurer of the royal navy, and sailed on. Soon thereafter Spanish colonial authorities, having conquered the mainland, claimed the islands and insisted that the English and French leave the South Atlantic. Unimpressed, Frenchman Louis Antoine de Bougainville established a settlement of twenty-nine people at Fort St. Louis on the eastern island in 1764 and claimed the islands for the French king, naming them the Illes Mallouines, from which the Spanish took the name that Argentines use today, the Islas Malvinas. A year later British Commodore John Byron surveyed the islands and claimed them for King George III, setting up a small colony on Saunders Island at Port Egmont. Meanwhile the Spanish protested the French intrusion and after some negotiation secured their agreement to depart. The English were less accommodating, so the Spanish evicted them by force in 1770. They were allowed to return in 1771, only to pull out of their own accord three years later, leaving behind them a plate inscribed with their claim of ownership.[2]

The independence of the Río de la Plata region in 1816 forced the Spanish to exit, leaving the islands to a new regime on the mainland that was too preoccupied with establishing its authority there to bother with the Malvinas. For a time no one but passing British and North American seal hunters set up camp there. Then in 1820 the new government authorized taking possession of the islands, though nothing came of it until 1826, when they sent businessman Louis Vernet to establish an Argentine colony and a few years later become its governor. The British, wanting the islands for themselves, protested Vernet's arrival only to be ignored by him. But the North Americans were less accommodating, refusing to comply when Vernet insisted that hunting fees be paid by everyone regardless of nationality. The governor responded by seizing three American fishing vessels on July 30, 1831. Enraged, the U.S. consul in Buenos Aires immediately dispatched the USS *Lexington,* then visiting the Argentine capital, to liberate the confiscated vessels, which its crew did with relative ease, blowing up the governor's powder magazines and packing Vernet and his staff off to the mainland. That is when the British stepped in. Not ones to pass up the chance for a long-sought acquisition, British authorities sent Captain John James Oslow and the HMS *Clio* into the vacuum created by Vernet's expulsion just in time to block the Argentines when they tried to set up another government on the islands. Renamed the Falklands, they were settled by British shepherds, who supplied wool to the

Falkland Islands Company, which was protected by the British government until the Argentine army went ashore in 1982.[3]

Dead-End Diplomacy

Argentine dependence on the British for their economic development during the next century forced them to postpone confrontation on the Falklands/Malvinas issue. Until World War II the English consumed Argentina's beef, built the railways that transported commodities from its prairies to its ports, and financed most of the country's trade. As late as the 1930s, a time when the world depression had weakened Argentina's markets abroad, its government was forced to grant the British substantial trade concessions in order to retain a consumer for its exports. Not until World War II tore Britain's economic empire apart and nationalist Juan Perón reached the Argentine presidency did Argentines feel confident enough to demand the islands' return.

Perón made colonialism an evil, Great Britain the devil, and its occupancy of Argentina's Malvinas a mortal sin. He observed the British relinquishing India and insisted that they do the same in the South Atlantic. But they refused categorically, claiming that the islands were not a foreign land ruled as a colony as India had been but an empty territory colonized by British citizens working for a British enterprise. It was not until 1963 that his successors finally began to make some progress on the issue, though without any help from the British. In that year President Arturo Illia, elected from the nationalist Radical party, took the matter to the United Nations, where he made a persuasive case for U.N. endorsement of British withdrawal, arguing that its possession of the islands was an anachronism in a postcolonial era that had witnessed the British withdrawal from almost every land they had governed in the southern hemisphere. Two years later the Twentieth General Assembly passed Resolution 2065, which endorsed binational negotiation of sovereignty over the islands, intending that it should lead eventually to their return to Argentina.[4]

Negotiations between the two countries were begun soon after the U.N. resolution was adopted, but little real progress was made initially. The British simply refused to discuss the issue of sovereignty, claiming as before that since there was no native population on the islands, it was not a colony. The residents had to decide their own fate, and they wanted nothing to do with Argentina. The fundamental impasse was obvious from the first meeting, but the Argentines returned time and again throughout the 1970s, going through the motions of demanding a discussion of sovereignty only to be refused each time. The British did offer a few minor concessions, such as when the Heath government signed a communications agreement with Argentina in 1974, granting it a monopoly over air access to the islands as well as responsibility for the supply of most of the islands' fuel; in return Argentina gave island residents free access to its schools and hospitals. Such measures were said to be the first step toward building trust between the Falklanders and the Argentines, but the closer they came together the more the islanders feared their abandonment by the British government and the harder they lobbied in London to prevent further progress.

British diplomat Nicolas Ridley gave it another try starting in 1979, working from inside the Foreign Office. He was quite aware of the political problem he faced and was determined to avert a confrontation with the infamous Falklands lobby. The latter, calling itself the Falkland Islands Committee, consisted mainly of Falkland Islands Company officials, some members of Parliament, and islanders, only 140 of whom had British passports, the rest of the 2,000 residents having only commonwealth status. They had begun their campaign in 1968, when, with the help of Conservatives who were then in the opposition, they launched an attack against the Labour government of Prime Minister Harold Wilson to halt its considering the transfer of sovereignty over the islands to Argentina. Their protests paid off, for Wilson not only dropped the issue but also pledged that no transfer would occur against the "wishes" of the islanders. The U.N. resolutions had always referred to the "interests" rather than the "wishes" of residents, and by changing the language used within Britain, he made it virtually impossible to carry forth any real transfer. Knowing this, Ridley chose to ignore the lobby from the outset and go directly to the cabinet, hoping to sell it a new proposal which, once approved, could be rammed through Parliament.

His solution was quite simple: give Argentina sovereignty over the islands on the condition that they agree to lease them back to the Falkland Islands Company, an arrangement similar to what had been done long ago in Hong Kong. Foreign Secretary Carrington carried the proposal to Prime Minister Thatcher, but she immediately rejected it. Then, after further consideration, she reversed herself and authorized Ridley to go ahead, but only on condition that he start out with a presentation of his proposal to the islanders, a requirement which, whether intended or not, threw him to the Falklander wolves. He dutifully gave it a try, going to Port Stanley in November 1980 to make his case to a hostile audience. But when he returned to report his mission to the House of Commons he was ravaged by critics, most of whom had been alerted to his enthusiasm for the lease-back solution by the Falkland Islands Committee. Shattered by the experience, Ridley resigned his post, leaving his colleagues in the Foreign Office to wonder about why he had ever risked his career on such a "trivial" matter.[5]

The Argentines continued to push for a diplomatic solution, nevertheless. In February 1981, at their annual talks in New York, they promised to guarantee the islanders a democratic form of government, retention of their legal system, their customs office, and schools in exchange for British recognition of Argentine sovereignty over them. Predictably they were refused and returned home angrier than ever, though initially with no plan for further action. Later in the year the Argentine Foreign Ministry turned to preparing new demands for their next meeting in February 1982, among them an insistence on more frequent talks, something they knew the British would not welcome. But while diplomats drew up proposals for another round, a less patient admiral persuaded his colleagues to take matters into their own hands and invade the islands.

The Invasion

The invasion caught the British by surprise, so much so that distinguished Foreign Secretary Carrington had to resign in embarrassment. Why they were so startled has been the subject of substantial investigation in Great Britain, but from all of the inquiries the same explanation emerges, namely, the bureaucratic inertia of officials who never believed that they had reason to take the threat of invasion seriously. British diplomats, like most others, predict future behavior from their knowledge of previous conduct. They knew that the Argentines were unhappy with Prime Minister Thatcher's refusal to discuss the sovereignty issue, but they also knew that it had never provoked a serious threat of invasion. Nor did they believe that the decision to withdraw the HMS *Endurance,* their major ice patrol ship stationed in the South Atlantic, would convey to the Argentines a message of disinterest in the islands' defense, which apparently it did. Its withdrawal was discussed in the mid-1981 defense review as part of a larger effort to save money, and though some opponents of the move in London pointed out the risks involved, they were never taken seriously in the Foreign Office or by the austerity-minded prime minister.[6] The British knew that the Argentines were becoming more impatient, yet past experience taught that invasions do not usually begin until after a gradual escalation of hostilities, which in this instance meant more intense diplomatic protests followed by the Argentines cutting off the islands' fuel supplies and air transport. Until such steps were taken, an invasion seemed improbable.[7]

In reaching such conclusions British officials were unduly influenced by the huge gap that had always existed between Argentina's threatening noises and its military passivity. Sovereignty over the islands was a popular cause in Argentina and its politicians profited from its exploitation, but their rhetoric had never generated anything but an occasional publicity stunt, like someone flying to the islands, planting an Argentine flag, and then rushing home to cheers. Equally important was the Argentines' preoccupation with settling their dispute with the Chileans over the Beagle Channel, something the British thought would distract them from taking any military action on the eastern front. So confident were the British in their analysis of Argentine behavior that they did not even try to monitor movements of Argentine military units when they were preparing for the invasion.[8]

The British also suffered from painting themselves into a corner from which there was no easy exit. Unwilling to concede sovereignty and unable to convince the islanders to allow more Argentine governance of them, they were locked into defending the status quo while keeping the negotiations going, a dead-end approach to bargaining that held no promise of a solution. As the British ambassador in Buenos Aires protested to the Foreign Office on October 2, 1981, this was no strategy at all "beyond a general Micawberism." And it left Argentines with only two real options: either they could resign themselves to living with the status quo, or they could do something more drastic to force the Foreign Office to bargain, which, of course, they chose to do in their own clumsy way.[9]

The Argentines misjudged the British as well. The invasion's small cadre of military planners were convinced that Britain would not go to war over the islands. They took Thatcher's budget cutting in the South Atlantic to mean that she had given up any notion of protecting the islands against attack. General Leopoldo Galtieri would later claim that the Argentine ambassador to London had assured him that the Thatcher government would not respond militarily to an invasion, swearing in his self-defense that "such a stormy reaction as was observed in the United Kingdom had not been foreseen."[10] Perhaps he was naive, but it is just as likely that he believed what he did because he had been given an exciting idea by navy planners and he wanted it to work. Once committed to it, he quickly turned his attention to its execution and winning the confidence of a handful of fellow officers on whom his presidency depended. He had neither the time nor the desire to find out how risky a project he had chosen to advance.

Invading the islands was not something dreamed up in 1982, of course. Plotting had been going on secretly within the armed forces since the early 1970s, one of its enthusiasts being Navy Captain Jorge Anaya, who became the navy's member of the junta when General Leopoldo Galtieri ascended to the presidency at the end of 1981. Impressed by how easily the Indian government had seized the Portuguese colony of Goa in 1961, Anaya tried to convince his colleagues that they could do likewise in the Malvinas. But preoccupied with fighting terrorism at home and unconvinced that they could supply the reconquered islands given British submarine superiority, President Jorge Videla and his junta tabled the idea for the time being when they took over in 1976.

It was not until December 1981 that the proposal resurfaced. It was a tumultuous time for officers, who had begun to lose their grip over the nation as their five-year economic rescue operation went awry and protests demanding the restoration of democratic government rose. The scheduled transition from one military president to another in March 1981 had not gone as smoothly as it was supposed to, some members of the junta being unhappy with the army's insistence on the choice of General Roberto Viola to replace his friend General Jorge Videla. It became even worse when Viola appeared to soften in the face of criticism from the business community by refusing to reappoint the people who had designed Videla's economic reforms. Desperate to reassert its authority, the junta gave up on Viola after eight months and forced him to resign against his will, appointing Army Chief Leopoldo Galtieri in his place.

Galtieri was more soldier than politician, previously never exhibiting the kind of ambition common among officers who made their way to the presidential palace. Of Italian heritage and born fifty-five years before to a middle-class family in the Buenos Aires suburbs, he had risen up the ranks more on his enthusiasm than his intelligence. Had service commanders not been replaced so often, Galtieri would never have risen so high within the army. But as others were forced out, he floated up the hierarchy, becoming popular among colleagues in the late 1970s, and well known for displays of emotion, showing rage one moment only to turn off his anger and charm people the next with his simplicity of phrase. Drinking whiskey was his favorite pastime, on the job as well as off, and visitors to his office occasionally found him "stretched out in his chair in shirt sleeves with a scotch in his hand and his feet on the table."[11] As president he talked tough from the beginning, promising to see the military's original economic and political reconstruction program through to its completion. To make his point to doubters he appointed fiscally conservative businessman Roberto Alemann as economics minister and authorized him to get on with the painful opening of the nation's economy to competition from abroad and the paring down of the public sector.

Meanwhile, Admiral Anaya showed up with his invasion plan, hoping to convince the capricious new president that it was exactly what the military and the country needed. It is not clear when Galtieri actually authorized him to go ahead with the invasion's preparation. Questioned by the military's Rattenbach Commission after the war, Galtieri claimed that he could not recall the date of his decision, though there is evidence that before his first month was completed he had announced the plan to Air Force Chief Lami Dozo and secured his agreement. It would be another three months before the fleet departed, and in the meantime Argentine diplomats, unaware of what the new president was up to, went about their business of preparing for another round of negotiations with the British on February 27 and 28.[12]

They approached the 1982 meeting hoping to secure concessions by threatening to escalate the controversy in unmentioned ways if the British again resisted. On January 27 the Argentine Foreign Ministry issued a document that announced its new demands, among them insistence on the creation of a binational commission of one year's duration that would meet the first week of every month to plot the restoration of the islands to Argentine control. No invasion was threatened, but three days before the document's release *La Prensa* newspaper columnist Jesus Iglesias Rouco, citing "high-level sources," warned that the military had made up its mind that if Argentina's demands were not met at the February meeting it would take "firm and clear" actions, hinting an escalation of some kind.[13] Characteristically the British Foreign Office disregarded the threats and sent officials to the meetings in New York to refuse Argentina's principal demands and return home. Argentine diplomats, disappointed and without anything to show for their efforts, flew back to Buenos Aires, where they were greeted by a furious Galtieri, who ordered the invasion's planners to accelerate their preparation of the scheme.

Galtieri and Admiral Anaya would testify later that they had intended to carry out the invasion in June or July, in the depth of winter, when a counterattack from sea would have been the most difficult. It was also their intent to wait until the British had withdrawn the remaining naval defenses of the islands as they had announced their intention to do. Yet, on March 26, long before invasion planning was completed and its diplomatic defense prepared, they decided to strike on April 2. It would later prove to be a major blunder to accelerate the initiative, even if as they claimed they had been forced to do so by unanticipated British aggression. We shall never know for certain why they felt so compelled to move up the date, but it is obvious that their own impatience and bad judgment had as much to do with it as anything else.[14]

The sequence of events that led to the decision taken on March 26 began 700 miles to the southeast of the Falklands in the South Georgia Islands, also held by the British. Why it did remains something of a mystery. One theory holds that Admiral Anaya had wanted to test the British resolve to defend their possessions in the South Atlantic before he went after the larger prize. If the Argentines took the South Georgias and the British did nothing but protest diplomatically, it would be easy to convince officers worried about provoking a war that nothing of the sort would be caused by their taking the Falklands. On the contrary, it would only confirm Anaya's contention that Thatcher had given up any notion of defending British interests in the region any longer. There was a certainly rationality to Anaya's incrementalism, but his colleagues rejected it nevertheless, for reasons never explained. That was at the beginning of March. But then on March 9 a businessman named Constantino Davidoff asked permission to take forty-one workers to the South Georgias to fulfill a contract he had signed with the British to pick up some scrap iron at an old whaling station, and he was given it by Anaya. When he arrived on March 19, however, Davidoff immediately raised the Argentine flag, causing resident British scientists with the Antarctic Survey to protest and insist that he lower it and stop work until permission to proceed was granted by the British ambassador in Buenos Aires. Davidoff lowered the banner but refused to seek new authorization. Galtieri later denied being party to the provocation, as did Anaya, but their defenses are not very convincing given Anaya's known desire to test the British before mounting the big invasion. But if it was their intent to demonstrate British passivity to their colleagues, they failed dismally. The British were provoked and acted accordingly. While Davidoff stood his ground, the ambassador in Buenos Aires asked London to show force immediately, and the next day Prime Minister Thatcher ordered the HMS *Endurance*, then visiting Port Stanley, to take two dozen marines to the South Georgias and sit offshore while the British ambassador tried to persuade Argentine Foreign Minister Costa Mendez to pull Davidoff out. The swift and hostile response took the Argentine government by surprise and Costa Mendez stalled, asking the British to hold their marines back while he looked into the matter.

Panicked by the prospects of a British buildup, the junta deliberated and made their fateful decision, dispatching three warships to the South Georgias that forced the *Endurance* to the ignominy of an embarrassed retreat. Had they been true to their experimental design, the Argentines would have taken that data given them by the British response and concluded that they were not yet complacent enough to allow an easy conquest of the islands and, therefore, the invasion should be postponed until they were. But it was confirmation not the invalidation of their assumptions that they wanted, and when it did not come, they chose to go ahead anyway, convinced that their only chance to avoid a war was to move quickly before the British augmented their defenses and made a real fight necessary.[15]

Calling off the invasion was not as easy as it might seem in retrospect. Galtieri had gone to great lengths to build support for it among a handful of officers who had put him in the presidency, and to admit miscalculation threatened to weaken their confidence in his leadership. Moreover, he needed Anaya's backing to keep the navy behind him and knew that he would lose it if he canceled the admiral's pet project. That left only one choice: to invade immediately. So, without an adequately prepared plan to guide the invasion, he decided on March 26 to go ahead with it, confident that he could somehow improvise a diplomatic strategy that would prevent reprisals by the British Foreign Office. Galtieri hoped that with the world now aware of how much the issue meant to the Argentines and how wasteful a war between the two countries would be, the British would have no choice but to respond to third party pressures by negotiating a settlement with the invaders.[16]

The decision to strike was also encouraged by events totally unrelated to strategic considerations, Galtieri's denials of playing politics with the issue notwithstanding. The armed forces were desperate for popular support at a time when the economy was deteriorating and politicians were taking advantage of growing public discontent to mobilize opinion in support of new elections. No single event made the invasion necessary politically; in fact, the largest public protest came a few days after the decision had been made to move in on April 2. But Galtieri and his colleagues were aware that the people the armed forces had rescued from Peronism and terrorism in 1976 no longer needed them to run the country, especially if it meant more economic austerity, bankruptcies, and recession. To ignore their discontent was politically impossible and sustained repression counterproductive, especially when so many of those who were unhappy came from the middle class. Authorities needed a popular cause, and the Malvinas issue was the best that they could find. Though Galtieri and Anaya will never admit that such considerations entered their minds—no military officer could make such an admission—their denials are unconvincing. The plot was hatched in response to diplomatic frustration and fueled by military hubris, but its political value made it compelling.

When Galtieri, Anaya, and Lami Dozo met with the fifty-four-member Comite Militar on March 26, they announced their decision to land on the Malvinas on April 2. Simultaneously they asked civilian Foreign Minister Costa Mendez, who had been aware of their plotting for over a month, to prepare as quickly as possible a diplomatic strategy for defending their bold initiative internationally. Two days later the Argentine fleet left Puerto Belgrano for the islands.[17]

As politically compelling as the decision was, one cannot help but wonder why they thought they could get away with it. Did they not know that the British would fight back, that the United States would abandon them, and that Europeans would take reprisals against them in support of their NATO ally? If they did, they clearly denied it to themselves, preferring instead to believe that they could pull it off. At what point commitments to a cause prevent realistic assessments of how one's adversaries will respond to aggression is never all that apparent, but such points do exist, and never more obviously than in Argentina in 1982. Galtieri and his colleagues were aware of the provocative nature of their actions, and they knew that Britain's Falklands were not Goa and that Margaret Thatcher was the "iron lady" and not the prime minister of Portugal. Nevertheless they were convinced that the British would no more likely go to war over the islands than the Portuguese did over Goa. Galtieri has stated that it was obvious to him and his colleagues that the British would never pay the price required to send their fleet to the South Atlantic and keep it there long enough to launch an invasion of their own. Had he believed otherwise, he never would have acted as he did, he now says. And in fairness it should be recalled that the British Foreign Office had for some time given the impression that they were losing interest in the Falklands, the cabinet having already received a commissioned study that recommended against new investments there.[18] Cuts in the naval budget followed, leaving Argentine geopoliticians to reason that the British were abandoning the South Atlantic strategically, creating a vacuum which they could fill. The only problem with this logic, of course, is the fact that the British did make clear their hostility toward Argentine seizures of their holdings in the region during the South Georgias incident. Galtieri, of course, persuaded himself that they were bluffing and that, if he pushed on he could call their bluff and force them to concede sovereignty to Argentina. That an invasion of territory the British had occupied for 150 years might discourage their bargaining with the aggressor never seemed to register with Galtieri. He could understand how national pride and commitment to a principle could lead him to act as he did, but he never really understood that it might make the rather aloof and complacent British fight back with even more determination.[19]

Galtieri also miscalculated President Ronald Reagan's response to the invasion. In retrospect it may seem strange that Argentines would expect the United States to stay neutral when its old ally was at war. But during the two years that preceded its move the military government was courted by the American president, responding enthusiastically to his friendship after four years of criticism from President Jimmy Carter for the repression of their subjects. Galtieri wanted to think that his rapport with Reagan would make it hard for the Americans to judge him harshly for doing what he thought everyone knew was inevitable. They had, after all, joined in Reagan's anticommunist crusade within the hemisphere, sending advisors to Central America to assist in counterinsurgency efforts in El Salvador and in the training of the Nicaraguan *contras* to fight the Sandinista government. Previously reluctant to join with the United States in any kind of hemispheric adventure, officers, delighted with their warm reception in Washington and basking in their own victory over terrorists at home, did not hesitate to sign up with Reagan.[20] Galtieri liked to refer to himself as the "North Americans' pampered child," and he wanted to believe that they would assist with the diplomatic solution of the issue.[21]

That was why he was so disappointed when, just as his ships set sail, he learned of Reagan's objections to his plan. When British intelligence finally picked up the movement of the Argentine fleet toward the islands on March 31, British Ambassador to the United States Sir Nicolas Henderson asked Secretary of State Haig and President Reagan to stop the Argentines before it was too late. Galtieri refused to meet with the U.S. ambassador in Buenos Aires, so Reagan called him at 10:10 PM Argentine time on April 1. We do not know for certain what was said, but three Argentine journalists have published a transcript that they claim comes from Galtieri's office. It reveals that each president spoke at least seven times in a dialogue that lasted about fifteen minutes, each repeating his basic argument often. Galtieri was stubborn and defensive throughout the conversation and Reagan firm in his warnings. For example, to justify his actions Galtieri stated:

> Argentina has always been in favor of a peaceful solution to this matter. But that is possible, Mr. President, only with Britain's recognition of Argentina's sovereignty over the Malvinas Islands. And it must be explicit and public.

Later Galtieri added:

The Argentine government, Mr. President, values its relations with the United States very much. That is why I want you to know that it is not my country that has brought this about; we want a solution and it can be found if tonight Great Britain will recognize Argentine sovereignty over the Malvinas Islands.

Reagan responded:

That is impossible at this moment. If the only option is a military invasion, I assure you, Mr. President, that the British will respond militarily. What will happen to the 2,000 islanders, Mr. President?

Galtieri replied:

You can be confident that the Argentine government will assure the safety of all residents of the Malvinas. They will still have their liberty, their free will, and their property. They can stay on the islands or move to Britain, whichever is most convenient. They can be Argentine or British citizens or migrate to the United States if they want.

To which Reagan again responded:

Mr. President, I believe that it is my obligation to warn you that Great Britain will respond militarily to your invasion. I know Great Britain. Moreover, Ms. Thatcher, my friend, is a very decisive woman and she will have no choice but to fight back. The war that follows will be tragic and will have grave consequences in the hemisphere.

Later Reagan added some thoughts about what it might cost Argentine relations with the United States:

I understand your words to mean that Argentina intends to go ahead and use force, Mr. President. I do not want to fail to emphasize pointedly that the relationship between our two countries will suffer seriously. North American and world opinion will oppose Argentina's use of force. Moreover, my efforts to rebuild good relations between our two countries will be gravely harmed. Great Britain, Mr. President, is a very close friend of the United States, and the new relationship that we have established between Washington and Argentina—initially against American public opinion—will be irremediably damaged.[22]

If the transcripts are as accurate as their publishers claim, it is clear that Galtieri went to war knowing, perhaps for the first time, where the United States stood and how convinced Reagan was of British retaliation. That the Americans waited so long to confront Galtieri is tragic, though not surprising, given how hard it was for them to believe that the Argentines would do something that might undermine Reagan's affection for his new ally. He had worked hard to recruit Viola and

Galtieri to his hemispheric crusade and could not believe that either of them would be so foolish as to force him to choose between them and Thatcher.

When it finally came, the invasion was almost anticlimactic. Informed that the Argentine fleet was approaching, Falklands Governor Rex Hunt announced to the startled islanders on radio the night before that Argentines were about to come ashore. Eighty British marines and a territorial defense force of one hundred twenty resisted the landing briefly, killing four invaders while suffering no casualties themselves since the Argentine troops had been ordered to spare lives, but one half-hour after they had landed Hunt surrendered and the islands' new rulers took over and sent the British marines home.[23]

Back in Buenos Aires Galtieri swiftly announced the triumph, and celebrations erupted in the streets of the capital. He spoke to euphoric crowds who gathered before the presidential palace in the same plaza where police had broken up a massive antigovernment demonstration three days earlier. When told that the junta had done it for them they cheered Galtieri louder and longer than they had any military officer since Perón. Little noticed at the time, however, were the signs that expressed the truer sentiment of most Argentines: "Malvinas sí, el gobierno militar no!" (Malvinas yes, military government no). People were happy, but a call for elections would have made them even happier, for while they loved what Galtieri had achieved, it did not make military government any more appealing to those who had suffered from its autocratic ways for six years.

Diplomacy and War

Galtieri has always claimed that diplomacy, not war, was his primary objective. Somehow the seizure of the islands was supposed to force the British to do what they had always refused to do: negotiate a settlement that recognized Argentine sovereignty over the islands. In other words, his intention, he has since argued, had never been to station 10,000 troops on the islands to defend them against British retaliation, but only to hold onto his conquest with a few hundred troops while pressure was put on the British by third parties in Latin America and Europe to give up the pretense of owning islands that many in its Foreign Office were ready to abandon. Such logic seems quite naive in retrospect, yet given their impatience with the British and their belief that the British could not afford to dispatch a fleet to fight a war in the South Atlantic, it is not hard to understand why a few patriotic, ambitious, and simple-minded

Argentine admirals and generals might conclude that the time had come for them to push the British to a decision.[24]

Immediately after securing possession of the islands, the Argentines went to the United Nations in order to diffuse predictable British efforts to mobilize world opinion against them. If they blocked the British in the Security Council, they would have little choice but to sit down with the Argentines and a mediator to resolve the matter to Argentina's liking. Though intensely anticommunist, officers were confident that they could secure a Soviet veto of the British resolution that asked for their withdrawal. The two countries had become close trading partners in the past few years, the Soviets providing a market for Argentina's grain after the United States chose to boycott sales to the Soviet Union in punishment for its invasion of Afghanistan in 1979. Economic necessity and not ideology dictated Argentine trade policy, just as it had in the past, so at the same time that they were helping the Reagan administration make war on Marxist guerrillas in Central America, they saw nothing wrong with looking to the Soviets for assistance in their contest with the British. Two days before the invasion, on March 31, Argentine Foreign Minister Nicanor Costa Mendez had asked the Soviet ambassador in Buenos Aires to request his government's veto to an inevitable British resolution after the invasion. The Soviets listened with interest, as did the Chinese when the same request was made of them, but when the showdown came in New York they surprised the Argentines by abstaining from the Security Council vote, allowing passage of a resolution that demanded the immediate withdrawal of all Argentine troops. So rather than confront a British government that was unable to mobilize sanctions against Argentina, Galtieri suddenly faced a belligerent Prime Minister Thatcher, who claimed that justice was on her side, making it unnecessary for her to do anything until after the Argentines complied with the Council's Resolution 502 by taking their troops home.[25]

Third World nations were supposed to become another source of support for Argentina, if only because of their expected delight that a blow had been struck against a colonial power by a fellow underdog. But they too failed to live up to expectations. While some vocally defended Argentina, very few did so enthusiastically. Argentina was not really one of them, and never less so than in 1982, when its military government was cozying up to the United States and waging war against liberation movements in Central America. But Argentina was desperate for support and tried hard to cultivate it wherever it could. Most amazing was Costa Mendez's trip to Havana at the end of May. Himself an old-fashioned conservative, the foreign minister swallowed hard and flew to Cuba to ask Fidel Castro to help with his wooing the nonaligned countries, who were meeting there at the time. Castro went along after portraying it as part of the poor nations' war against the imperialists, and he took a majority of the delegates with him to pass a resolution endorsing the Argentine position. But few were really comfortable doing so, for as one African diplomat noted: "Costa Mendez was a man who came to a place in which he did not believe, said things he did not believe, and we, his interlocutors, did not believe them either."[26]

Costa Mendez did not do as well at the Organization of American States, however, and his government never really recovered diplomatically. If there was any place a Latin American nation in danger of going to war with a European power expected support, the OAS was it. The 1947 Rio Treaty had bound the region's nations to the defense of any member, which to the Argentines meant protecting them against an invasion of their islands by the British. Nevertheless, when the time came to vote for an endorsement of Argentina's position, several OAS nations held back, paying lip service to Argentina's cause, but refusing to assist Galtieri in his defense of Argentine territory. In desperation, Costa Mendez asked for a resolution that demanded the withdrawal of the British naval task force then on its way south, but again he failed to get the necessary two-thirds to vote in his favor. The best he could get, it turned out, was the last thing he needed: an OAS endorsement of U.N. Resolution 502, which called for the withdrawal of both sides.[27]

Latin American recalcitrance revealed a schizophrenia in their attitude toward Argentina, being as they were sympathetic with its attempt to regain what everyone recognized as its legitimate territory, while privately being pleased to see the pretentious Argentines punished for their belligerence. Moreover, few governments believed that it was in their interest to condone the use of force to settle territorial issues since nearly all Latin American countries were plagued by border disputes with their neighbors. So when it came time to sign up with Argentina, many held back, guaranteeing their neighbor nothing more than a little economic aid and some help in mediating the dispute as President Belaunde Terry of Peru tried to do on several occasions but with no success.

The European nations did not help either. Thatcher set the example by freezing $1.4 billion in Argentine assets in Britain, prohibiting new loans by British banks, cutting off imports from Argentina, and then asking members of the European Common Market to impose a six-week ban on exports to Argentina, which they did with more alacrity than was customary. By themselves such measures could not force

Argentina to back off since Europe was no longer its principal market, but they hurt nevertheless, hitting the country at a time when it was already in deep economic trouble. All that Argentina could do in return was suspend payments on its debt to British banks that had syndicated half of the $20 billion debt held in Europe.[28]

The U.S. government, having failed to stop the invasion, tried immediately after it to bring its two allies together to revolve the matter peacefully. Secretary of State Alexander Haig shuttled back and forth, searching for an agreement that would secure Argentina's withdrawal in exchange for British promises to negotiate more sincerely. He went to London on April 8, then to Buenos Aires on April 10, and back to London on April 12. He returned to Washington on April 14 to brief Reagan and arrived in Buenos Aires again on April 15 with a "five-point" plan. In it he asked for withdrawal by both sides, the creation of a three-flag administration for the rest of the year made up of Britain, Argentina, and the United States, followed by year-long talks leading to a final settlement arrived at in consultation with the islands' 1,800 residents. But when he presented it to the Argentine junta on April 18 Admiral Anaya tossed it aside arrogantly, insisting that he was confident that Thatcher was bluffing since it was impossible for her task force to withstand the South Atlantic winter long enough to win a war. Galtieri agreed, leaving Haig with no choice but to return home with nothing to show for his efforts. A few days later President Reagan made public the poorly kept secret of his intention to give his old British allies whatever support they needed to expel the recalcitrant invaders.[29]

Later when he wrote of his experience Haig, not averse to either hyperbole or blaming his woes on others, complained that his efforts in the Falklands controversy had cost him his job as secretary of state by giving his enemies in the Reagan administration an issue on which to challenge his competence as a diplomat. But true or not, it was obvious that his failure to secure a peaceful resolution of the conflict was a major disappointment, and he blamed it, not surprisingly, on the Argentines. His discussions with them never went as well as he had hoped, the results changing almost hourly. On at least two occasions he prepared to leave Buenos Aires with what he thought was an agreement to withdraw troops and begin new negotiations only to be given a note by Costa Mendez as he boarded his plane explaining that they had changed their mind and that without Thatcher's acknowledging Argentine sovereignty over the islands neither withdrawal nor negotiation could begin. More than once Haig bemoaned Galtieri's "bad faith," something that he thought was due less to the president's desires than to his getting trapped by Admiral Anaya into a position that promised a loss of support among his military colleagues if he yielded to Haig's demands.[30]

Throughout the episode confusion surrounded everything that authorities did when Haig was in town. He was told one thing at the Foreign Ministry only to learn that the country's bargaining position was not what he thought it was when he spoke to Galtieri, and still different when Costa Mendez bid him farewell. As Haig observed: "On every decision, the government apparently had to secure the unanimous consent of every commander in the army and their equivalents in the navy and air force. Progress was made by syllables and centimeters, then vetoed by men who had never been part of the negotiations."[31] But Haig should not have been surprised, given the character of military government in Argentina, for unity had never been its primary strength. The highly politicized yet almost feudal character of the interservice command structure has always been its curse when it tried to govern for very long, and despite the need to stay together to wage a war, old habits were too ingrained to allow it.

While the diplomats labored in vain the British fleet moved southward, regrouping and refueling at Ascension Island with supplies provided secretly by the United States on orders of Secretary of Defense Caspar Weinberger. The British submarine *Spartan* arrived on station off Port Stanley, the islands' capital, on April 12 to begin to set up an exclusionary zone around the islands in order to discourage Argentines from supplying them by sea from the mainland. The first British landing was made at South Georgia on April 25 by commandos who quickly took it from a small Argentine garrison. Then on May 1 a Vulcan bomber flown from Ascension struck the airport in Port Stanley as did guns fired from ships and Sea Harrier jet fighters. It was then that the British pulled off what would become the most controversial incident of the war. On May 2, on order of the British cabinet in London, the nuclear submarine *Conqueror* torpedoed the Argentine cruiser *General Belgrano* just outside the exclusionary zone as it was heading back into port on orders of the Argentine command. The *Belgrano* sank swiftly in the freezing waters, taking 368 sailors with it. The sinking shocked Argentina and the rest of the world and gave Galtieri an excuse for rejecting the revised version of Haig's five-point plan presented this time by Peruvian President Fernando Belaunde Terry. But it did force the Argentine fleet to stay in port for the rest of the war as Thatcher and her commanders wanted. It was not until long after the war that she would admit that the *Belgrano* was outside the exclusionary zone, just as the Argentines had contended. But even then she claimed that the attack was justified because the British believed that the ship was giving navigational assistance to aircraft that were sent from shore to attack the British fleet. But whatever the reason, right or wrong, it did little to build support for the British war effort in world opinion.[32]

For the next twenty-five days the battle was fought in the air and on sea as the British awaited the arrival of the forces and equipment they needed for their landing (see Table 1.1). The fleet was quite vulnerable to attacks from the air, though their distance from the mainland where the Argentine fighters were based seldom allowed more than a single pass over targets at sea. Nevertheless, the Argentine pilots hit hard, sinking the destroyer *Sheffield* on May 4, the *Antelope* on May 24, and the *Coventry* and *Atlantic Conveyor* transports on May 25. The *Sheffield* and the *Atlantic Conveyor* were hit by radar-guided, sea-skimming Exorcet missiles launched at long ranges by Super Entendard fighters. The British were fortunate that the Argentines had only a few Exorcets on hand; had there been many more the fleet might have been devastated long before the invasion had begun. Several ships were bombed from the air, but to their good fortune many of the Argentine bombs were duds. In the air war both sides fought intensely but the Argentines paid the most for their efforts, losing seventy Skyhawk, Mirage, and Dagger jets compared with the British giving up only nine of their Harriers, the difference resulting largely from the Harrier's very

1.1   Chronology of Falklands/Malvinas War, April–June 1982

April 2	Argentine invasion of islands
April 5	British carrier group sails from Portsmouth
April 10	Secretary of State Haig visits Buenos Aires
April 12	British declare exclusion zone around islands
April 25	British recapture South Georgia Islands
April 27	Haig's final truce proposal sent to London
April 30	President Reagan declares U.S. support for Britain
May 2	Argentine cruiser *General Belgrano* sunk on orders of British war cabinet
May 3	General Galtieri rejects Peruvian peace plan, citing *Belgrano* sinking as reason
May 4	HMS *Sheffield* sunk
May 8	British war cabinet dispatches landing force from Ascension Island
May 18	Argentine junta rejects U.N. Secretary General de Cuellar's peace proposal
May 19	British war cabinet authorizes landing
May 21	Landing at San Carlos begins
May 25	British ships *Coventry* and *Atlantic Conveyor* sunk
May 28	Battle of Goose Green won by British
June 11	Battle of Port Stanley begins
June 14	Argentines surrender

successful use of its American-made AIM-9L heat-seeking Sidewinder air-to-air missile, which often confounded and shot down the brave but less experienced Argentine pilots.[33]

One last effort was made to settle things diplomatically just before the British forces landed at San Carlos Bay on May 21. But when U.N. Secretary General Javier Perez de Cuellar asked Thatcher on May 19 to hold off the invasion a little longer so that he could press the Argentines to withdraw, she refused and went to the House of Commons to announce amid great cheers that her forces were about to recover the Falklands. Galtieri was no more cooperative with the secretary general, insisting as before that the British agree to discuss the sovereignty issue before Argentina withdrew its forces. The issue was moot when on May 20 the British cabinet authorized Rear Admiral John Woodward to go ashore and get the job done.[34]

Galtieri never has explained why he refused to seize this last opportunity to prevent war. Perhaps he had grown convinced that Admiral Woodward was coming ashore regardless of what Argentina offered at the bargaining table, seeing as how Thatcher was more desirous of revenge than peace. Or maybe he was afraid to appear the coward, knowing that if he did his military colleagues would never accept it. Whichever it was, he could not get out of what had become a no-win situation: if he brought the troops home without much to show for the original invasion, he would look the fool for having sent them on April 2, but if he left them they were certain to be humiliated in battle with a stronger force.

The British landed at San Carlos Bay on the opposite side of East Falkland Island from Port Stanley, where most of the Argentine troops were concentrated. Not anticipating their coming ashore there, the Argentines were caught off guard, unable to marshal their forces for a swift counterattack against a very vulnerable advance force. And fortunately for the British, cloud cover made detection of the invasion by air impossible at its inception, depriving the Argentine air force of a chance to strike before the expedition could set up minimal air defenses on shore. When they came the second day, Argentine pilots fought bravely and inflicted damage on the invaders, but the latter's firepower proved too much for the flyers and their losses were heavy. Quickly the British set up a base and sent expeditionary forces inland, attacking first at Goose Green a few miles away. The battle lasted nearly a day as the Argentines fought tenaciously, but they were no match for the very professional British paratroopers, 450 of whom secured the surrender of 1,200 Argentines after killing 50 of them and losing 17 themselves.[35]

In the end the Argentines' fortress mentality and British skill at

warfare dictated a swift victory. Authorities in Buenos Aires made no
effort to improve the chances of their troops once the British landed,
leaving Major General Mario Benjamín Menéndez and his troops to
draw together around Port Stanley in the hope that they could somehow
hold off the rapidly moving British forces.[36] When forced to defend
themselves the Argentine soldiers fought hard, but the initiative belonged to their enemy and one after another they either surrendered or
pulled back after brief battles. Later, after discharge from the service,
many Argentine soldiers would boast about how brave they had been,
giving most of the credit to the noncommissioned and younger officers
who led them in the field. Their assessment of senior officers was less
kind and filled with bitter complaints about how arrogant officers had
abused their army of draftees, treating them like serfs whose well-being
mattered little. Horror stories of food shortages and bitterly cold weather
for which they were unprepared became common, as was admission
that morale fell quickly when it became apparent how vulnerable they
were. As British victories accumulated, Argentine soldiers could think
of nothing but their disadvantages and how they had been betrayed by
their own leaders. As one of them reflected when the war ended:

> After some hours watching the English troops preparing for battle the picture
> became clear. Helicopters took them from the front to San Carlos or Darwin to eat
> or be treated by doctors, or to get anything else they needed. We, in contrast, were
> stuck at the same places all the time, freezing and hungry. We had spent sixty days
> on the islands and they only fifteen or twenty. We were fed up with the place and
> could not take it any more. Some of us had lost feeling in our feet to frostbite. But
> the English had incredible outfits and impermeable boots. The difference was just
> too much.[37]

A rationalization for a humiliating defeat? Perhaps, since the British
troops were never as well off as they appeared to be to their foes, but
there was enough truth to it for thousands of Argentine soldiers to
question the wisdom of those who had sent them to a war they could not
win. At least that is how they told it when they returned to a nation
embarrassed by having cheered them into battle.

Public disillusionment with Galtieri and his colleagues came
quickly, provoked not only by the defeat itself but also from recognition
that he had been lying to them about the war's progress right until the
end. Argentines were, for example, told that the British had been immo-
bilized at San Carlos and "were awaiting their Dunkirk." And frequently
anonymous military sources were quoted in the press and on radio and
television dismissing reports of a large British landing anywhere, insisting that the number involved was no more than 500 and that they were
no match for Argentine forces. Some newspapers, like the daily *Clarín*,

did publish British accounts and contrasted them to Argentine ones, but only the most skeptical discounted the accuracy of what they were being told by their own government. That is why the loss came as such a shock when it finally occurred twenty-four days after the San Carlos landing. While the rest of the world watched and waited for the inevitable British triumph (more confident of victory than the British commanders were, given their vulnerability to air attack), Argentine citizens were certain that their new fortress was being defended. When the end suddenly came they did not want to believe it, but when they finally did the nation fell into a quiet stupor from which it took several weeks to recover.

They learned later that exhausted British forces had laid siege to Port Stanley on June 14 and demanded that Major General Menéndez surrender in order to avert what would surely become a bloody last stand. To his credit he gave in without a fight, and within just a few days nearly all of the 11,313 soldiers who surrendered were herded onto ships and sent home. When they arrived the public was kept away, as if hiding evidence of their humiliation would make the whole debacle more bearable, at least for Galtieri and his service commanders. But soldiers eventually went home to tell their tales, and within a couple of months the entire country came together like never before in its hatred of those who had taken their youth into battle. And though few would admit it, they were ashamed of themselves for having gone along with it so enthusiastically and unskeptically.[38]

Undoubtedly much of the credit for the triumph belongs to Britain's highly trained officers and soldiers. Theirs was a volunteer military whose squadrons and companies thrived on rivalries among their respective units, much like athletes who take great pride in besting their competitors. They were served well by such attitudes throughout the conflict.[39] They also benefited from the supplies they received from allies like the United States since they were not well prepared to fight a sea war in the South Atlantic. To begin with, their capacity for air surveillance and satellite communications in the region was weak. Moreover, they were short of the high-quality air-to-air missiles needed to hold off the Argentines' Super-Entendard and Mirage aircraft as well as bases in the vicinity where they could store the aviation fuel essential to fight an extended battle. At Defense Secretary and Anglophile Caspar Weinberger's insistence President Reagan went to the rescue early in the conflict, supplying fuel at the American Wideawake air base on Britain's Ascension Island, 200 Sidewinder AIM-9L air-to-air missiles—probably the most decisive weapon of the campaign (they claimed as many kills as all other weapon systems together)—8 Stinger anti-air-craft systems, and several Shrike air-to-ground radar-seeking missiles. But most indicative of U.S. determination to assure a British victory was Weinberger's controversial decision to move a military satellite from its Soviet-watching orbit over the northern hemisphere to the south, where it could keep an eye on the Falklands area in order to assure Britain maximum information about Argentine movements. If we accept the notion put forward by the British at the time that the strategic balance in the region was extremely close at the outset, then it is fair to assume that U.S. assistance was most helpful to their victory. Neither the British nor the Americans want to discuss the matter, of course, the former because Thatcher prefers to credit her own troops with the triumph and the latter who want to avoid recriminations from the Argentines at a time when both countries have much more to gain from a renewal of their friendship. Argentines want U.S. assistance in arranging new negotiations over the islands as well as help with the financing of their huge foreign debt, while the Reagan administration needs as many friends as it can get in a time of controversy over its interventions in Central America.[40]

Not to be overlooked in any assessment of the war's outcome is the performance of the Argentine military in combat. Though their adversay's military skill and modern arsenal made defeat probable from the start, the refusal of the Argentine navy to fight after the *Belgrano* was sunk cost them dearly. So did their sending draftees without cold weather training to defend the frigid islands. Fearful that the Chileans might take advantage of their military adventure, they left their best troops on the border to discourage intrusions. Their biggest problem, however, was their inability to work closely together. Interservice rivalries were supposed to have been set aside when the military took over the country in 1976, giving the impression for the first time that the army, navy, and air force were ready to put national politics over their own contests for prominence. But their new-found unity was of short duration, and in 1980 a rift between the army and navy developed over the army's selection of General Roberto Viola to become president in 1981. Soon thereafter army commanders divided over Viola's performance as president, with the winners of the dispute replacing him with Galtieri in December that year. War is supposed to unite armed forces, but it seldom does, and never less so than in Argentina in 1982. The navy that had launched the plot panicked after the loss of the *Belgrano* and refused to lend much support to the air force or the army, who fought the navy's war for it. And the air force pretty much proceeded on its own, never ignoring the battle plan but seldom submitting entirely to the army's control. By the time the war ended no one was really in charge.

Nearly everything that could go wrong with the retaking of the Malvinas actually did. Galtieri and Anaya had underestimated Thatcher's resolve and Reagan's commitment to his country's old ally, and they failed to understand that their South American neighbors' support of their cause was not enough to make up for their resentment of Argentines as a people. But saddest of all was their naiveté about what it took to force an adversary to negotiate with them on their own terms. After having been kept in tow for almost a century by British merchants and bankers, they, like Perón before them, wanted desperately to turn the tables on the British and were convinced by British lethargy in military matters that they could get away with it. In a very Argentine manner they set out to get some justice the easy way only to discover that nothing came cheaply or easily for them anymore. As rudely as the British had treated them over the years, negotiation was the only way out, but Galtieri never quite understood what bargaining really meant. In a rare admission of failure General Menéndez later confessed as much when he was asked to assess the whole affair. Testifying before the military's Rattenbach Commission in 1983 he mused: "My final impression . . . well . . . I guess it is that we really did not know how to negotiate with the flexibility necessary to avoid the kind of defeat that became inevitable at the hands of an enemy stronger than ourselves."[41]

A Blessing in Disguise?

It was some time before Argentines recovered from the shock of defeat, but as they began to assess their betrayal by the armed forces their hopes for the military's leaving office increased. At first they could do nothing but watch as Galtieri's junta was replaced by another whose members busied themselves bickering over what to do next, evidently finding it impossible to hide interservice conflicts and recriminations from public view. Political party leaders quickly seized the opportunity to campaign for an end to military dictatorship, but when the decision to pull out came it was the military's own loss of confidence, not public protest, that provoked it. Ruling the country required agreement among service commanders on political strategy and tactics, but after the war they never reached such agreement. With nowhere else to go they announced their intention to hold elections before the end of 1983, not even bothering to rig them this time.

On October 30, 1983, Argentines went to the polls and voted for the first time in ten years, choosing a president, provincial governors, and national legislators. They thus secured for themselves another opportunity to test their capacity for democratic politics. It was cause for unprecedented celebration by a population that had suffered through a decade of violence and repression and now welcomed relief from both. Of course, everyone knew that the military was still with them and that the new president's tenure would be no more secure than his predecessors' had been. But that was no reason not to embrace political liberty warmly when it finally came.

It was left to Argentines to discover whether or not they could live together under the rules of constitutional democracy. One could not be faulted for thinking that they would fail the test once more, given how many times they have done so in the past. Perhaps democracy's proponents expect too much of them, erroneously associating literacy and affluence with civility and political accommodation. It is not inconceivable that Argentines may have grown accustomed to pushing and shoving each other, mixing military coups with elections in a manner that allows competing forces the means to defend themselves against aggressive rivals. Perhaps they want to keep it that way. Perhaps—but such assumptions risk selling the Argentines short by underrating their capacity for political reconciliation. It is not inconceivable that they really covet the liberty that comes with a constitution and are willing to pay a price for it after living under authoritarian governments for fourteen of the past seventeen years.

Whichever it is, we are left to wonder why they came to suffer such political miseries in the first place. Just why is it easier to govern Spain and Italy than it is this New World land of Spaniards and Italians? Is Argentina another Latin American country that is too weak and too penetrated by outside forces to manage its own affairs amicably, as some of its own people contend? Or is its condition more the product of mind than matter, something that Argentines have created for themselves?

We need to look into the past to find answers to these questions, starting long before the Falklands/Malvinas War. Argentina is a country that got off to a slow start in the nineteenth century and then rose to unexpected prominence in an incredibly short time. But new problems accompanied sudden prosperity and the way in which politics was used to promote and protect it. The result has been a twentieth-century tale of high hopes and repeated disappointments.

Notes

1. Argentine troops were ordered to hold their fire in order to avoid the kind of provocation they feared would come from killing islanders and the marines who defended them. They really believed that the British would take a kinder view of the whole thing if bloodshed were avoided.

2. Fritz L. Hoffmann and Olga Mingo Hoffmann, *Sovereignty in Dispute: The Falklands/Malvinas, 1493–1982* (Boulder, Colo.: Westview Press, 1984), chs. 2–4.

3. Ibid.

4. Guillermo Makin, "Argentine Approaches to the Falklands/Malvinas: Was the Resort to Violence Forseeable?" *International Affairs* 59, no. 3 (Summer 1983): 291.

5. *The Economist,* June 19, 1982, p. 37.

6. The debate in Parliament over the removal of the *Endurance* included an exchange between Labourite James Callahan, prime minister until 1979 and supporter of the ship's retention, who on February 9, 1982, argued that its return then could have "serious consequences," and Prime Minister Thatcher, who responded that the government "felt that other claims on the defense budget should have greater priority." See Peter J. Beck, "Britain's Antarctic Dimension," *International Affairs* 59, no. 3 (Summer 1983): 433.

7. A brief but excellent summary of British diplomacy before the invasion is available in *The Economist,* June 19, 1982, pp. 35–43. The British government's review of prewar diplomacy reaches much the same conclusions about expectations of gradual escalation. See the "Franks Report" issued on January 18, 1983, excerpts of which are published in Max Hastings and Simon Jenkins, *The Battle for the Falklands* (New York: Norton, 1983), pp. 361–372.

8. These errors of judgment are reported in the so-called Franks Report made by the British government on January 18, 1983.

9. Beck, "Britain's Antarctic Dimension," p. 434. On this and other aspects of British diplomacy during the war, see Peter Calvert, *The Falklands Crisis* (New York: St. Martin's Press, 1982).

10. The Argentine ambassador has denied that he ever gave Galtieri such an assurance. On Galtieri's self-defense, see *Buenos Aires Herald,* April 3, 1983, p. 13.

11. O. R. Cardoso, R. Kirschbaum, and E. Van Der Kooy, *Malvinas: La trama secreta* (Buenos Aires: Sudamericana-Planeta, 1983), p. 35. This volume, which is cited often in this chapter, is the work of three reporters from the daily newspaper *Clarín,* who prepared it from interviews with participants in the episode in Buenos Aires, London, and Washington, D.C. Popular in Argentina, it sold over 140,000 copies within its first year of publication.

12. Ibid., pp. 77–78.

13. *La Prensa,* January 24, 1982, p. 1.

14. General Galtieri, Foreign Minister Costa Mendez, and Admiral Anaya defended their decisions before what became known as the Rattenbach Commission, a military investigative body that held secret hearings in 1983. Excerpts from their testimonies were published in *Gente* magazine, December 8, 1983.

15. The incident is told from the British point of view in *The Economist,* June 19, 1982, p. 43.

16. Cardoso et al., *Malvinas,* ch. 4.

17. Ibid., pp. 87–89.

18. The most recent of these being the Schackleton Report made just a couple years before to the British prime minister, leading even some in the British government to believe that Thatcher would use it to usher in a gradual abandonment of the islands.

19. This interpretation of Galtieri's perceptions of the British is drawn primarily from his testimony before the military's Rattenbach Commission in 1983. Far less cunning in his response to questions than the more duplicitous Foreign Minister Costa Mendez and Admiral Anaya, Galtieri revealed his own naiveté time and again when he tried to explain himself. See *Gente,* December 8, 1983.

20. For a more detailed analysis of this collaboration, see Gary Wynia, "Argentina: Rebuilding the Relationship," in *From Gunboats to Diplomacy: New U.S. Policies for Latin America,* ed. Richard Newfarmer (Baltimore: Johns Hopkins University Press, 1984).

21. Buenos Aires Herald, April 3, 1983, p. 13.

22. Cardoso et al., *Malvinas,* pp. 96–100. This and all other translations of works in Spanish cited in this book are the author's.

23. Hastings and Jenkins, *The Battle for the Falklands,* pp. 72–74.

24. This interpretation draws heavily on testimony by Galtieri and Anaya before the military's Rattenbach Commission. See *Gente,* December 8, 1983.

25. Cardoso et al., *Malvinas,* pp. 120–123.

26. Ibid., p. 122.

27. Hastings et al., *The Battle for the Falklands,* pp. 139–148.

28. The Economist, April 10, 1982, p. 26.

29. Hastings et al., *The Battle for the Falklands,* pp. 108–111.

30. Alexander Haig, *Caveat: Realism, Reagan and Foreign Policy* (New York: Macmillan, 1984), pp. 261–302.

31. Excerpt from ibid. published in *Time,* April 9, 1984, p. 61.

32. See Arthur Gavshon and Desmond Rice, *El hundimiento del Belgrano* (Buenos Aires: Emece, 1984).

33. On the air war, see Jeffrey Ethell and Alfred Price. *Air War South Atlantic* (New York: Macmillan, 1984); and B. H. Andrada, *Guerra aerea en las Malvinas* (Buenos Aires: Emece, 1983).

34. New York Times, May 24, 1982, p. 7.

35. The battle is described in detail in Hastings et al., *The War for the Falklands,* pp. 233–253.

36. Menéndez later testified to having been given lame excuses or having been ignored altogether when he asked for more potent weapons and ample supplies, blaming the refusal of Galtieri and Anaya to deliver on their promise to make his defense of the islands anything more than a bluff. See his testimony before the Rattenbach Commission in *Gente,* December 8, 1983.

37. Daniel Kon, *Los chicos de la guerra* (Buenos Aires: Galerna, 1982), p. 37. Also see Nicolas Kasanzew, *Malvinas: a sangre y fuego* (Buenos Aires: Abril, 1982); and Carlos M. Turolo (h), *Así lucharon* (Buenos Aires: Sudamericana, 1982). Many collections of war stories telling of gallantry as well as suffering were published immediately after soldiers were discharged, and in 1984 *Los chicos del la guerra* was made into a powerful and popular antiwar film.

38. On Argentine coverage of the war, see *New York Times,* May 24, 1982, p. 7.

39. Hastings et al., *The War for the Falklands.* This interpretation of soldier behavior comes from Hastings but is repeated in several other works.

40. These details were revealed in *The Economist,* March 3, 1984, pp. 29–31.

41. Gente, December 8, 1983, p. 82.

2

The Price of Prosperity

It is tempting to blame Juan Perón for Argentina's woes, if only because so many Argentines do. But the country's economic infirmities and political rancor began much earlier. He exploited the hostility of the poor toward the rich but he did not invent it. The upper class had supervised the creation of a society over which they enjoyed immense social control well into this century. But as it changed and they did not, opposition to them grew, especially among nationalists in the middle class and the leaders of an alienated urban working class whose numbers increased rapidly in the 1930s. The oligarchy's stubborn refusal to share anything but the symbols of power with their adversaries is what gave Perón the opportunity to launch his provocative reformist effort in 1946. That they should have hung on so tenaciously is not all that surprising, however, given how much power they had accumulated while running the country for almost a century.

Enjoying a Late Start

When the Spaniards reached the sparsely populated prairies of the Río de la Plata river basin in 1536, they found none of the gold, silver, and abundant indigenous labor that had made Mexico and Peru so attractive to colonization and economic exploitation. Pedro de Mendoza established an outpost at what is now Buenos Aires only to abandon it promptly and settle up river in Asunción, the current capital of Paraguay. Few people followed him to the southern end of the New World during the next two centuries, however, and not until the early eighteenth century when the Treaty of Utrecht (1713) allowed the British to sell slaves and merchandise there and to export hides from the region did Buenos Aires become a trading post of some significance, rising to a population of 20,000 by 1776, when it was made a viceroyalty. But it would be another century before its economic development really got underway, several decades after independence in 1816 and two unsuccessful experiments in constitutional government in 1819 and in 1826 that were followed by a series of civil wars that did not end until 1853.[1]

Disputes over who would pay for the nation's development divided its citizens in the nineteenth century and still do today. Although they were happy to see their wool, hides, and salted beef sold in markets abroad, cattlemen did not want to expend their surpluses to build the nation's infrastructure or finance the immigration that would be needed to supply labor to the countryside for the development of grain production. Such "private-mindedness" set a standard of conduct that would become a way of life, inhibiting the creation of "public goods" from then until now. The elitist, constitutional governments that succeeded one another after 1853 tried to raise funds and build roads and railways, but their budgets were meager. So they turned to foreigners, who welcomed opportunities for investment when they saw how rapid markets for the country's grain and beef were growing in Europe. As consumption of its commodities abroad increased and railways were built ever farther from the coast into the interior, additional land was put into production, and by the turn of the century this isolated, sparsely populated country of feuding cattlemen was transformed into the breadbasket of an industrializing Europe, quickly becoming the most prosperous nation in Latin America and one whose per capita income surpassed those of most European countries at the time.

Argentina was blessed by land and climate that allowed it to produce an abundance of meat and grain using little technology, its *pampas* being one of the most fertile humid grasslands in the world. But it also had much more, most notably a small but ambitious landowning class that was able to adapt its cattle breeding and grain production to rising demand more swiftly than might have been expected from a people accustomed to modest success with sheep raising, breeding horses, and slaughtering low-quality native breeds of cattle for their hides and salted beef. Some had acquired their lands during colonial times, while many others took advantage of the Conquest of the Desert campaigns (1879–83) that cleared the interior of nomadic Indians and doubled the amount of available land on the *pampas*. The added territory was supposed to be distributed by authorities in modest parcels, but the plan was subverted easily by wealthy people who sought to expand their holdings or acquire new ones. As a result, when settlement was completed around 1914 nearly 80 percent of the *pampas* was owned by just 8 percent of the families who held property there. Production grew nevertheless, the area sown to grain increasing by 1,600 percent and the volume of exports by 2,000 percent between 1860 and 1914. Comparative advantage worked for the Argentine oligarchy, allowing the accumulation of great wealth from the exploitation of the nation's rich soil with the help of enthusiastic foreigners.[2]

New technology, like the refrigeration process introduced by the English River Plate Fresh Meat Company in 1883, made it possible to export frozen meat rather than salted beef. Soon cattlemen improved the quality of their stock using Herefords and Aberdeen Angus brought over from England. An added boost came with the invention of beef "chilling" in 1908, a process much preferable to freezing since it preserved more of the taste in the best meat. As processing and shipping (handled almost entirely by American and English companies) developed so did the division of labor within the beef industry, with cattle breeders starting production and "fatteners" completing it on their rich pastures near markets in and around Buenos Aires. As demand rose, herds grew steadily, and by 1920 stock had increased by 50 percent over the 1890 total.[3]

Grain production rose simultaneously thanks to an influx of immigrants who were eager to labor as tenant farmers on the still sparsely populated *pampas*. It also helped that Argentina had never been turned into a land of *haciendas* during colonial times because of the shortage of labor then. Had it, rapid adaptation to new export opportunities would not have been possible, but because cattlemen only needed immigrant labor to turn their lands into huge granaries, the transformation came easily.[4] Tenant farmers and cattlemen complemented each other perfectly. The latter needed their pastures upgraded to raise high-quality stock for slaughter and sale in European markets so they required tenant farmers to sow their holdings with alfalfa after raising grain on it under the standard three-year contract. Tenants leased from 240 to 600 acres, often through oral agreements which necessitated their sharing a specific portion of their profits with their landlord, generating investment-free income for the landlord while gaining access to some of the country's best land for themselves. Renting land was no substitute for owning it and grievances accumulated, but at the time it was a workable arrangement that swiftly transformed Argentina from one of the world's least developed pastures into one of its richest farm lands.[5]

Agriculture allowed some people to acquire great wealth very quickly much as minerals had done in other countries. People "struck it rich" because they held the right property. Land was a commodity that was retained for its value or leased and traded for profit much like gold and silver were. Even the tenants were not very attached to pieces of property since they had to move from region to region every few years to sustain themselves, seldom building homes or joining in the formation of permanent communities anywhere. Unlike places like Iowa or Illinois, where small towns sprung up and became county seats and service centers for farmers, in Argentina all government and trade were confined to Buenos Aires and a few provincial capitals. Even today, long after the emergence of a rural middle class, the visitor to the countryside is struck by how empty of towns it is.

Unlike the United States, where 63 percent of the farmers owned the land that they worked in 1914, only 40 percent did in Argentina. Had Argentines been allowed to acquire it more easily, their society would have become much different than it did. But without a large rural middle class leading movements for populist reforms this very agrarian nation entered the second quarter of the twentieth century under the control of a small but powerful rural elite who, along with their British customers, refused to share real power with those below them. Theirs was not the kind of society Alexis de Tocqueville described in *Democracy in America,* filled with yeomen farmers whose individualism was sustained by their access to new land; instead it was a productive economy owned and managed by a few thousand people who controlled the nation's primary source of wealth, people who resisted any innovation that threatened their social status and economic power. If social change were to come, it would not be in the countryside, where nothing resembling a large community of modern farmers with a stake in modernization developed until the mid-twentieth century.

It is necessary to appreciate how bound Argentina became to one source of wealth and economic development to understand why it never emulated the United States, a nation to which it was similar in natural resources. Everything depended on the *pampas* and its production, and other possible modes of development were either ignored or subordinated to it. In addition, just one city monopolized all decision making and communication with the rest of the country as well as the outside world. Argentina's ruling class had a good thing going, and the immigrants who came over had no choice but to subordinate themselves to them. The late James Scobie described it so well when he wrote: "It was as if, long before the Civil War, the South had emerged as the dominant and only area of United States expansion with its capital at Savannah or Charleston, an economy based entirely on cotton exported to British mills, and an oligarchy composed of plantation owners and merchants."[6]

The role the British played in all of this would become quite controversial, but to the oligarchy it seemed nothing less than natural. Never mind that the British had wanted to lay claim to the region's economies since colonial times and had sent a few thousand soldiers to liberate Buenos Aires from the Spanish only to be roundly defeated not long before independence. Argentines evicted the Spanish on their own, but after they did they could hardly wait to welcome the British back, wanting all the trade and investment that Britain had to offer. It came slowly at first since Argentina had little to sell, but when their industrial revolution caused the British to look abroad for grain to feed its growing working class, it was to Argentina, among others, that they turned. Thanks primarily to British investment the railways grew from 6,500 kilometers of track in 1889 to 31,100 by 1914, and the national product rose at record rates. To all accounts it was a mutually beneficial partnership that fed British workers while making Argentine cattlemen and traders wealthy people. Argentines would one day change their minds about it all and rebel against British patronage, but that would not happen until after World War II, when the British no longer had much interest in shopping there.

A Nation of Strangers

North Americans pride themselves on being a nation of immigrants, a land where millions began anew after escaping the poverty and political persecution they suffered in their homelands. Argentina too was a nation of immigrants, the number of which is smaller than North America's, but as a proportion of the resident population it was actually much larger, nearly 30 percent in 1914 compared to 15 percent in the United States.[7] It is one of the seldom told stories of massive demographic change in the modern world. The Canadian and Australian experiences resemble it, but because Argentina's population was so small when immigrants started arriving in 1870—only 2 million—the demographic impact of the 6 million who had arrived by 1915 was enormous.[8]

When the Spanish conquered the River Plate region in 1553, an estimated 400,000 Indians lived there, half in the northwest (now the provinces of Jujuy and Salta) at what then was the southern tip of the Inca empire, and only 30,000 on the *pampas*. Just 1,200 Spaniards stayed behind after the conquest, but by 1778 their number had grown to 70,000. As happened elsewhere in the region, the indigenous population was decimated by disease and cohabitation with the Spaniards, and by 1850 about 70 percent of the population was mestizo or mixed blood. It was this largely mestizo society of 2 million people ruled over by cattlemen that the immigrants joined after 1880.[9]

They came in four waves, the first beginning in the 1880s, when cattlemen and land companies recruited colonists, tenant farmers, and people to harvest grain during the European winter and spring. Italy supplied most of them, giving Argentina the Italian veneer that it exhibits today, and Spain many of the rest, the annual number reaching a peak of 220,000 in 1889. Some were peasants, but most came from small towns. They did not consider themselves "Argentines" at first, many of them intending to accumulate wealth and then return to their native lands and set up a small business or buy a house. Eventually many would stay, but there was always a steady flow back to Europe; nearly one-fourth of those who arrived before 1915 exchanged their pesos and returned home.

Jews were among the members of the first wave, nearly all of them from Russia, some being brought over by the international Jewish Colonization Association in order to create farm colonies in Entre Rios and Santa Fe provinces, and others coming to make homes in Buenos Aires, where by the turn of the century they had created a large barrio several blocks square just north of the city's most prominent plaza. Today an estimated 400,000 Jews live in Argentina, most in Buenos Aires, where third-generation descendants of migrants are involved not only in industry and commerce but also in education, the professions, and politics. Their integration into society has not prevented charges of anti-Semitic persecution, the most recent being made when a military government ruled in the late 1970s. Jewish Argentines disagree about how seriously threatened they really are by anti-Semitism. Some Argentines delight in blaming Zionists for all of their problems, and a few use violence to make their point, but most Jews insist that there is nothing systematic or immanently dangerous about it. Yet, the mere fact that it troubles some of them indicates that anti-Semitism cannot be dismissed as casually as many people try to do.[10]

Economic depression in 1890 slowed the flow of immigrants to a trickle until a second wave began in 1904, again made up primarily of Italians and Spaniards, the largest number, 323,000, reaching Buenos Aires in 1912. Though some of them settled in the countryside as intended, two-thirds stayed in cities, where they set up small shops or worked in construction and on the railroads. By 1914, according to one source, the foreign-born owned 66 percent of Argentina's industries and 74 percent of its retail stores.[11] Immigration fell off during World War I only to pick up again afterward, albeit at a slower pace than before with most people coming from Central Europe, especially Poland, and Russia, whose revolution many were fleeing. With little room left for them on the *pampas*, they were encouraged either to colonize the northeast to develop tropical fruit and lumber industries or to go south of the *pampas* to develop deciduous fruits in mountain river valleys. The last and smallest influx began after World War II, when a half-million fled the hardships created by the war in Europe. Nazi criminals like Adolf Eichmann were the most notorious of this group, but they were the exceptions. Contrary to popular mythology, Argentina never became a refuge for thousands of Nazis, most of its Germans having come earlier, forming a community of 45,000 by World War II.[12]

The Boom Ends

Good times were over far sooner than was expected. Reliance on agricultural exports for the achievement of economic development is always risky since customers can find other suppliers, natural disasters can wipe out crops, war can cut off trade, and tastes in food can change. The wisdom of hindsight makes the vulnerability of the Argentine enterprise obvious, but life was too good to believe that it would end soon. Not unlike oil-producing Third World nations in the 1970s, Argentines, after decades of meager development, had discovered that they had something that nations richer than themselves wanted, and they took full advantage of their good fortune. But the enterprise was never all that secure, being hit first by a world recession in the 1890s and then by World War I. But each time it was struck, the oligarchy rode out the recession, convinced that they would make up for their losses when better times returned. And they did for several decades, but in the 1930s it finally caught up with them.

The economy behaved erratically after World War I, its peaks and valleys coming ever closer together. For example, commodity prices fell when the war ended then rose again in 1922; a bad harvest followed in 1924 and world prices fell once more in 1925, only to rise in 1926. Still, Argentina managed to become the world's second largest exporter of wheat by the end of the decade (20 percent of the market), and the largest of corn (66 percent), linseed (80 percent), and meat (61 percent). Four cereal companies, owned predominantly by foreign capital, handled the grain trade, and five meat packers (three North American and two English) made sure that beef and mutton were sent in good condition to markets in Europe.[13] The operation ran well, absorbing occasional setbacks and then responding quickly to good markets when they appeared, convincing even doubters that Argentina could withstand the vicissitudes of the world market well enough to sustain its newly achieved high standard of living.

But economies do not always cooperate with those who direct them, and never less so than in 1929, when a depression that started in the industrial nations spread to the rest of the world. South American economies were especially vulnerable because of their heavy reliance on foreign markets and suppliers of industrial goods for their sustenance. The shock was unprecedented not only to their economies but to their politics as well. Ruling oligarchies panicked everywhere. After having tolerated the rise of urban middle classes and their political movements, they closed the door on them, fearful that they would permit economic disaster to provoke dreaded social upheavals, calling in the armed forces to keep the order in Chile, Brazil, and Argentina.

After evicting the Radical party, whose election it had permitted fourteen years before, the Argentine oligarchy responded to the depression pragmatically, proving themselves capable of abandoning some of their most sacred free trade doctrines when the preservation of their export economy required it. They begged the British not to abandon them and secured new trade agreements after granting their benefactors unprecedented concessions. Argentina was guaranteed a quota for chilled beef and the elimination of British tariffs on cereal imports in return for reduced tariffs on imported manufactured goods and a promise to spend sterling on goods and financial services from Britain. To complete the package the British helped Argentina create its first Central Bank.[14]

Essential to recovery was the government's initiating regulation of commodity markets and the sale of foreign exchange. A national meat board was created in 1933, membership on it being divided between public officials and cattlemen, and it was allowed to set minimum and maximum livestock prices, something previously forbidden by free marketers but now demanded by cattlemen as a means of protecting them against the world market and exploitative foreign meat packers. The grain trade was even more vulnerable with 70 percent of it exported, compared to only 33 percent of the nation's beef, so a grain commission was also created to operate much like the meat board. But instead of pushing up prices by withholding supplies from the market as the Canadians and North Americans were doing (a tactic prevented in Argentina by insufficient storage facilities), the Argentines chose to cover the losses borne by producers by financing the margin between the official and world market prices out of government profits on newly established exchange controls.[15] Thousands of vulnerable farmers were saved, and after declining by 11 percent between 1929 and 1932, the national product started growing again, helped by a drought in the United States that began in 1933 and lasted for four years, giving Argentina a virtual monopoly on the international grain market until the United States came back and caused grain prices to fall in 1937.[16]

Agriculture was not the only beneficiary of the rescue operation. Industry also profited. Manufacturing had been going on since before the turn of the century, and by 1920 it accounted for almost 20 percent of the national product. Enterprising immigrants and foreign investors had gone into food processing, and during the 1920s firms were added in chemicals, metals, and electrical products, some of them financed by North American investors bent on getting into the Argentine market.[17] Despite the ruling oligarchy's hostility to industry they had little choice but to tolerate its growth, and by 1940 its share of the national product had risen to 28 percent.[18]

Before Argentines had finished congratulating themselves on their recovery from the depression they were hit again, this time by World War II. At issue was whether Argentina should limp along, mixing a little more industrialization with continued reliance on the export economy, or devote far more public and private resources to industrialization. Finance Minister Federico Pinedo tried to settle the debate early by taking to Congress in 1940 a modest proposal designed to strengthen the country's economic position. He contended that massive industrialization was too expensive but some was necessary in order to increase economic independence. He argued for more food and textile industries and pursuing new markets abroad, especially in the United States. Unfortunately it was never tested since the opposition blocked its passage in the Chamber of Deputies largely on partisan grounds, the Radicals and their allies hoping to embarrass the incumbents as an election approached. But his ideas did not die; they merely languished until military politicians much less sympathetic to the oligarchy came along a few years later and adapted the notion of further industrialization to their own nationalistic objectives.[19]

A new generation of officers who were convinced that the oligarchy was losing touch with wartime economic realities took it upon themselves to prepare Argentina for its uncertain future, starting with their seizure of power in 1943. Untrained in economics and new at governing the country, they viewed development in basic, concrete terms, concentrating their energies on promoting the development of oil, iron, and steel industries. It was from among them that Colonel Juan Perón later emerged, taking the initiative away from his colleagues by using the support of the working class to put his notions of nationalism and populism to work in 1946.

A Society Divided

During all of this time, Argentine society was developing its current structure, one that is noted more for its divisions and antagonisms than its integration. The nation's founders had hoped it would be otherwise, of course. The oligarchy had always set the standard for good life in the country, giving it a reputation for extravagant wealth. Its members were rich, educated, and cosmopolitan. They owned three- and four-story villas in Buenos Aires that were overfurnished and overstaffed. When the heat of summer made the capital unbearable, they retreated to their chalets in the Córdoba hills and beach houses in Mar del Plata or vacationed in Europe.[20] With the help of English engineers and French architects, the oligarchy transformed Buenos Aires in a few years' time from a muddy old port town into one of the hemisphere's most elegant cities. They were a ruling class of agrarian entrepreneurs, who believed that Argentina was theirs to dispose of as they wished. Never did they doubt their right to rule over the several million immigrants who kept the enterprise going for them while they prospered.

The Argentine upper class lacked the cohesion characteristic of most elites in Latin America at the turn of the century. Although many old families increased their wealth in boom years, there was always room for others who made fortunes in real estate, banking, and trade. Competition among them for economic advantage was quite common. Rivalries grew, like the one between cattle breeders in the interior provinces and "fatteners" on the pampas near Buenos Aires, whom breeders accused of using their proximity to markets to rig them to the breeders' disadvantage. Similarly, fatteners contested with foreign meat-packing companies, which they claimed were always exploiting their oligopolistic control over the export market to deny fatteners fair prices. Gradually both were challenged by industrialists who resented the economy's direction by free-trading agrarian elites.

Labeling the upper class an "oligarchy" might seem wholly inappropriate given their diversity and lack of affection for one another. Yet calling them anything else risks ignoring their strength as a ruling class that defended its power quite successfully until World War II. They were elitist to the core, convinced of their superiority to those beneath them socially, and were always willing to go to great lengths to protect their privileges. Their economic competition and disputes over government policy were intense, but the oligarchy seldom allowed them to stand in the way of defending their kind against critics in the middle and lower classes who sought larger shares for themselves. Tariff policies, commodity prices, and trade strategies were legitimate issues for dispute, but the redistribution of real power never was. The oligarchy tolerated the election of candidates from the middle-class Radical party in 1916 only because they knew that the Radicals understood the rules of the game well enough to abstain from tinkering with the wealth and power of the rich. When the world depression struck and Radical control over the protesting masses weakened, members of the oligarchy once more united long enough to direct the armed forces to evict the Radicals and return the government to the upper class for another decade.[21]

The oligarchy's panic and grab for political control in the 1930s proved very costly to the country's maturation. Coming after the middle class had begun to accumulate some power of its own, it deepened antagonisms between the two classes. Nothing that happened during the first half of the twentieth century did more to retard the development of a politics built on accommodation for mutual advantage that is so important to democratic government. At the precise moment that the society's growth and increasing diversity made a broad political consensus essential to political stability, the oligarchy chose to solidify divisions among social classes and increase middle- and lower-class resentment of their exclusion from politics. The result was a renewed provocation of an interclass conflict that the populist Juan Perón would rush to exploit before his rivals on the Marxist left could do likewise. By the time World War II arrived, Argentines did not need to be told that their subjugation by an unpaternal upper class would persist unless a more aggressive effort was made to end it.

The wealthy are not the only ones who are blamed for the failure to fashion stable, constitutional governments after 1930. Many fault the middle class and its habit of emulating the rich rather than reshaping society along bourgeois, moderate lines. With prosperity and immigration, the middle class had grown rapidly; by 1920 nearly one-third of the nation's urban dwellers were in the middle class. They never enjoyed much cohesion as a social force, however, sharing as they did little more than a desire to "make it" in the New World much as the upper class had done. The fact that the middle class was large and its members were of diverse origins made collaboration difficult. Despite the leadership of the Radical party, it proved weak and ineffective as a governing class, exhibiting the kind of woeful division and vacillation that now seems endemic to the Argentine political scene.[22]

Perhaps it is too much to have expected the middle class to fashion a democracy in such an elitist society. Immigrants learned quickly to live by the existing rules of the game. For many it was a small price to pay for what they gained materially, some of them becoming quite affluent in their new home. It was an exciting place to be for the immigrant accustomed to the immobility of traditional European village life, since few restrictions were placed on how he earned a living. Buenos Aires was truly the city of opportunity at the turn of the century, and taking advantage of it was all that preoccupied many people until they had settled in and discovered how little power they really had. As one Spanish observer noted on a visit to the Argentine capital in 1910, "The city is forever remaking and altering itself and everyone seems to live in a constant state of alert as if at war, stimulated by the preoccupation of enriching himself as quickly as possible."[23]

Today Argentine society resembles European ones more than it does others in Latin America. Its upper and middle classes are large and culturally sophisticated, and its working class has become one of the most urban and highly organized of any in the hemisphere.

Today only a minority of the upper class derive their income from the land, most having turned long ago to finance, commerce, and industry. They store much of their wealth outside the country and remain as worldly as before, traveling frequently to Europe and the United States to be among equals. Most still believe in their superiority to the rest of the nation, being as certain as their grandfathers that the country needs to be under the firm control of an enlightened elite in order to prosper. They have little good to say about the politicians who have ruled the country during the past forty years, and though more accepting of the armed forces and the necessity of their policing an unruly population, class differences make it impossible for them to welcome middle-class officers into their social circles. In short, they know that too much has changed since Perón came on the scene to allow them to control everything again, but that does not prevent their retaining substantial wealth and social prestige with the help of the investments they make abroad in more prosperous and reliable economies.

Just how many people are wealthy no one can say with any certainty, for nowhere do people disguise their lack of wealth so successfully. Argentines take great pride in pretending that they are more affluent than they really are; for them faking prosperity is not a sin, but a talent much admired. The worst examples of such pretensions have a seedy, rather pathetic quality to them, but the best are hardly distinguishable from the real thing. It is because so many of them are so good at exhibiting a veneer of affluence that Argentines seldom seem to suffer as much as they should from deep recessions and other calamities. It is hard to believe that the people one meets on the streets of Argentina's largest cities are members of a nation whose per capita income is only $2,000. Income is higher in cities than small towns, of course, and a visit to working-class suburbs and the poorest provinces makes one less incredulous, but discovery of the nation's regional poverties takes nothing away from the fact that there are few peoples anywhere who are more adept at convincing one that affluence is their normal condition.

The middle class is larger and more diverse ethnically and professionally than it was a half-century ago, and its incoherence as a social class continues. Most of middle-class Argentines eat well, own homes or apartments, and drive their own automobiles. Although they are among the nation's most productive farmers, the vast majority work in small businesses, government bureaucracies, or as professionals in cities. They take their recreation in private clubs, wear the latest fashions, and avoid all forms of heavy labor.

Many of them strive for personal economic independence, inspired by examples from the past—the cattleman's enrichment and the immigrants' success in business. It is to become a *propiocuentista,* or owner of the firm, that many enterprising people work so hard. Because of them, small businesses abound throughout the country. In difficult times many of them go bankrupt, but that seldom stops the ambitious from trying time and again. They are economic survivalists, forced to invent creative methods to operate as independent entrepreneurs, often taking great pride in their dexterity and defiance of the odds. Society pays a price for it, of course. The *propiocuentista* does not want to be reigned in by anyone, dedicated as he is to retaining independence by avoiding social control. Civic responsibility holds little appeal to a mentality that fears the consequences of conforming to standards set by authorities with societal concerns. Government can serve as a necessary protector and provider by giving business to entrepeneurs who are unable to make it on their own in unregulated markets, but few *propiocuentistas* believe they incur obligations to return the favor by paying taxes or obeying regulations intended to benefit the larger community. As far as they are concerned, Argentina is the land of opportunity not conformity. After all, that is why their ancestors came to this faraway land in the first place.

When it comes to politics, members of the middle class exhibit little coherence or consistency. They are downcast and pessimistic one moment and hopeful and cautiously optimistic the next. Many things bother them, from the imagined and real conspiracies of oligarchs and foreigners to the belligerence of a proletariat whose militancy earns it rewards at the expense of the middle class. They occasionally appeal to the armed forces to defend their interests, but they are fickle collaborators, welcoming protection for a time and then demanding that government be returned to them before the military has completed its assignment. In brief, the middle class is an essential part of the nation's power structure, one that supplies most of its bureaucrats, party leaders, and military officers, as well as the people who manage most of its businesses, yet it cannot run Argentina by itself. The nation's upper and lower classes have made certain of that.

It is the power of the working class that has grown the most in the past half-century. During the construction of railways and the building of metropolitan Buenos Aires, immigration changed the composition of the working class and rapidly increased its size. Industrialization added even more to its ranks. Just before the turn of the century, labor unions began forming to defend working-class interests, led primarily by European immigrants, who brought their proletarian ideologies with them. For a time they met repression, but migration to the cities from small provincial towns created a working mass living in close proximity, thus facilitating organization and political mobilization. It was General Juan Perón, and not the socialist and syndicalist leadership, that did the organizing, however, and Argentine labor has remained powerful and ideologically nonconformist ever since.

Nowhere else in Latin America has organized labor become as aggressive and politically potent nor labor's confrontations with authorities as routine. It is true that many Argentine workers do not belong to unions and that the 3.4 million who do lose as often as they triumph when they challenge the economic power structure. Nevertheless, nobody can rule the country for long without blue-collar collaboration, since so many of the nation's public and private enterprises depend on a highly skilled work force for their operation. That is why today few things preoccupy authorities more than finding ways to secure the conformity of a still dissatisfied work force.

Taken together, Argentina's social classes form a community whose members share no common understanding of what membership in a national community demands of them. The wealthiest members of society look abroad for their sustenance and comfort. The middle class would like to follow them, but its members must instead devote their energies to dealing rather atomistically with permanent economic insecurity. And the working class relies on its power of intrusion as an organized force to extract just rewards from employers and the nation's governments. The country is more European in ancestry than any Latin American country except neighboring Uruguay, yet its economic development has fallen far behind that of the once-poor countries from which its immigrant population came. And, though Buenos Aires is one of the world's most Caucasian, middle-class cities, Argentina's poorest provinces resemble poor regions of Chile or Colombia more than they do those of Spain or Italy. Regionalism survives within the country despite a pretense of nationality. Argentines love the same flag and proudly sing the same anthem, but the sophisticated Buenos Aires *porteño* has no doubts about his superiority to his provincial compatriots.

Demographically life has changed little for some time. Most people live in cities, 83 percent of them in towns with over 2,000 people, and 47 percent in cities of more than 500,000, the three largest being Buenos Aires (10 million) and Córdoba and Rosario (1 million each). By Latin American standards they are a well-educated people, though not as well educated as they pretend: only 32 percent of those over fourteen years of age have completed primary school, 10 percent secondary school, and just 3.3 percent have university degrees. The Argentine middle class, though proportionately the largest in Latin America, is not really a highly educated one, but rather one that has profited from the nation's scarcity of skilled labor, abundance of public employment, and the low cost of such necessities as food.[24]

Argentine women are the most educated in Latin America. In 1980 almost half of the university graduates were women, among them one-third of those from law school and one-fourth of the new doctors. Many women work full time and now compose 27 percent of the national work force, spread nearly equally among domestic employment, office work, schoolteaching, and sales. Is this evidence of the Argentine woman's "liberation"? Not really, since male dominance remains strong in the home as well as almost everywhere else in society. The scarcity of labor opened the door to female employment long ago, and economic decline and lower real wages in recent years have made two incomes more necessary than ever in order to maintain the standard of living previously enjoyed by middle- and lower-class families. Some women are trying to promote greater equality between the sexes and it is no longer considered as alien an issue as before, but progress is slow.[25]

Argentina today is a remnant of its glorious past and much more, a nation that has continued to mature economically and change socially despite losing much of its momentum fifty years ago. Its people are proud of their past, but they do not revel in it the way Mexicans do. They have no roots in an ancient pre-Colombian culture, nor did they fight a revolution that gave them a new political purpose in the twentieth century. Monuments to those who led the war for independence are evident in most city plazas, but there are no large museums of real quality anywhere in the country or "statues of liberty" that celebrate the arrival of millions of immigrants. For a long time those who came to its shores had trouble making up their minds about whether to settle there, and today their descendants seem too worried about the future to devote much time to celebrating their ambiguous past. When they tell their history, they do so in a very partisan manner, each version filled with short lists of heroes and long ones of villains. The Radical party faithful claim credit for breaking the oligarchy's monopoly and worship the memory of Hipólito Yrigoyen, the first Radical president (1916–22), and for them democracy's founding father. Peronists, in contrast, have little use for Yrigoyen, believing as they do that popular democracy began with the liberation of the working class by patrons Juan and Eva Perón in 1946. And not to be left out, conservative members of society show no respect for either view of history, convinced as they are that Radicals and Peronists have done more harm than good to what was once a rich nation. In short, they all love their country but can agree on little else.

An Aversion to Legitimacy

Argentine politics mystifies foreigners, who cannot comprehend why so many literate and sophisticated people find it so hard to live in peace with each other. They insist that abundant food, high employment, and a large middle class should guarantee greater civility and accommodation. The Argentines know otherwise, yet they also know that their politics is not as chaotic as it appears to people unfamiliar with it. Although military and civilian governments rise and fall according to no constitutional plan, the nation's power structure has changed very little during the past four decades. As a result, politics is quite repetitive, the military coming and going at almost regular intervals and civilian governments doing much the same. It is as if Argentines designed their own way of doing politics many years ago, and though it seems bizarre to others, they have stuck with it because it is what they know best.

When change has come it has been in the form of additions to the national power structure rather than subtractions from it. Periodically a movement has risen up, moved in, and ruled for a time before being forced out of office. There were three of them during the first half of this century, the Radicals governing for more than a decade starting in 1916, the oligarchy returning in 1930 and staying the same length of time, followed by the Peronists from 1946 until 1955. Each thought itself superior to its rivals only to be deposed by them with the military's help before consolidating control over society. The oligarchy engineered the removal of the Radicals in 1930, the Radicals celebrated the eviction of the oligarchy in 1943, and both of them cheered when Perón was tossed out in 1955 (see Table 2.1).

After they sent Perón into exile, his enemies within the armed forces set out to destroy his movement by forcing the working class into other parties. But the masses would not permit such house cleaning,

2.1 Elections and Presidents, 1916–83

Year	President	Party	Percentage of Popular Vote
1916	Hipólito Yrigoyen	UCR	45
1922	M. T. Alvear	UCR	48
1928	*Hipólito Yrigoyen	UCR	57
1931	General A. Justo	Concordancia	39
1937	*Roberto Ortiz	Concordancia	54
1946	General Juan Perón	Laborista	52
1951	*General Juan Perón	Peronist	62
1958	*Arturo Frondizi	UCRI	45
1963	*Arturo Illia	UCRP	25
1973	Hector Campora	Peronist	49
1973	*General Juan Perón	Peronist	62
1983	Raul Alfonsín	UCR	52

*Government overthrown by military coup

Party Identifications:

  UCR = Unión Civica Radical (Radical party)
  UCRI = Unión Civica Radical Intransigente
  UCRP = Unión Civica Radical del Pueblo

Sources: Cesar Reinaldo García, *Historia de los grupos y partidos politicos* (Buenos Aires: Sainte Claire, 1983); and *La Semana,* November 3, 1983, p. 69.

and when elections were held again in 1958 and Peronist candidates were prohibited from participating, the exiled Perón instructed his followers to vote for Radical candidate Arturo Frondizi without pledging their loyalty to him. Frondizi promised Perón that he would legalize Peronism after his election in defiance of military wishes, a bold gesture that caused many within the Radical party to bolt and form their own separate People's Radical party (UCRP) to contest the election with Frondizi's Intransigent Radicals (UCRI). Frondizi won easily with Peronist support, but he lost Perón's backing immediately afterward over his choice of economic austerity measures that were damaging to the labor rank and file. Nevertheless, despite military opposition, he went through with the legalization of Peronism, inviting the movement's candidates to contest with his own party in gubernatorial elections in March 1962, which they did, triumphing in the largest provinces and provoking another coup by anti-Peronist officers.

What to do next was determined after a year of conflict within the military between legalists who wanted to give elections another try and others who aspired to some form of permanent military rule. The former prevailed and authorized new elections in mid-1963, though again they prohibited the Peronist party's participation. This time UCRP candidate Arturo Illia won, though with only 25 percent of the popular vote since many Peronists cast blank ballots in protest of the entire process. Illia governed for three years, suffering congressional losses to Peronists when he too legalized them in 1965. A year later the military took over once more, though this time they did so inspired by much more ambitious objectives. Encouraged by many in the business community who longed for less politics, the same "legalist" officers who had called for elections in 1963 deposed Illia and took complete control for themselves, creating an authoritarian government devoted to accelerating the nation's economic growth and reorganizing its politics from the bottom up. Politicians were made unwelcome while military officers and civilian technocrats ran the nation, delivering on their promises to accelerate economic growth. But in mid-1969 the public protested massively, shaking General Juan Carlos Onganía's government to its foundations. A year later his colleagues removed him and began a slow process leading to the holding of new elections in 1973.

The temptation to invite Perón back to subdue the country's contumacious labor movement was great in 1973. The seventy-five-year-old exile cultivated confidence in his ability to restore order and was brought home after eighteen years abroad to lead his party to victory in the 1973 elections. Prohibited from candidacy himself, he endorsed stand-in Hector Campora, who won easily only to be pushed aside so that Perón could be elected president six months later. The elderly general's tenure was brief as he died of natural causes before his first year had ended, leaving the presidency to his wife and vice-president Isabel. Argentina reached a low point during the next two years as terrorism grew while the economy plummeted. To no one's surprise and to the relief of almost everyone the armed forces took over again in mid-1976.

Service commanders, as they had done in 1966, promised to reconstruct the nation's economy and politics, convinced that it was the only way to avoid repetition of the Peronist disaster. While their civilian advisors went to work on the economy they unleashed a brutal, secret war against terrorists and leftists of almost any stripe. They kidnapped and killed over 9,000 persons and boasted of having saved the nation from destruction while their subjects cowered in fright. But when General Jorge Videla turned the presidency over to General Roberto Viola in 1981 as planned, the authoritarian edifice began to crack. Protests against its punishing economic policies grew in the business community, and confidence in the government dropped when foreign debts rose astronomically and the peso collapsed in value. An attempt to shore up the regime was made in late 1981 by General Leopoldo Galtieri, but when he went to war in the Falklands and lost, he took military dictatorship with him. In 1983 officers departed for their bases and gave civilians a chance to start all over again.

A bemused but troubled Argentine observer summed it up well when he concluded, "We have created a system that permits all sectors to alternate in power despite continuous interruptions of the formal political process. It is as if there is a tacit agreement that no government should be allowed to endure. In this each sector can take its turn in power without ever having to share it."[26]

But there was no real tacit agreement on how or when to exchange office, only determinations by each "sector" to avoid succumbing to its rivals entirely. The result was a cyclical politics in which civilian and military governments rose and fell at regular intervals without anyone planning it that way. The regularity is stunning: during the last twenty years there were two civilian governments that lasted three years, each time separated by two military ones that ruled for exactly seven years each.

If the country's political history is marked by additions and cycles, it also reveals an obvious irresolution of fundamental problems of political legitimacy. Time and again Argentines have found it impossible to agree on how they are to be governed. It started with the oligarchy's desire to make politics a reflection of the distribution of economic power in the country rather than allow it to become a means by which those less well off could compensate for their economic disadvantages. When they finally allowed the middle class into the government in 1916, it was understood that the latter's elevation was only to be a partial one. It was also a brief one, for the oligarchs returned in 1930, trying harder than ever to rig elections and exclude the masses from politics. However, their doing so provoked a rebelliousness that would remain long after they were evicted in 1943. Thereafter it seemed that anyone who governed the country invited rebellion whether or not he ruled repressively, succumbing to opposition before his tenure had expired.

Argentines cannot help but wonder why they have gone through all of this. There was nothing inevitable about it. Mexicans have not suffered a military coup in seventy years, and after a century of dictatorship the Venezuelans adopted a multiparty democracy that has operated without interruption since 1959. Even Brazil, after two decades of military government, found the restoration of constitutional politics a smoother and more dignified process than the Argentine military every has.

Compromise and consensus have not come very easily in Argentina at any time in its history. Those who ruled the country when its modernization began were averse to sharing real power with those below them.

And when the oligarchs were finally forced from office in the 1940s by the Peronists, they were shown little more respect than they had shown their victims previously. And on it went, with the Peronists popularizing authoritarian politics and reinforcing antagonisms in society and partisanship in government. How they managed the feat and what it has meant to contemporary politics is our next subject. Juan Perón tried twice to transform his country, once beginning in 1946 and again in 1973, but he came up short each time. His death in 1974 ended his quest, but his politics survive him, a little weakened by the loss of its founder but still enthusiastically embraced by millions.

Notes

1. For a compact summary of the nineteenth century, see James R. Scobie, *Argentina: A City and a Nation* (New York: Oxford University Press, 1971), chs. 1–4.

2. Detailed accounts of development on the pampas are given in James R. Scobie, *Revolution on the Pampas: A Social History of Argentine Wheat 1860–1910* (Austin: University of Texas Press, 1964); and Roberto Cortes Conde, *El progreso argentino, 1880–1914* (Buenos Aires: Sudamericana, 1979).

3. Horacio Giberti, "Granos, carnes, y tierra," *Primera historia integral 42* (Buenos Aires: 1980), p. 35. Demand for Argentine beef rose when hoof and mouth disease in France cut live shipments from there to Great Britain and British involvement in the Boer War increased demand at home for frozen beef.

4. Scobie, *Revolution on the Pampas*.

5. Jorge Federico Sábato, *La pampa prodiga: Claves de una frustración* (Buenos Aires: CIESA, 1980), chs. 1–2. Immigrants were also attracted to the countryside by land developers who tried to create new enterprises outside the pampas region. In Córdoba, Entre Rios, and Santa Fe, land companies established colonies in the 1880s and attracted Europeans to them by advertising abroad. See Manuel Bejarano, "Inmigración y estructuras tradicionales en Buenos Aires," in *Los fragmentos del poder: oligarquía a la poliar44ía argentina,* ed. Torcuarto Di Tella and Tulio Halperin Donghi (Buenos Aires: Jorge Alvarez, 1969), pp. 101–147.

6. Scobie, *Argentina,* p. 232.

7. Oscar Cornblit, "Inmigrantes y empresarios en la política argentina," in *Los fragmentos del poder,* pp. 394–401.

8. Gobierno Argentina, Dirección de Estadisticas y Censos, *Censo-Serie B,* 1983, pp. xi–xx.

9. Ibid. It has been estimated that in 1870 Indians formed 12 percent of the population, mulattoes 14 percent, and pure Europeans only 3 percent, the other 71 percent being mestizo.

10. For a recent history of Jewish migration to Argentina, one should consult Eugene F. Sofer, *From Pale to Pampa: A Social History of the Jews in Buenos Aires* (New York: Holmes & Meier, 1982). The most recent controversy over anti-Semitism was touched off by journalist Jacobo Timerman, editor of *La Opinión* newspaper, when he was jailed and tortured by the armed forces and then released under foreign pressure and allowed to migrate to Israel. Timerman blames anti-Semitism for his persecution and criticizes Argentine Jews for pretending that the problem does not exist in order to get along as best

they can. Many of them, in turn, complain that Timerman glorified his own suffering by cloaking the whole episode with memories of the Holocaust. After Alfonsín's election he returned to Argentina in 1984 to edit the daily *La Razón*. See his *Prisoner Without a Name, Cell Without a Number* (New York: Knopf, 1981).

11. Cornblit, "Inmigrantes y empresarios en la política argentina," p. 405.

12. Dirección de Estadísticas y Censos, *Censo-Serie B*, 1983. The data on German residents is taken from Ronald C. Newton, *German Buenos Aires, 1900–1933: Social Change and Cultural Crisis* (Austin: University of Texas Press, 1977).

13. Arturo O'Connell, "La Argentina en la depresión: los problems de una economía abierto," *Desarrollo económico* 23, no. 92 (January–March 1984): 479–488.

14. Javier Villanueva, "Economic Development," in *Prologue to Peron: Argentina in Depression and War: 1930–1943*, ed. Mark Falcoff and Ronald Dolkart (Berkeley: University of California Press, 1975), pp. 56–82.

15. See Gary W. Wynia, *Argentina in the Postwar Era* (Albuquerque: University of New Mexico Press, 1978), pp. 26–27, for more details.

16. O'Connell, "La Argentina en la depresión," pp. 488 ff.

17. Villanueva, "Economic Development," pp. 67–68.

18. Livio Guillermo Kuhl, *Una política industrial para la Argentina* (Buenos Aires: Club de Estudio, 1983), p. 73.

19. Juan J. Llach, "El Plan Pinedo de 1940, su significado histórico y los orígenes de la economía política del peronismo," *Desarrollo económico* 23, no. 92 (January–March 1984). Llach argues that the "internal market" strategy advocated by Peronists at their formation in 1944 was an adaptation of the ideas put forward by conservative Pinedo three years before. Pinedo was appalled by the Peronists' abandonment of free trade, but that did not stop them from turning his critique of the primary product export economy and advocacy of industrialization into a nationalist and protectionist justification for industrial development.

20. Scobie, *Argentina*, p. 173.

21. On divisions within the rural oligarchy, see Peter H. Smith, *Politics and Beef in Argentina* (New York: Columbia University Press, 1969); and on politics during the 1930s, Peter H. Smith, *Argentina and the Failure of Democracy: Conflict Among Political Elites: 1904–1955* (Madison: University of Wisconsin Press, 1974); and Mark Falcoff and Ronald Dolkart, *Prologue to Peron*.

22. Scobie, *Argentina*, p. 175.

23. James R. Scobie, *Buenos Aires: Plaza to Suburb, 1870–1910* (New York: Oxford University Press, 1974), p. 232.

24. Dirreción de Estadísticas y Censos, *Censo B*.

25. Ibid.

26. Guido Di Tella, *Perón–Perón 1973–1976* (Buenos Aires: Sudamericana, 1983), p. 319.

3

The Peronist Invention

"I am a Peronist, fanatically Peronist," Eva Perón loved to tell anyone who would listen. And when she did she spoke for millions of Argentines who were equally proud of their newly found fanaticism. Together they helped Juan Perón create a politics that was impatient with complexity and suspicious of foreigners and oligarchs and one that revered the *descamisados* (shirtless ones), as Perón called his masses. No labor movement in Latin America has become stronger or more contentious than Argentina's, not even those in "revolutionary" Mexico or highly industrialized Brazil. That is why authorities who persecute the working class continually fail to subdue it.

A General's Ambition

Juan Perón was an enterprising politician who wanted to make Argentina a powerful nation at a time when its future was in doubt. He was not a revolutionary but an audacious opportunist, whose personal ambition and good timing led him to use the working class to break the oligarchy's grip on the nation. But it was the oligarchy's profits and not its property that the Peronists confiscated, committed as they were from the outset to making the state the patron of entrepreneurs and workers alike rather than the nemesis of either. Their failures were many, and the country is still paying for them, but however great and costly they were, few Peronists regret what they did.

It is not hard to understand why something like Peronism would arise in postwar Argentina. The nation's spectacular economic boom had begun to taper off before the 1929 depression. Conservative efforts to patch up the economy during the 1930s were moderately successful, but they did not dispel concern about the country's economic vulnerability or prevent rising anxiety about how to cope with the adverse effects of a new world war. On the political front things looked even less inspiring. The Radical party, plagued by internal division and embarrassed by its collaboration with the ruling oligarchs before the war, seemed to have lost its drive and originality. And ruling conservatives inspired little confidence in their ability to offer anything new when conditions demanded it.

Argentina was changing but no one appeared ready to meet the challenge. Industrialization had progressed substantially after 1930, supplying more of the national product than agriculture by 1940. With the growth of industry came a larger working class, causing a new political concern for military officers who were determined to prevent its radicalization by socialist and anarchist intellectuals and labor leaders who led the attack against capitalism. What to do about all of this was unclear at first, nationalist officers having decided only that it was a problem far beyond the capacity of the lethargic oligarchy to solve. Finally the armed forces took it upon themselves to set things right, deposing the ruling oligarchs in June 1943.

Their objectives were never very clear, and that is why it was relatively easy for one among them to seize the initiative and offer solutions of his own. Juan Perón adroitly exploited fear of working-class radicalization, offering to take care of the nation's proletariat if others would give him the authority he needed to accomplish the task. No one fully understood where it would all lead, but that was to Perón's advantage, as it would be in virtually everything he did. He was determined to win the allegiance of organized labor and use it to the state's advantage as well as his own. If it worked, the government would become the patron rather than the oppressor of a compliant working class that had discarded its revolutionary ambitions in exchange for a host of new economic and political privileges. It would require substantial change in the function of government, beginning with its transformation from just a regulatory mechanism into a beneficent provider that guaranteed the economic security of those in its care. But Perón managed it, needing only three years to make his way to the presidency and three more to win over millions of people who were delighted by the attention and affection he gave them.

Argentines will never agree about how much Perón actually accomplished. Too much is at stake, even today, to permit anything resembling objectivity. Even scholars are not certain about the politics he practiced, some finding it fascist in character, others simply *caudillismo* in modern dress, and some an innovative version of populist democracy. Fascination with it is matched by frustration with its refusal to fit neatly into familiar categories of politics. But its ambiguity and unconventional character was of no concern to Perón; he delighted in being unique, seeing himself the creator of an innovative political synthesis that he boasted was neither capitalist nor socialist, neither authoritarian nor liberal democratic.

It was his political practice and not political theory that distinguished Perón from his peers, however, for his grand synthesis was always more something of mind than deed. He was a military officer who liked politics, one who matured in an organization whose fatuous nature tutored its members as much in bureaucratic conspiracy as in weaponry. He was also the kind who believed that leadership involved commanding the loyalty of people much like the general did his troops by leading them in conquest and sharing its bounty with them afterward. There was always something Romanesque about him, no doubt due in part to his admiration for the style of Benito Mussolini, whom he observed at first hand while stationed briefly in Italy just before the war. He was not the country's first military politician, nor would he be the last, but he quickly proved himself to be the most adroit at outwitting civilians at their own game.

There was nothing in Perón's early life to predict his becoming the nation's most powerful leader. His grandfather was a physician and senator, but his father turned to farming, never rising above the middle class. Born in the small town of Lobos in Buenos Aires province on October 8, 1895, Perón was of Sardinian, Basque, and Scottish ancestry, nothing at all unusual in this country of European immigrants. He went to school in Buenos Aires, his parents hoping that he would become a physician, but when the time came he chose the military academy, claiming later that he did so primarily to stay with friends. An average student, he received his commission as a second lieutenant in 1913 and began what should have been a normal career in the increasingly professionalized, German-trained Argentine army.[1]

He rose through the ranks without particular distinction, developing a reputation for industry, lack of pretension, athletic ability, and success as a teacher of noncommissioned officers. It was to teaching and writing military history that he devoted his energies during the 1930s, spending some time as an instructor at the military academy, where he became a lecturer admired by students for his ability to simplify complex matters of history and military strategy for audiences lacking in university educations. This experience served him well when he later chose to become the nation's "instructor" from the presidential podium, the first leader ever to speak directly to the working masses in language inspiring to them, at his most effective when appearing before them as the enthusiastic officer intent on leading them into battle against the oligarchy and British imperialists.

Critical to Perón's political education was his being stationed in Italy from July 1939 until December 1940, where he watched Mussolini and the Italian fascists at work. He was not so naive as to believe that he could simply imitate the Italians back home, but the idea of building a stronger nation using bold and popular leadership to mobilize people and resources was quite appealing to him and seemed to be exactly what Argentina needed at the time. Many people worried about the economy's decay after the war, and in his militaristic way Perón convinced many of them that he, like Mussolini, could cure the nation's ills by mobilizing its people for the pursuit of common objectives much as the fascists had done in Europe a decade before. He was not the first to take his inspiration from such sources, of course. Lieutenant General José Uriburu, the leader of the coup that removed Radical party president Hipólito Yrigoyen in 1930, also believed that fascism was the answer to depression-related problems, and only the oligarchy's fear of losing control over him prevented Uriburu from carrying through with his plot. But in 1943 the military had turned against the oligarchy, and to many people, frustrated as they had been by a long depression and a slow recovery that had revealed their frightening vulnerability to decisions taken in European capitals by bankers, generals, and prime ministers, Perón's bold approach to the country's reconstruction was inspiring.[2]

He started his quest a few months before the coup, when he and some colleagues formed the Grupo de Oficiales Unidos (GOU), a secret military "lodge" intended to bring officers of like mind together to formulate their solutions to the nation's problems and prepare a strategy for securing their implementation by military superiors should they take over the government. Lodges had been common within the army for a couple of decades, serving as secret seminars for would-be conspirators, most of whom were devoted more to advancing each other within the army than to political matters.[3] The creators of the GOU had both objectives in mind, but it was their political ambitions that would distinguish them. To begin with, they were disturbed by the army's loss of public esteem as a result of its close association with the corrupt and increasingly incompetent Castillo administration, itself the unexpected result of more tolerant Roberto Ortiz being forced by illness to relinquish the presidency to his reactionary vice president Castillo in 1940. Equally influential was their fear that Castillo or his soon-to-be-elected pro-British successor would yield to U.S. pressure to end Argentine neutrality, something nationalists like Perón abhorred doing. Some of them favored the Axis powers, but whether they did or not, they felt Argentina had more to gain by staying out of the war than it did from endorsing either side. And finally, they were concerned that a decade of the oligarchy's repressing the working class would prompt communist and syndicalist mobilization of the urban masses toward the achievement of radical change, something that they, committed as they were to the essentials of mixed capitalism, could not tolerate. Since the conservatives had lost their touch, they had to go, but their eviction in 1943 was never intended to allow anything but the creation of a new ruling class that was even better equipped to prevent the radicalization of national politics. Even Perón agreed with that. What his colleagues lacked at the outset was a concrete plan for accomplishing the task, and it was to creating one that he devoted himself while superiors took charge of the nation's governance.[4]

His three-year assault on the presidency was the kind from which legends are made, and the Peronists love to recite it.[5] It was indeed a spectacular triumph, but there is little in his good timing and tactical maneuvering that envious politicians would find all that mysterious. He was just better than they were at taking advantage of the anxieties caused by the country's isolation during the war and its hostility toward Great Britain and more adept at exploiting the desire of the working class for recognition and favor than some of its own leaders were. He knew that Argentina would never be the same again after the war regardless of who led the nation. But he, more than most, had some idea, albeit a very crude one, of where the nation might go in the postwar years. Most important, he knew how to communicate his popular message to everyone who needed to hear it, using some of the same talents that had made him a popular teacher of noncommissioned officers.

Peronizing the Proletariat

The coup's leaders rewarded Perón with an undersecretaryship of war, a position which he exploited to advance his GOU colleagues within the army, but it was his work in the obscure labor secretaryship that contributed the most to his political triumph. His strategy was daring though quite simple. Rather than repress organized labor as the conservatives had done, or allow them to be led by parties on the left, as would surely happen if the country were governed democratically, he set out to incorporate labor leaders into ruling circles, making the federal bureaucracy their patron and them wards of the state. The idea was not new; European fascists had tried it and so had Mexico's revolutionary leaders like Lazaro Cárdenas a decade before. The scheme was corporatist in nature, based on the linking of private economic interests in capitalist economies to the state in an organized and centrally supervised manner in order to save capitalism from self-destruction.

The labor movement was not eager to sign up at first. Perón was a stranger to them, an officer with no obvious affinity for unions that had been led for over fifty years by civilian anarchists, socialists, and syndicalists. They were born when working conditions were deplorable and wages low, prompting agitation for reform. In 1895 there were 23,000 industrial enterprises in Argentina, primarily in furniture, food, printing, metal work, and construction, which employed 170,000 persons. Most of the latter were foreign born, having migrated there a few years before, bringing their proletarian ideologies with them from Italy and Spain. Typographical workers were the first to organize in 1877, but it was not until 1901 that a group of unions launched the country's first national labor federation. Their exclusion from politics by the ruling oligarchy and maltreatment by their employers made revolutionary doctrines popular among workers. But they were divided from the beginning over matters of political strategy, some preferring the Socialist party practice of accommodation and others mass protests intended to force concessions by authorities. Neither strategy achieved a great deal, however, since authorities, be they Radicals in the 1920s or conservatives after 1930, refused to concede much to the working class. Typical was the way acclaimed populist Hipólito Yrigoyen, elected president by the Radical party in the country's first real democratic elections in 1916, responded to his working-class critics. When strikes escalated into unprecedented mass protests in 1919, Yrigoyen turned the police loose on them. Then he signed legislation granting them the eight-hour workday and pension programs, promising the working class more if they would stay in line and accept his paternal rule over them. It was a mixed blessing, obviously, but never enough to compensate for their losses after being hit by economic depression, unemployment, and renewed repression in the 1930s.[6]

Disputes among its ideologues also weakened the labor movement during the depression years. Nevertheless, socialists and syndicalists united long enough to launch a new national federation in 1930, the General Confederation of Labor (CGT), modeling it on the French CGT, then Europe's most prominent labor organization. It was dominated initially by the railway workers and included only a few industrial unions, but by taking advantage of proletarian discontent with the oligarchy's heavy-handed ways, its leaders converted many to the cause of mass protest against capitalism itself. Though their ability to affect the government's behavior was slight thanks to its power of repression, fear of their mobilizing the working class toward such ends worried military officers like Perón as much as it did the nation's wealthy when they witnessed unprecedented growth in the industrial work force as the country entered the 1940s.

The migration of thousands of unskilled laborers to Buenos Aires during the war had created an immense base for mass organization. Laborers in some of the new industries were incorporated into existing unions, but most remained unorganized during their first few years of employment. The challenge for anyone eager to take the proletarian cause away from its more radical champions was to deal with unorganized labor before CGT unions did while at the same time dividing and weakening the CGT. It was a monumental task, and few in the Argentine bourgeoisie could even conceive of it being done, let alone carry it out. Laborers were not sitting outside their factories waiting for a Perón to lead them. They had organizations eager to mobilize them that were led by men with a half-century of experience, albeit a rather disappointing one, but one that had taught them what they were up against in the nation's well-entrenched and reactionary upper class. Still, Perón, undeterred by the odds, went after the labor movement and did not stop until he had completed one of the greatest robberies anyone had seen. It is doubtful that even he knew exactly where it would end or the tactics that he would employ along the way. But the more his presidential ambitions rose and his success at wooing labor leaders grew, the more confidence he gained in his ability to ride them to the top.

There are many "critical moments" in Argentine history when decisions were made whose consequences are still felt today, but few were more consequential than a little-known event that occurred on May 24, 1944. Until that time most labor leaders had spurned Perón's overtures, making it clear that they had no intention of cooperating with the military regime. Some among them, including the leadership of the two largest organizations, even went so far as to announce a "liberty march" to be held on May 1, 1944, to protest the government's authoritarian ways. But just as they were preparing for their protest they received invitations from the government to join with it in the celebration of a national independence day on May 24. It was a clever move aimed at dividing the labor movement and securing for the government whatever popular support its seduction of labor bosses could deliver. To the government's delight it worked. Union leaders found themselves trapped between a call for a demonstration of their patriotism and their desire to represent class interests. By a vote of six to four they chose to call off their protest, allowing their cooptation by authorities then advised by Perón.[7]

Perón solidified his ties with labor by securing for them government decrees that guaranteed the members of responsive unions retirement benefits, social security programs, paid vacations, and the like. He also appealed to their nationalism, adroitly attracting wartime neutralists away from socialists and communists who campaigned for taking the side of the Allies. Step by step he drew one union after another from its old ideological stance to a new, pragmatic one that put them under the supervision of an increasingly paternal state. In doing so he also elevated labor leaders long ignored and persecuted by authorities to membership within the government. It meant a great deal to the working class, not just because they had so long been denied respect, but also because it was obvious that their inclusion within the government meant that they, as a political force, would attain the power needed to guarantee their remaining at the center of national politics thereafter.

Winning the Prize

The cultivation of working-class support was only one part of Perón's presidential campaign. He also had to prevent his military colleagues from blocking his quest, a distinct possibility since he and his GOU friends were a small faction whose ambitions were resented from the outset by senior officers. Though Perón secured appointment as vice president in July 1944, rival officers did not give up their attempts to stop him until he had defeated them in a direct confrontation fifteen months later in October 1945. Fearful that his popularity among the working class would catapult him into elections planned for 1946, they had him arrested in mid-October and carted off to prison on Martin Garcia Island just off shore from Buenos Aires. Unfortunately, they allowed him to bid farewell to his followers over radio just before departure, touching off unprecedented labor protests that culminated on October 17, when thousands came out of the working-class suburbs to concentrate before the Casa Rosada to demand that then president General Edelmiro Farrell release Perón from prison, which he reluctantly did. The army always finds it hard to deal with mass demonstrations; they can break the back of union strikes but popular rebellion frightens them, so on October 17 they yielded, bringing Perón to the presidential balcony to receive the cheers of the masses, as he would do often during the next decade.[8]

U.S. paranoia and the Radicals' high principles also contributed to Perón's triumph four months later. From the outset foreigners appeared to be more worried about him than most Argentines were. The U.S. government feared after war broke out in Europe that Germany would extend its influence into South America if no resistance was put up by local authorities. Argentine neutrality had frustrated their efforts, and the creation of a government whose members exhibited sympathy for the Axis powers seemed to confirm their worst fears in 1943. The latter was encouraged by the dispatches of sensationalist correspondents like Ray Josephs, who warned Americans about Perón, insisting that his

> strong sense of showmanship, his Goering-like uniforms and his constant smile hide a relentless drive which insures getting him what he's after. . . . The colonel's speech bore the old Nazi-flavored refrain that employers, workers and the State were the parties to all social problems and that they and nobody else would arrange the solution "avoiding the useless squandering of energies and values."[9]

He continued:

> His methods have a familiar ring; he believes in striking the enemy with audacity, taking advantage of his opponents' errors, gaining time and then advancing quickly. He speaks the language of the *calle* [street], likes good eating and hearty living, and goes to workmen's *boliches* [bars] to talk to them and convince them he is their true pal.[10]

Hardly the portrait of an Adolf Hitler or Benito Mussolini, yet one that nevertheless was cause for worry in Washington. No matter that Buenos Aires was farther from New York than was Paris; anyone who was not a U.S. ally was a potential enemy that might give strategic advantage to the Germans in a war that included battles for control of the Atlantic, North and South. But such reports, when read in Argentina, were just what Perón needed to promote nationalism. Nothing helped him more than U.S. Ambassador Spruille Braden's delivery of the same message. Braden has made up his mind before arriving in Argentina in mid-1945 that Perón had to be stopped, convinced that he and his military colleagues were "bred by the Nazis." At his urging the State Department issued a "Blue Book" just two weeks before the 1946 election warning Argentines of the mistake they would make by electing him. Characteristically Perón turned it to his advantage, blaming the Americans for trying to replace Great Britain as Argentina's subjugator.[11]

The Radical party was the only remaining obstacle. It was the nation's largest organized party prior to 1945 and one that expected to triumph over conservatives when elections were held. Perón's opponents within the military knew this and were tempted to conspire with the Radicals to lend them what additional help they might need to assure victory. But true to their high principles, the Radicals refused military overtures, a decision no doubt bolstered by unjustified confidence in their ability to defeat the newly mobilized Peronists. When they finally realized what their chances really were they had no choice but to turn to the conservatives and several minor parties for help, forming an electoral alliance behind a Radical presidential candidate that called itself the Unión Democrática. But it was too little and too late: when the votes were counted 52 percent had gone to Juan Perón.[12]

The Peronist State

Mobilizing the working class against the nation's powerful oligarchy hardly seemed the best way to unite the nation. But the contradiction never bothered Perón, for it was really a mock battle that he fought with the oligarchy. He had set out to prevent a class struggle rather than advance one, and winning the favor of labor and then taming it was how he intended to do so. Critical to success was his making the *"oligarquia"* the enemy while promoting industrial development by lending assistance to private industry. He and Evita railed against the rich, attacking their ostentatious wealth, ridiculing their love for private clubs and horse racing and their affection for the British, feeding the *descamisados* (shirtless masses) on the illusion that they were taking control of the country from its richest members. Actually, nothing of the sort occurred. What he took from the oligarchy was its government, not its property. It was good populist theater, not revolutionary politics, and ten years later, when Perón fled, the oligarchy was still there, bruised and vengeful, but not seriously damaged by Peronism.

The Peronist state never became as corporatist as Perón wanted, nor did it unite social classes as much as he intended. It was partisan and favored the working class while advancing Argentine capitalism by making government as much the benefactor of industry as organized labor. Its organization began with the formation of the Partido Laborista and its nomination of Perón for the presidency on October 24, 1945. Labor leaders organized the party, but they were joined in it by dissident Radical party politicians from the Unión Cívica Radical–Junta Renovadora, many of them critics of their own party's leadership for its collusion with the ruling oligarchy during the late 1930s. The Centros Independientes formed the party's third constituency, including within its ranks people from all over the political spectrum, among them provincial conservatives who detested the Radical party and die-hard nationalists who hoped that Perón would become a New World fascist.[13] Its organization left much to be desired, but that did not matter for the numbers were there. Later he would reorganize it as the Partido Peronista, transforming it into an instrument of personal control. Ostensibly a democratic party that drew its authority from its grass-roots *unidades basicas,* or basic units, it was actually a hierarchy commanded by Perón in the role of supreme leader. Military concepts, not democratic ones, defined its operation, with "tactical commands" being made responsible to "strategic commands." Unlike the Radical party, which was created by outsiders who used it to agitate and campaign their way into the government, the Peronist party became primarily the instrument of authorities, who drew on their control over the state and the resources it allowed them to keep the party going.

Essential to Perón's success was his sustaining control over organized labor after it had elected him president. It was never automatic since labor leaders occasionally found themselves torn between their deep, and often radical, political ambitions and the conformity Perón demanded of them. He insisted that they forsake their old ideological motives for more pragmatic ones that fit into his design for the country and that they remain loyal to a military officer who lacked their proletarian origins. Not one to take chances, Perón had secured the decree of a new labor law in October 1945, a law that would prove invaluable to his domination over unions in later years. Modeled on Mussolini's legislation, it forced a concentration of power within the labor movement and thrust government into the supervision of its compliance with a very politically motivated plan of reorganization. In essence it required that authorities recognize only one national labor organization in each industry, effectively eliminating dissident unions that defied the orders of the "official" ones. Some resistance to him remained within the CGT, however, and it was not until February 8, 1947, when he secured the removal of Luis Gay from the secretary generalship of the confederation, that he felt secure. Though supportive of Perón, Gay had resisted complete subordination to him, committed as he was to an "independent" labor movement in principle. Perón gave up on winning Gay's allegiance and replaced him with a more subservient Aurelio Hernández, thus finishing the creation of his "verticalist" command structure within the CGT.

The government's domination over the CGT, though great, was never as complete as Perón would have liked, despite his best efforts to assure it. It is no secret that he had to intervene many times to terminate unauthorized strikes by locals, whose leaders took it upon themselves to improve salaries and working conditions. But, each time they defied him, Perón struck back, jailing rebels and replacing them with new leaders whom he authorized to reward loyal members with more pesos. Such methods corrupted and divided the labor movement often, always presenting union bosses with difficult political choices. Their loyalty to Perón and the unity that it gave the entire movement was a source of immense power which they needed to defend themselves in a society where most power had been concentrated at the top. However, it was often in their own interest, especially after Perón fled, to ignore his orders and pursue a more self-aggrandizing strategy aimed at satisfying their own political and economic needs, sometimes by cooperating with governments he opposed. There would never be an easy way out, for even though unity brought power, it invited the kind of subjugation that many individual unions found disadvantageous to their local interests.[14]

Eva Perón added something special to her husband's arsenal of instruments for staying popular. She was the perfect populist propagandist, thriving on the adoration of the masses:

> To her followers, she was Evita, a selfless woman who worked tirelessly to improve the lives of workers, destitute women, and needy children, totally dedicated to the downtrodden because she was born poor like them, and so committed to them that she sacrificed her life on their behalf. To her enemies, however, she was only an ambitious actress, a trollop who rose to the top by using countless men, a hypocrite interested in money, jewels, and luxurious clothes, and a vengeful woman intent on accumulating power to make Argentine society pay for the shame heaped upon her because of her background.[15]

Her political career began just before his election in 1946. They had met a year before when they participated in fund raising for victims of an earthquake in the northern provinces, she a twenty-four-year-old actress of very modest fame, and he a forty-eight-year-old widower and rising power within the army. She moved in with him and watched as his campaign for the presidency began to develop, and then joined the protest when he was arrested in October 1945. She did not march the masses from their homes to the Casa Rosada as myth would have it, but was one of several from the general's inner circle to speak up for his release. It worked and they were married four days later.

He took advantage of her oratorical skill and sudden fame, making her a special liaison with the masses. For her fans she became a direct link to authorities, one that allowed them to bypass the CGT hierarchy whenever she agreed to carry their messages to cabinet ministers. She was also a very unique social worker, the director of her own Fundación Eva Perón, from which she launched projects for the young, aged, and poor in barrios around Buenos Aires. She was especially fond of holding court with poor ladies who would stand in line for hours to make their requests to her and receive money or goods in return. The Fundación's responsibilities and capital grew rapidly. By 1950, it was constructing schools, workers' resorts, and union headquarters and was one of the biggest spenders in the government. Many people benefited from its projects, but its value was always more symbolic than substantive, for it reinforced the notion that the masses had acquired benefactors whose name was Perón.[16]

Evita's projects brought inspiration to the needy, especially women, but her goal was never their "liberation" as understood by feminists today. While she thrived on the masses' adoration, she always subordinated herself to Perón publicly. He was her leader as well as theirs, she told women when she launched the Partido Peronista Feminina, the party's women's branch, in 1949. She encouraged political activism among women, but insisted that it not come at the expense of their fulfilling their duties to their husbands. This message of devotion to the masculine leader was sent into schools through the required reading of her book *La Razón de mi vida* (The Purpose of My Life), which called on children to be as dedicated to him as she was. Always feigning a humility that was transparent to all but her most devoted followers, she delighted in playing the role of the humble companion of the greatest man Argentina had ever known.

Her death in 1952 hurt Perón and his government. But it would be incorrect to blame his downfall on her absence. The working class remained loyal to him until the end, and the officers who eventually overthrew him made their first try in 1951, when she was still alive. It did take some of the glitter away, however, at a time when the economy was in trouble and he was forced to impose austerity on his supporters to deal with the crisis. For many it was like a movie ending with a tragic finish while life carried on. At the same time it gave Peronist propagandists the material for a legend of great and tragic proportions with which to remind Peronists of their origins and purpose. It was for Evita as well as themselves that they had to fight on, if only to justify her faith in them and vindicate the price that she had paid for her people. It was powerful stuff and the Peronist leadership knew it. The military's theft of her embalmed body and secret transport of it to Milan, Italy, in 1955 only helped the myth makers who made the return of their saint a cause for unifying the flock. And it eventually paid off: Evita was brought home in 1974 when the Peronists ruled again.

A Populist Paradise Never Reached

Perón's nationalism and his populist economics were not simply the wild ideas of an unscrupulous politician out to accumulate mass support. There was much to be concerned about in Argentina at the end of World War II. After recovering some from the depression, the country's economic future remained in doubt. Great Britain was gone as a trading partner and capital was needed to advance the nation's industrialization, but Argentines were not certain where it would come from after the war; moreover, Radical party politicians and the military opposed relying as heavily as before on foreigners to supply it. Nor were they certain how much of the European market they could capture at war's end, especially if the United States took it upon itself to supply the damaged nations the grain they needed. Some even warned of another world war that would isolate Argentina again, this one fought by the United States and the Soviet Union. Because Argentines did not want to be caught unprepared for more isolation, they felt compelled to strengthen their position economically as best they could.

Perón chose to prepare the country for the unknown by making it more independent of its trading partners with additional industrialization fostered by mass consumption. His approach was akin to that of the American New Deal except for his greater reliance on the expropriation of foreign-owned utilities and market regulation. Backed by substantial gold reserves built up during World War II, he used his authority to turn the state into the economy's manager. Crude in design and execution, the approach consisted of taking over most utilities and all banking, purchasing railways from their British owners, imposing state control over the export of commodities, and supervising labor–management relations. He also raised tariffs to protect industries from foreign competition and stimulated domestic consumption by raising real wages almost 50 percent between 1946 and 1948. In essence, he made the state more responsible than ever before for public welfare, increasing its powers and inflating its budget, guaranteeing the nation thereafter a budget deficit in which nearly everyone developed a stake.[17]

The operation relied on the country's farmers and cattlemen to finance import substitution industrialization. Cleverly adapting to his nationalist needs the system of production and price controls created by the conservatives during the 1930s to protect producers from the vicissitudes of the international market, Perón confiscated some of the farmers' profits and used them to pay for the subsidization of industry, the employment of thousands of his supporters in government jobs, and the building of the nation's infrastructure. He required farmers to sell their grain to the government at prices lower than those paid in the world market, keeping the difference to pay for his projects. The rural sector became his unwilling collaborator, and as long as they kept producing and prices stayed up, it worked. But it made him the farmers' prisoner, for by relying so much on them he placed the fate of his effort in their hands. Like all Argentine presidents after World War II, Perón wanted to exploit the country's most valuable resource in order to rebuild the economy. And like them he learned how risky this "easy road to development" really was, discovering the hard way how agriculture, though rich and bountiful, could never live up to the exaggerated demands that urban politicians placed on it.

In the short run he needed to sell grain at good prices in order to finance his scheme, but, as feared, increases in U.S. exports cut into potential markets, especially after the Marshall Plan began in 1948, when the Truman administration sent an abundance of grain to help allies in Europe with their recoveries. Then two successive droughts in Argentina reduced farm production, making it impossible to take advantage of the rise in world demand for commodities touched off in 1950 by the Korean War and economic recovery in the industrial nations. This especially hurt since income from exports was desperately needed at the time to pay for increased imports of capital goods and raw materials for industry. Consequently Argentina staggered after 1950, failing to "take off" as Perón had wanted. Peronism had brought a three-year boom, followed by a bubble that burst before it had achieved its primary objectives. In the end it was Perón who had to adjust, backing away from his nationalism and inviting foreign firms into the country again while taking away many of the workers' income gains in order to deal with unwanted recessions.

Was the Peronist solution a colossal bungle, done in by policies totally inappropriate for Argentina? It was certainly ill-timed, for at the moment that the world economy was beginning a thirty-year period of incredible growth that opened hosts of new opportunities for trade, he was coddling an industry whose high costs denied it a chance to advance through the export of manufactures, making the mistake of fighting an economic war using battle plans more appropriate to past ones.[18] Nevertheless, his making the state a grand economic patron was not really all that unique. Brazilians, Chileans, and Mexicans were doing much the same thing at the time, though a bit more efficiently than Perón did. In each country the defense of a highly protected industry became synonymous with industrialization per se; no one was concerned about its costs since the mere fact of industrialization brought so much with it, not the least of which were greater independence from the industrial nations and the employment of an expanding work force. That protection would one day make industrial exports less competitive in world markets was the least of their concerns when they started.

Ironically he proved more adept at compensating for adversity than at creating new wealth. When expansion ended he responded with tough austerity measures in 1952 that gradually restored an equilibrium of sorts and led to 5.5 percent average growth rates during his last two years. Moreover, he persuaded workers to put up with the real decline in wages induced by his stabilization policy. It is the latter that sustained the belief, even among some non-Peronists, that only he could ever get the working class to conform to austerity measures in the future and contributed to the military's bringing him home to pacify his followers in 1973.

The Peronist experiment left Argentina with a host of new problems. The public sector was bloated and the Argentine upper and middle classes even less willing than before to pay their tax bills. Industrialization had proven far more expensive than expected, and Peronist farm policy had discouraged the expansion of production at a time when ever increasing amounts of foreign exchange were needed. And infrastructure deteriorated when the Peronists found themselves unable to carry through with their construction plans after 1950. But most important, people lost what little confidence they had in government during the Peronist era, all of them, that is, but the die-hards of the Peronist movement, who would never lose theirs. Instead of bringing a new coherence to society, Perón deepened old conflicts and added new ones. Government was intensely partisan before he had come along, and was even more so after he left. The notion that authorities governed for the entire nation, balancing one interest against another, favoring some but not to the total exclusion of the others, never had taken hold in Argentina before 1945, and Perón and his successors saw to it that it did not thereafter either.

How Fascist Was It?

Histories of Perón's government abound, but satisfactory descriptions of the exact nature of Peronism remain scarce. Some contend that its original design was largely fascist, among them Marxists who see Perón as the instrument of a bourgeoisie that used him to establish state control over the proletariat in order to prevent its radicalization.[19] They are correct to some degree, for he and his military colleagues began with the idea of making the state the patron of unorganized laborers in order to block their mobilization by revolutionaries. But Marxists try too hard to demonstrate that because many of his cabinet ministers were from the middle class and were supported by small business and tenant farmers his regime was under the control of the bourgeoisie. What they neglect to note is that people from the middle class were on both sides of the Peronist divide, more of them opposing him and his scheme than joining it once its true character was known.

Others, among them prominent political sociologists, emphasize differences between the Argentine social structure and those of European nations, arguing that what distinguished Peronism was its greater reliance on the working class for its power than on the petit bourgeoisie, as was the case in fascist Europe. Had the Argentine social structure been farther along in its development, Peronism might have taken the form of European fascism; as it was, the closest that it would come was in its desire to replace the bogus liberalism of the oligarchy with a corporatism in which a strong central government imposed itself on all social sectors.[20]

There may be an even simpler explanation of what Perón wanted to do if one recalls that he took inspiration from Mussolini not Hitler, having observed the latest Italian renaissance at first hand just before the war. Italian fascism was always a bit nebulous, and the state that it established was built as much on words as it was on deeds. Of course, it did exhibit a mania for spectacular projects, most of them made from cement and steel, but what made it work as long as it did was Mussolini's determination to turn a disorderly and weak Italy into a proud and strong nation run by a popular authority. To someone like Perón who rejected bolshevism and had lost what little confidence he had in liberalism, Italy's rebirth under Mussolini was enviable and worthy of imitation. If the Italians had made a mistake, it was in going to war, something that he had no intention of doing. Working out the details of Argentina's renaissance and its corporatist organization did not really concern him much at the outset; instead, what mattered was getting the whole process started, which is what he thought he was doing when he marched Argentina forward in 1946.[21]

His treatment of opponents was as repulsive to democrats as Mussolini's had been. He drew the masses into a single party, mixing radical rhetoric with conservative, autocratic methods of direction, and when frightened by his opponents, encouraged its thugs to rough them up, steadily raising the cost of criticism and protest. The intervention of hostile newspapers and the burning of churches whose priests protested his legalizing divorce and prostitution became commonplace during his second term. Still, his operation was even less well organized than Mussolini's had been. It was, as most political innovations in Argentina are, a hastily contrived and deficient imitation of the original.

Especially frustrating was his failure to win the full confidence of entrepreneurs whom he thought he was regulating for their and the nation's own good. But they were never desperate enough to accept him as their savior, and only the most economically vulnerable and opportunistic saw advantage in going along with him. Equally troublesome was the fickleness of his colleagues in the armed forces. He had tried to penetrate the services and create a hierarchy loyal to him, but no president had managed it before and he was no exception. Nor did he find it advantageous to challenge them directly by creating an Argentine SS, fearful as he was that so provocative a step would surely prompt direct retaliation. In the end he had little choice but to rely on military friends, whom he never entirely trusted, to keep their colleagues in line.[22]

Perón was always less comfortable working on policy with the nation's industrialists, farmers, and laborers than Mussolini had been. A corporatist in spirit, he was never much of one in practice. Instead, he preferred to be everyone's commander, who ruled over them in the country's best interests. Doing otherwise was too much work and involved too many people in high circles for his taste.[23] Nevertheless, he went through the motions, twice creating government councils on which private interests were represented. But fearful of their interfering with his supervision of the country, he ignored them when critical decisions were made, preferring to rely almost entirely on conventional fiscal, monetary, and regulatory devices to induce desirable behaviors.[24]

Ambiguity not consistency characterizes Peronism as a political phenomenon. For example, Peronists competed in elections with other parties, winning a free one in 1946. But that did not stop them from abusing the rights of their critics, forcing some to flee the country and others to go underground. They favored organized labor in disputes with industry, yet they protected industry from foreign competition and came to its rescue when the economy went sour in 1952. They attacked the oligarchy and took some of the farmers' profits from them with taxes and price controls, yet they took none of their land away. They talked of corporatism, claiming to be a movement whose goal was the unification of the nation for a common purpose, but they divided it even more than before. And though Peronism was born within the military establishment, it was the Argentine army that sought to stop Perón's ascendancy in 1945, staged unsuccessful coups against him in 1951 and 1955, and finally deposed him later in 1955. He lived off ambiguity, determined to succeed in a society where a constitution and popular support did not guarantee him tenure. The oligarchs had struck back in 1930 to end the life of an elected government, and it was quite conceivable that either they or one of the opposition parties would work with the armed forces to do so again. That is why Perón's treatment of the opposition is not really surprising; he wanted to prevail in a society where one dealt harshly with one's rivals before they were able to retaliate.

It was not only popularity with the masses and intimidation of the opposition that sustained Peronists in power. To keep their powerful machine going, Peronists also relied heavily on the state's resources. It is easy to forget that Peronism was not a spontaneous phenomenon but something created by people in government to keep themselves there. As such, it relied on the government's resources as much as on union dues to sustain its operation. The idea of becoming just another political party competing in a democratic system was alien to the movement's founders. In their view the government belonged to them, and they expected its prompt return after it was taken from them in 1955.

Peronists were rapacious monopolists when they ruled the nation, never as neat or well organized as fascists are supposed to be, but nearly as disrespectful of their critics. Still, despite their verbal and physical intimidation of opponents, they never came close to taking real control over Argentine society. And throughout it all Perón worked not just for his own glory but also to make Argentina powerful and more widely appreciated, determined to recover the respect lost when authorities had gone begging to the British after the depression. He also created the country's first welfare state, which, if not as massive as he promised, was enormous for a nation of Argentina's public resources. The country would never be quite the same again, though it was not until several presidents had tried and failed repeatedly to dismantle his highly regulatory welfare state that his achievement was fully appreciated.

The New Generation

Life did not cease for Peronists after the 1955 coup, even though their party was closed, many of its leaders were jailed, and most CGT unions were intervened in by military officers. As one of his first objectives, General Pedro Aramburu had set out to purge the CGT of Peronists, hoping to superintend the election of less politically ambitious union officials in their place. But individual federations resisted, and a new generation of Peronists emerged to lead most unions in a prolonged effort to resist persecution. With Perón gone they had to rely on their own devices to survive, developing new political strategies and tactics. Standing their ground against hostile authorities became the order of the day, as they tried to buy enough time to reorganize and mobilize the masses in campaigns to secure Perón's return from exile. It would be eighteen years before they succeeded, however, and in the interim this new generation of labor leaders learned to play a new game, opposite the one Peronists had played in the past. Now, they were defenders of the working class but were not its well-financed benefactors, and they sustained themselves by attacking governments rather than protestors.

It was never easy, but they fought hard and long, weakening some governments and undermining others until the armed forces had little choice but to invite the old general back, in 1973, to restore order to the nation.[25]

The Peronists' strength came as much from their numbers as from their tactics. It is worth recalling how massive an organization Perón had created when he reorganized the CGT. By 1950 the employees of nearly all but the smallest enterprises had been drawn into the organization, and with the government's assistance, they built huge treasuries from funds extracted from employer and employee alike. In the 1960s nearly one-third of the nation's labor force still belonged to unions, far more than in any other Latin American country.[26] Of even more importance politically, more than half of the union members lived in or around Buenos Aires; this concentration facilitated mobilization for strikes and protests against authorities. Although size and concentration were no guarantee of victory in conflicts with governments that fought back, they did serve to make the complete subjugation of labor unions impossible.

What Perón's absence cost the CGT was not its power but the unity it had enjoyed while he was there to discipline rebels in its midst. No one but he could enforce the principle of *verticalidad* on the labor movement. Without him the various federations of the CGT had to settle their differences on their own, something that never came easily to so aggressive a group of labor leaders. Disagreements arose over how to respond when their party was excluded from elections and over what to do about government efforts to coopt unions into alliances that dealt harshly with those that did not join. As a result, divisions within the CGT became common, and it was often impossible to know exactly who commanded the confederation. This pattern of fragmentation emerged as early as 1957 at the CGT convention that Aramburu had called to launch his de-Peronization effort. Although Aramburu failed, divisions did result, as federations that had never enjoyed being party to Perón's exploits rushed to escape Peronist control. When the convention ended there were three factions instead of one. The largest, calling itself the "62," claimed loyalty to Peronism. A second, the "32," separated itself from Peronism and expressed a commitment to less politicized unionism. The third faction was formed of a few remaining federations whose leaders said that they were Peronist but called themselves "independents" to indicate their desire to escape the control of Peronist politicians. During the next two decades anywhere from 50 to 80 percent of the nation's union membership belonged to the "62," sustaining its leadership of the largely Peronist working class, even though it too was often torn apart by disputes among its own members.[27]

Typical was the rivalry that arose between José Alonso, leader of the garment workers who was elected secretary general of the CGT at its convention in February 1963, and Augusto Vandor, head of the nation's powerful steelworkers union. Alonso was committed to the CGT's old line, espousing loyalty to Perón and and his cause as the movement's unifying principle. Vandor, in contrast, was more independent, never entirely separating himself from Perón, but always reaching out to non-Peronist unions to form alliances devoted more to the immediate interests of labor than to the long-term ones of Peronism. He reminded one of Luis Gay, the CGT secretary whose defiance caused Perón to remove him in 1947. Calling his faction the "Azopardo" (after the street on which its headquarters was located), he charted his own strategy, ignoring orders from Perón in Spain when they conflicted with this own intentions. For example, when loyal unions decided to aim for some accommodation with the military regime that took over in 1966, Vandor led his followers into battle with the armed forces, staging massive strikes which provoked a violent response from authorities that broke their back and resulted in the government's intervention of Vandor's metallurgical workers union. Later, in 1969, he was assassinated by terrorists determined to liberate workers of their "bourgeois" leaders; Alonso was killed a year later by the same people, but their deaths only led others to sustain divisions within the movement that owed more to a growing independence among member federations than to rejection of Peronist ideals.[28]

Conflicts between individual unions and CGT leaders also resulted from changes caused by the country's further industrialization in the 1960s. Large enterprises that manufactured automobiles, chemicals, and plastics were built with the government's encouragement, most of them owned by multinational corporations. Many were placed inland, some as far north as Córdoba, where workers were housed in neighborhoods alongside factories. Their cohesion as communities was greater than was traditional in the older, leader-dominated unions, and being new and distant from the capital, they demanded more autonomy organizationally, often moving to the left ideologically to distinguish themselves from the old CGT in Buenos Aires. Some of them participated in the massive protests that occurred in Córdoba in May 1969 against the military regime; protests which, though put down by the army, led to the armed forces pulling out of the government and letting the Peronists back in four years later. The rebellion gave the Córdoba unions a new sense of power that would make them increasingly defiant of the CGT, as Perón would discover when he returned to the presidency in 1973.[29]

Whether united or working separately, labor leaders concentrated their attention as much on confrontations with authorities over their policies as on collective bargaining at the local level. This was natural since wages were so much affected by government interventions in the economy and by the implementation of successive anti-inflation stabilization programs. It also followed from the CGT's determination to make governing the nation impossible for anyone who attempted to exclude it. Using a "rubber band" strategy, which had them yielding to hostile governments one minute and then fighting back the next, CGT leaders managed to keep most governments on the defensive, making it impossible to build any foundation for post-Peronist politics. They were simply too numerous to be destroyed by force of arms and too consumed by a desire to restore Perón to power to roll over and die as a movement.

In other countries similar persecution might have radicalized the working class, but this never happened in Argentina. Most unions refused invitations from the left to vent their frustrations on capitalism itself. Perón's popularity had something to do with it, but very practical political considerations were just as influential. Peronism had given labor leaders a taste of power and it remained the shortest route to regaining it. To forsake it for more revolutionary causes would remove them even farther from their objective; moreover, alliances with ideologues would have proved uncomfortable for the organization men of the CGT. The Peronists were power politicians who knew what they wanted. And it was not socialism or communism but control over the social services and wage policies that populist politics had given them. Theirs was the narrowest of visions but that was no embarrassment to them, and the more that ideologues on the left attacked them for selling out the proletariat, the more stubborn they became in defending themselves. Their success in denying Marxists and anarchists access to the working class has never been complete, but it is remarkable nevertheless and remains a source of great pride to regulars in the labor hierarchy.[30]

While all of this was going on, Peronist white-collar politicians, many of whom had been senators, deputies, judges, and cabinet officers, busied themselves discovering ways to buy time until they, too, would return to power. They worked hard to assume a new respectabilty, although, since they were from middle- and upper-class families, this did not require much on their part. Often they went into business, helped by the entrepreneurs whom they had made wealthy when they were in office. They retained friendships with military officers who shared their nationalist beliefs, each helping the other to advance economically while plotting with and against the other politically. In short, Peronist entrepreneurs and professionals clung to their positions at the edge of the national economic establishment, advancing as best they could while waiting for Perón to come home. When they were assaulted, it was by the youthful left and not by anti-Peronist authorities. Increasingly after 1969 they were terrorized by extremists who resented their very bourgeois behavior. To defend themselves, they joined labor bosses in creating little armies of their own, which made war on terrorists, initially just out of public view. By the early 1970s, however, this violence had spilled over into the streets. With the situation getting out of control, it seemed that only Perón could bring peace to a nation in which both sides claimed to be fighting in his name. Thus it was to Perón that the nation turned in desperation in 1973.

El Retorno

The decision to let Perón return was a long time in coming. Only after military officers intent on imposing order on the country failed to do so after six years of trying did they decide to call elections. But even then it was not their intention to stand by and watch a Peronist replace them in the Casa Rosada. Instead, they hoped that either a new party led by a military officer would hold the Peronists off or that, if this failed, a coalition of non-Peronist parties would do the job. But neither alternative attracted much support, and when elections were held in March it was Juan Perón who would prevail one last time.

He campaigned for his FREJULI party, first from Spain and then during a brief visit home at the end of 1972. He promised national unity not division this time, claiming that after years of battle between the government and organized labor, only he could end the fruitless struggle and bring everyone back together again. But that was not all; while preaching unity he promised each interest that appealed to him for support exactly what it wanted: order for the military; a healthy investment climate for business; and a social revolution for the strident Peronist Youth. It was all rhetoric and everyone knew it, yet they wanted desperately to believe that he would deliver on all of his promises. Even some in the armed forces resolved that the time had come to give the seventy-seven-year-old populist a final try at ruling his people.

In retrospect it looks preposterous, of course, the old, ailing general coming home and making everything right again. But Argentines longed for order, and after nearly two decades of failing to subdue one another, Perón was all that was left, it seemed. That is why 49.5 percent of them voted for his stand-in candidate Hector Campora in March. A runoff was required, but the second-place Radicals with only 21 percent conceded and it was all over. As expected, the working class had voted Peronist, as had some in the middle class. The more laborers there were in a district and the lower their average income, the more it went Peronist, just as in the old days. The only difference this time was the addition of many young persons from the middle class who saw Perón as a vehicle for reform.[31]

Campora's presidency began on May 25, but it lasted only fifty days. He did make the most of it, however, to the displeasure of the party's old guard. He took Perón's call for reconciliation more seriously than was intended, declaring an amnesty for all "political prisoners," turning loose 370 persons, some of them well-known terrorists. A military that had seen some of its prominent members assassinated by those released took a dim view of the exercise, as they did Campora's authorizing the destruction of police files. Orthodox Peronists were no happier, fearing that Campora was starting something that he would not be able to control. So when Perón returned on June 20, they demanded Campora's removal and he gladly complied.

On July 13 Campora was ousted and Raul Lastiri, then president of the Chamber of Deputies, announced new elections for September 23, which Perón then won with 62 percent of the vote. Peace did not follow immediately, however. Instead José Rucci, secretary general of the CGT, was assassinated by terrorists who accused him and his CGT colleagues of betraying the proletariat with their bourgeois unionism. Perón did nothing at first, demanding peaceful reconciliation by all of his friends, but within a few weeks he lost his patience and turned the police and the military loose to battle with the terrorists.[32]

It was on the economic front that the Peronists seemed most at home when they began. Even before Perón returned to assume the presidency, Campora's advisors were preparing another neocorporatist solution for handling conflicts over policy among rival economic sectors. Its design was the work of nationalist businessman José Gelbard, leader of the General Economic Confederation that was founded in the 1940s and authorized by Perón to represent the nation's entrepreneurs before his first government. Gelbard believed that orderly policy making required advanced agreement between labor and management in all sectors of the economy. Concretely he proposed a *pacto social*, or social contract, that called a truce over wage and price policies for two years while authorities worked to reduce inflation, then hovering around 70 percent, prior to dealing in any significant way with progressive income redistribution, Peronism's most fundamental economic goal. To induce labor's cooperation he raised wages by 20 percent while freezing all retail prices. It worked, and reluctantly CGT leaders signed on, as did skeptical business leaders and representatives of most farmers' organizations.[33]

When Perón was elected in September, confidence in the *pacto* rose briefly. But it soon became obvious that even he was no match for the forces working against its completion. Labor unions had changed during his exile, many of them having secured greater independence from the CGT's leadership. As we learned, they had spent almost two decades on the defensive, fighting authorities who tried to discipline them, and now they had no intention to become docile again, even when the general demanded it of them. Moreover, some labor leaders, especially the younger ones from more recently industrialized cities like Córdoba, did not really trust him, having become convinced that he had compromised himself with the nation's economic elite and armed forces in order to be allowed back. Even conservative labor leaders were suspicious of him, fearful that he had neither the will nor the stamina to lead them against a revolutionary left that was challenging their control over the proletariat at the time of Perón's return. Whether he could have passed the test of either we shall never know, for just as he began to assert himself he died of natural causes on July 1, 1974, a year after coming home.[34]

Economically things went rather well during the first year. The economy grew by 6.5 percent in 1973, slightly faster than the previous year, and the rate of inflation was cut in half. But the price and wage freeze lasted too long, impairing business profitability and discouraging investment, eventually causing shortages of all kinds. Equally disturbing was a sudden scarcity of foreign exchange, a consequence of the Peronists' overheating the economy while maintaining a fixed exchange rate. Moreover, import prices rose by 35 percent in 1973 and in 1974, while export prices remained constant. And, unfortunately, the European Common Market decided to add to the country's woes by banning meat imports in July 1974 in order to protect its own beef industry.[35]

Perón's death could not help but set off a power struggle within the government, given his failure to pick successors or create the means for others to do so, but it could not have come at a worse time for a *pacto* that needed renewal. His wife and vice president, Isabel, succeeded him, but she relied heavily on close friend and Social Welfare Minister José López Rega for guidance during the next months. López Rega was Perón's personal secretary in Spain, an eccentric, conservative Peronist, known by Argentines as Isabel's unscrupulous "Rasputin" for his reliance on astrology to justify his capricious and vindictive behavior. He was tied to a cadre of Peronist businessmen, some of whom wanted organized labor brought back into line, using as much force as necessary. Most labor leaders, even an old guard whose affection for the rebels in their midst was no greater than López Rega's, wanted no part of it. Neither did the Peronist Youth, themselves an obvious target for persecution given their deep penetration by revolutionary cadres. Campora had allowed each of these groups a free reign after his inauguration, but Perón, acceding to the demands of conservatives and labor bosses, had begun purging the movement of its radical youth a few months before he died, forcing many of them underground. That left a struggle for power between the movement's right wing and rebel labor leaders, a conflict that might have been avoided were it not for López Rega's personal ambition and overconfidence, as well as his desire to make conformity with austere economic policies the test of loyalty to the movement.

He started by dismissing most of Perón's cabinet, including *pacto* designer José Gelbard.[36] That set the stage for a confrontation with the most aggressive labor unions over the renewal of the *pacto* in June 1975, one that López Rega sought and was convinced he could win. It began with the appointment of Celestino Rodrigo, a fellow member of the Peronist right wing, as economy minister. Rodrigo announced an orthodox economic stabilization plan, not unlike the one Perón had forced on his people back in 1952, aimed at taming inflation, which then was shooting up to an annual rate of 335 percent. Prices were freed, government spending cut, and wages kept under control. It was exactly the opposite of what laborers wanted after two years of *pacto* wage controls. When they protested, Rodrigo, on López Rega's advice, offered a "take it or leave it" 50 percent wage increase. But that was not enough: labor leaders balked at the insult and declared war on the government, touching off an all-out fight with López Rega and Isabel Perón. Who the winner would be was never in doubt to anyone but López Rega and his inner circle. Labor leaders mobilized the rank and file and nearly shut down the entire country from July 4 to July 8 at the cost of $66 million per day to the economy. Peronist deputies in Congress gave their support to the unions, and suddenly Isabel and López Rega found themselves isolated from the movement they were supposed to be leading. Isabel had no choice but to relent, and when she did her cabinet resigned and López Rega fled the country on July 18, not to be seen again in Argentina.[37]

Isabel Perón's government never recovered the authority that it lost from its defeat by the CGT. Efforts were made to patch up the economy but conditions only became worse, as did the level of violence caused by the intensification of warfare between terrorists and the government. By early 1976 no one was really in charge anymore. Peronism was a movement without direction, a collection of rival factions whose leaders had lost what little respect they had for each other. Everyone in society began to take cover as the country came apart, counting the days until the military took over on March 24, 1976.

The Montoneros and Liberation

The greatest tragedy of Perón's return was not his flawed economic policy or the self-destructive battles fought between labor leaders and the Peronist right but the violence that arose before his return and escalated after he died. It had never been his intention to lead his people into a civil war or even to provoke others to fight one. But he contributed to one nevertheless by encouraging young revolutionaries to believe that they could use him to advance their own cause of true revolution. When they finally realized that he was more their enemy than friend, they went to war against Peronism as well, lumping together the Peronist "forces of occupation" with their bourgeois coconspirators and military protectors as objects for clandestine persecution. The struggle that followed was a bloody one, and Argentina is still recovering, a decade later.

The violence that Argentines lived with in the 1970s was truly unprecedented. To be sure, political conflict had always been intense and brutality not uncommon, but never before had it bred so much personal insecurity, fear, and madness. Even in the last years of the first Peronist regime, when protests and repression rose, most people left their homes confident that they would return to them at the end of the day to spend a quiet night with their families. It was quite different in 1975 and 1976, when they feared becoming innocent victims of terrorist bombings or police reprisals. Violence had been infecting politics for some time, encouraged by the success of riots in bringing down General Juan Carlos Onganía's dictatorship in the late 1960s. Young and affluent recruits to leftist political causes embraced it with unprecedented fervor, determined to provoke a complacent society's rebellion against militarism and strong-arm Peronism. Their vision of the mass insurrection was romantic and naive, but that did not make them any less dedicated to pursuing it by terrifying a society unaccustomed to bombs exploding in public places.

The Montoneros sprung from this new generation of idealistic, self-disciplined terrorists. On May 29, 1970, they introduced themselves to the nation by kidnapping and killing General Pedro Armaburu, the president who had tried unsuccessfully to de-Peronize the masses in 1955 after Perón fled. They were punishing him for his misdeeds, they claimed, among them his authorizing the execution of twenty-seven Peronists and his hiding Eva Perón's embalmed corpse in Milan, Italy. But they also wanted recognition, letting the world know what they would do to the enemies of Peronism if they did not let Juan Perón back into power. Who these strange people were and why they claimed Peronism as their cause was something of a mystery at first, even to Peronist leaders, who denied any association with them.

Guerrilla warfare was not entirely new to the country, of course. As early as 1962 the Marxist-Leninist Armed Forces of Liberation (FAL) was trying to wage a rural war, and in 1967 the Che Guevara–inspired Revolutionary Armed Forces (FAR) set up its own *"foco"* in northwestern Argentina. Not long thereafter the Trotskyite Revolutionary Workers' party launched an armed unit called the People's Revolutionary Army (ERP), which functioned well into the 1970s. By the time the Montoneros came along each of these groups had tried to mount a war against Argentine authorities. Yet, it was obvious that none had met with much success as long as they were devoted to replicating rather classical guerrilla strategies.[38]

The Montoneros intended to do things differently. To begin with, they were very few in number, no more than twenty persons who operated in utmost secrecy at the time of the Aramburu operation. They had come together in 1968, some of them right-wing nationalists with fascist ideals and others advocates of their own versions of Christian liberation. Initially intent on little more than destroying authority in its existing forms, they would eventually claim revolutionary goals aimed at creating a new society, one built on the replacement of capitalism with a socialism untarnished by old-fashioned populism or the crudities of modern communism. But to do that they needed power and that is where their support for Peronism came in. Though it would later prove to be their undoing, at the time it seemed a reasonable strategy.

Like Peronist nationalists they saw Argentine history in simple terms, as a struggle between its landed oligarchy and the masses. The Peronists had led the masses into battle with the oligarchs only to be stopped by the latter's counterrevolution in 1955. To return to power the masses had to become more revolutionary than before, inspired by the likes of the Montoneros and other radical forces. The Montoneros had no illusions about winning the masses from their less revolutionary Peronist leadership overnight, but they believed that somehow they could expropriate them from Peronism, turning what had become a rather unrevolutionary, self-interested proletariat into a revolutionary force that they would lead toward the destruction of capitalism and the social structure that accompanied it. In the meantime they had to rid the country of its military government, and that required their devotion to the Peronist effort to achieve Perón's return. Short-term objectives not ultimate ones controlled their behavior initially, giving them no choice but to devote themselves to working with a Juan Perón who had no intention of releasing the masses to their care. For him they were not competitors but instruments to be used to undermine the authority of a ruling military and force their accepting his return to the presidency as the only way to restore order and legitimate government to the country. Liberation was his cause, too, but his version had little to do with socialism or revolution as Montoneros understood it.[39]

But that does not explain the Montoneros' preference for terrorism over the direct mobilization of the masses. It seems that their choice of tactics also derives from very practical considerations as well as a degree of romanticism. Little insight was needed to recognize that most workers were heads of families who could ill afford the personal sacrifices required to wage real war against the state. If battles were to be fought, less compromised youth would have to wage them, people in their twenties, some of them students. Moreover, Argentina was an urban country and it was in the cities that authorities had to be confronted; and it was there that terrorism worked best since it allowed sudden strikes followed by the perpetrators' immediate blending back into society, undetected by the police. The age of rural warfare was over in 1970, the victim of repeated defeats in Tucuman during the 1960s and the shock of Che Guevara's fiasco in Bolivia in 1968. A new kind of warfare was called for, one that could destroy authority by demonstrating the government's incapacity to protect its own members from violence. Evidencing an incredible vision, the Montoneros were convinced that by humiliating the oppressors of the working class they could win the latter to the cause of liberation no matter how bloody and disrupting their attacks on authorities became.[40]

Their daring kidnappings, robberies, and attacks on military installations as well as their celebrating the martyrdom of colleagues who "fell" to military bullets earned the Montoneros the attention they desperately sought in 1971 and 1972. They were also helped by the military's massacre of sixteen terrorists who had escaped from the Rawson Prison in August 1972. When the fleeing prisoners did not make it to an awaiting hijacked aircraft at nearby Trelew Airport in time to board it, they were captured, taken back to prison, and shot by officers embarrassed by their escape. Unintentionally, authorities made heroes of the men and women they killed, and they could do nothing but watch as Perón, seizing on the event for personal advantage, sent flowers from Spain to honor the victims.[41]

But just when the Montoneros' war was getting underway, it ended, at least temporarily. In mid-1972 General Alejandro Lanusse announced his intention to hold free elections the following year, giving the Peronists a chance to return to the offices from which they were evicted eighteen years before. When they won the election and Hector Campora was inaugurated on May 25 the Montoneros, now a few hundred in number, were among the celebrants, cheering wildly at the release of their imprisoned colleagues by the new president. It was a bizarre occasion, even in the annals of Argentine history, as the members of terrorist organizations danced in the streets, celebrating the inauguration of an elected government while the armed forces and the police they had been assaulting for over two years quietly looked on. Almost overnight the once reclusive Montoneros had become participants in constitutional politics, 8 of their members taking seats among the 145-person Peronist majority in the Chamber of Deputies.

What to do next was never all that obvious, however. Victory in elections for the cause they supported took them only halfway home, creating an opportunity to work directly with the masses without any guarantee that the new government would allow them to carry through with their plans. Moreover, they were trained in secretive, terrorist activities and not mass mobilization. To come above ground suddenly and lead the crowds did not come automatically to them. But they tried anyway, starting by rapidly expanding their influence within the Peronist Youth movement, itself the depository of a new generation of Peronist leftists. The Montoneros showed exceptional skill at recruitment, and they quickly captured leadership posts in the youth organization, to the displeasure of the government's more conservative Peronist leaders, who feared competition from a rival organization commanded by ideologues with whom they had little in common other than apparent concern for the working class. The more the Peronist Youth called on its members to "stamp on the old union leadership as if they were cockroaches," the more upset the latter became.[42]

It was obvious that the Montoneros' triumph was more apparent than real: they were heard within the new government but they were excluded from all of its most powerful posts. To compensate they threw their enthusiasm into organizing grass-roots social movements all over the country, in slums and university campuses, linking them together with something called the Tendencia Revolucionaria, an organization whose leaders promised to force the government to deliver on its revolutionary promises. But in doing so they invited an open conflict with the Peronist old guard that would doom them before they were prepared to go into battle. Peronist right wingers started the fight the day Perón returned, staging a shootout with the banner-waving Peronist Youth at Ezeiza Airport on June 20, 1973. Led by Jorge Osinde, a former security chief, Peronist thugs fired on their youthful rivals, killing 30 and wounding 300 more. Their message was clear: no matter how much Perón had egged them on before his return, revolutionaries were unwanted in the movement now that he was back.[43]

After he became president, Perón immediately declared war on the Trotskyite People's Revolutionary Army (ERP), always more avowedly anti-Peronist than the Montoneros. He also wanted to send a message to the Peronist Youth, making it clear that the time had come for them to get in line under his leadership, leaving their zeal for "liberation" behind them. But the message did not penetrate the Montoneros armor, and they continued with their calls for mass action, somehow convinced that when Perón discovered the magnificence of their efforts he would accept their achievement. The old general's patience with them was wearing thin, and then it ended abruptly at a mass rally on May Day 1974. After being interrupted several times by youthful chants of the names of slain Montoneros, Perón

> lost his self-control, abandoned his national unity speech, and unleashed an attack on the Peronist Left which amounted to a declaration of war. After just fifty seconds of praise for the quality of Argentine trade unionism, hearing slogans against union leaders from the Left, Perón made his first reference to "those stupid idiots who are shouting"; but the Tendency at first did not react. Peron continued, "I was saying that through these [last] 21 years, the trade unions have remained intransigent, yet today some beardless wonders try to claim more credit than those who fought for 20 years." Soon after, having heard Montonero propagandistic slogans about two assassinated labor leaders ("Rucci, traitor, say hello to Vandor"), Perón referred ominously to "comrades who have seen their leaders assassinated without punishment having been implemented yet." He lambasted the Revolutionary Tendency as "infiltrators who work within and who in terms of treachery are more dangerous than those who work outside."[44]

At long last it became clear to the Montoneros that Perón had abandoned them. If any doubts remained, López Rega dispelled them after Perón's death when he sent his own neofascist terrorist organization, the Argentine Anti-Communist Alliance, or Triple A, after them, instructing his men to liquidate suspected Montoneros. As part of its crusade the government closed the Montoneros' newspapers, denied them permission to hold rallies, and fiercely broke up their demonstrations. Locked out of the government and denied any opportunity to influence it, the Montoneros decided to go back underground in September 1974. Drawing on the reservoir of support they had created during the previous year among students and the poor, they began a new campaign of terrorism, commanding one of the mightiest urban guerrilla organizations ever to exist in Latin America.[45]

They raised money by kidnapping wealthy businessmen and holding them for ransom, securing $70 million in 1975, and then purchasing the weapons they used to assassinate labor leaders and right-wing Peronists. In mid-1975 they expanded operations to include attacks on military installations and police stations, and during 1976 killed or seriously injured 300 persons. Retaliation came, as they expected, but it was not until the military took over in March that it began to overwhelm them with its ruthlessness. In the past when terrorists were caught they were sent to prison, where they were tortured but usually kept alive. Not any longer. On orders from the highest command, military intelligence and paramilitary units abducted whomever they wished (averaging fifteen per day during the last quarter of 1976), took them to secret concentration camps, tortured them for information about their colleagues, and then killed them without even recording their deaths. Many of their victims were not terrorists but young people who had participated in the social works of the Tendencia Revolucionaria when the Montoneros had gone above ground to mobilize their mass movement during the first months of the Campora government. Some were also Montoneros who revealed the location of their colleagues while under torture, making it possible for the armed forces to rip their organization apart in one year. In early 1977 those who remained at large gave up, nearly one thousand of them fleeing abroad, most taking refuge in Mexico City, Havana, and Caracas.[46]

Many lessons were learned from the painful experience. The Montoneros knew that they had naively overestimated their ability to win Perón to their side and had waited too long to admit their mistake. They had also underestimated the average Argentine's aversion to terrorism of any kind and how easy it would be for the armed forces to convince even the working class that its acts of repression were all that separated society from chaos and destruction in 1976. Peronists also learned many things, the most obvious of which were the costs of forming alliances with people much more radical than themselves. Radical revolutionaries are incompatible mates for the rather bourgeois Peronist leadership. Most labor leaders are part of the nation's diverse and disjoined political "establishment," threatened as much as merchants and bankers by a radical redistribution of power. They will use whomever they can to reconquer government when they are excluded from office but once back they will not share power with such allies. The Montoneros, in their zeal to fashion an innovative kind of liberation, one that was supposed to join Peronist nationalism with their version of mass revolution, never accepted such realities of power and interest until they had been destroyed by their illusions.

An End and a Beginning

Perón's last presidency was the victim of its own contradictions, the most destructive of which was between his desire for political reconciliation and his need to promote political conflict in order to force the military to bring him back. He could not turn political violence on and off as he had done many years before. From exile he had promoted the growth of two conflicting movements, one run by labor leaders devoted to protecting their privileges and the other by youthful ideologues who wanted to give real power to workers. Always confident of his Machiavellian wisdom, Perón played with both, convinced that he could draw on their energies at will. But his political habits were those of another era, totally inappropriate for a new age of much more extremist politics. He had rediscovered a country that was beyond his power to govern. It was a land in crisis, both economic and political, one wracked by a war between the left and right, and one without a ruling class with enough power to restore order. Old age and ill health slowed Perón down, but it was Argentine society that defeated him in 1974, as it would have any other Peronist who tried to govern under such circumstances.

The Peronist return in 1973 proved a debacle for Argentina. It was also a boon to the movement's opponents within the upper and middle classes and to military officers determined to reconstruct the nation's politics according to their own design. The latter had tried and failed in 1966, but that did not weaken their desire to try once more in 1976. Why people in uniform should be so ambitious for themselves and their nation yet perform so badly each time they try to govern it is a question that cannot be answered without a closer look at the country's *partido militar.*

Notes

1. Joseph Page, *Perón: A Biography* (New York: Random House, 1983), pp. 22–23. Page's lengthy biography is the best compilation of events in Perón's political career yet available.

2. Ibid., pp. 34–35.

3. On the origins of lodges in the Argentine army and the purposes they served in the 1920s and 1930s, see Robert Potash, *The Army and Politics in Argentina: 1928–1945* (Stanford: Stanford University Press, 1969).

4. The controversial GOU is examined in ibid., chs. 7–8; and Page, *Perón,* ch. 5.

5. The most notorious example of such legend building was *La razón de mi vida,* a book ostensibly written by Eva Perón that was made required reading in all schools. In it Eva tells of Perón's magnificent rise to power to serve the Argentine masses and of her complete devotion to him and his cause, making herself an example of the loyalty expected of everyone else. Thousands of copies were burned by his enemies when Perón was overthrown in 1955, but reprintings in later years make it available today.

6. Hiroschi Matsushita, *Movimiento obrero argentina: 1930–1945* (Buenos Aires: Siglo Veinte, 1983).

7. Ibid., pp. 273–298. In his book Matsushita offers the most thoroughly documented study yet of labor politics before and during Perón's rise. He stresses the importance of fundamental changes in posture by the government and the old labor leadership in May 1944, claiming that opportunism won out over ideology on both sides and established the basis for Perón's capture of the labor movement during the following year.

8. Few events in Argentine history have more written about them than those that occurred in October 1945. Probably the most complete account is Felix Luna, *El 45* (Buenos Aires: Sudamericana, 1971). Also see Nicholas Fraser and Marysa Navarro, *Eva Perón* (New York: Norton, 1980), ch. 4.

9. Ray Josephs, *Argentine Diary: The Inside Story of the Coming of Fascism* (New York: Random House, 1944), p. 261.

10. Ibid.

11. Relations between the United States and Argentina between 1943 and 1946 were obviously more complex than described here, as recent research into State Department records reveals. See Carlos Escude, *Gran Bretaña–Estados Unidos y la declinacion argentina: 1942–1949* (Buenos Aires: Belgrano, 1983); and Mario Rapoport, *Gran Bretaña, Estados Unidos y las clases dirigentes argentinas: 1940–1945* (Buenos Aires: Belgrano, 1980).

12. On the election campaigns, see Luna, *El 45.*

13. Alberto Ciria, "Peronism and Political Structures: 1945–1955," in *New Perspectives on Modern Argentina* (Bloomington, Indiana: Latin American Studies Program, 1972), pp. 1–7.

14. Ruben H. Zorrilla, *El liderazgo sindical argentino: desde sus origenes hasta 1975* (Buenos Aires: Siglo Veinte, 1983), pp. 28–39.

15. Marysa Navarro, "Evita and Peronism," in *Juan Perón and the Reshaping of Argentina,* ed. Frederick Turner and José Enrique Miguens (Pittsburgh: University of Pittsburgh Press, 1983), p. 15.

16. Ibid., pp. 18–25. Also see Fraser and Navarro, *Eva Perón.*

17. On Peronist policy, see Gary W. Wynia, *Argentina in the Postwar Era: Economic Policy Making in a Divided Society* (Albuquerque: Unversity of New Mexico Press, 1972), pp. 47–80.

18. This point is made very effectively by Guido Di Tella, "La Argentina economica (1943–1973)," *Criterio* (navidad 1982): 746–763.

19. The latest attempt to portray Peronism as the fascist enemy of real proletarian revolution is Juan José Sebreli's *Los deseos imaginarios del peronismo* (Buenos Aires: Legasa, 1983).

20. See Gino Germani, "Fascism and Social Class," in *The Nature of Fascism,* ed. S. J. Woolf (London: Weidenfeld, 1968); and *Politica y sociedad en una epoca de transición* (Buenos Aires: Paidos, 1968).

21. I am grateful to Paul Johnson's insights into Italian fascism for this comparison. See *Modern Times: The World from the Twenties to the Eighties* (New York: Harper Colophon Books, 1985), pp. 96–103.

22. This comparison draws heavily on descriptions of European fascism offered by Renzo de Felice in *Interpretations of Fascism* (Cambridge: Harvard University Press, 1977), ch. 1.

23. Wynia, *Argentina in the Postwar Era,* pp. 52–61.

24. Ibid., ch. 2.

25. Marcelo Cavarozzi, "Unions and Politics in Argentina, 1955–1962," Wilson Center Working Paper, no. 63, pp. 4–12.

26. Data on employment are taken from Kuhl, *Una política industrial para la Argentina,* p. 117; and on labor membership from Zorrilla, *El liderazgo sindical argentino,* p. 129. The high percentage of union membership is explained in part by Argentina's lack of a large rural labor surplus.

27. Zorrilla, *El liderazgo sindical argentino,* p. 129.

28. Ibid., pp. 60–68.

29. On labor during this period, see Ruben Rotondaro, *Realidad y cambio en el sindicalismo* (Buenos Aires: Pleamar, 1971).

30. I am grateful to Eldon Kenworthy's comments on the Cavarozzi paper for having pointed out this retention of perspective and its causes. See Cavarozzi, "Unions and Politics in Argentina," p. 18.

31. José Enrique Miguens, "The Presidential Elections of 1973 and the End of an Ideology," in Turner and Miguens, *Juan Perón and the Reshaping of Argentina.* Also see Manuel Mora and Peter Smith, "Peronism and Economic Development: The 1973 Elections," in ibid.

32. The eventful year of 1973 is neatly summarized in Gerardo Lopez Alonso, *Cincuenta años de la historia argentina* (Buenos Aires: Belgrano, 1982), pp. 270–285.

33. The program is described in some detail in Guido Di Tella, *Perón-Perón 1973–1976* (Buenos Aires: Sundamericana, 1983), ch. 3; and Horacio Maceyra, *Campora/Perón/Isabel* (Buenos Aires: Centro Editor de América Latina, 1983), ch. 4.

34. On dissent within the Peronist movement during Perón's last months, see Jorge Luis Bernetti, *El peronismo de la victoria* (Buenos Aires: Legasa, 1983).

35. Guido Di Tella, "The Economic Policies of Argentina's Labor-Based Government, 1973–1976," Wilson Center Latin American Program Working Paper, no. 47, p. 14.

36. Maceyra, *Campora/Perón/Isabel,* ch. 7.

37. Lopez, *Cincuenta años de la historia argentina,* pp. 324–327; and Maceyra, *Campora/Perón/Isabel,* ch. 7.

38. The history of these and other guerrilla organizations is summarized in James Kohl and John Litt, *Urban Guerrilla Warfare in Latin America* (Cambridge: MIT Press, 1974), ch. 4.

39. Celia Szusterman, "Review and Commentary," *Journal of Latin American Studies* 16:157–170.

40. Ibid., pp. 79–84.

41. Kohl and Litt, *Urban Guerrilla Warfare in Latin America,* pp. 333–334.

42. Richard Gillespie, *Soldiers of Perón* (New York, Oxford University Press, 1980), p. 121.

43. Kohl and Litt, *Urban Guerrilla Warfare in Latin America,* p. 333.

44. Gillespie, *Soldiers of Perón,* pp. 149–150.

45. Ibid., pp. 160–163; Montonero leader Mario Firmenich announced their war against Peronist authorities at a secret press conference on September 6, 1974.

46. Ibid., p. 251.

4

El Partido Militar

Argentines are not fond of military officers and were never less so than in 1983, when they paused to contemplate the crimes that their soldiers had committed against them during the previous decade. Over 9,000 citizens had been killed by military and paramilitary security personnel since 1976, most of them after being tortured in secret detention centers. General Galtieri's taking the country into a war that he could not win only deepened antipathy toward his kind. Without a doubt, it was the lowest point in the history of the armed forces. Nevertheless, it did not mark their end as a political force. On the contrary, they still had to be reckoned with as President Raul Alfonsín reminded everyone only eighteen months after his inauguration, when he announced on national television that unnamed persons were plotting a coup to overthrow him. Obviously the *partido militar* was too much a part of the nation's politics to disappear very quickly.[1]

Nor should we expect it to vanish, for the military's political involvement is just as much a part of national life as party politics are. To begin with, officers

> have taken power repeatedly for the simple and actually rather banal reason that the civilians have not managed our affairs of state very adequately. Military coups are like artillery projectiles, which explode not on their own account but because of those who load and fire them. Thus our present [in 1981] "authoritarian" situation is not the responsibility of the military but of all of us.[2]

Politicians for years have readily accepted corporals, generals, and admirals as "colleagues in a complex and at times byzantine game."[3] The script and the cast of characters changed often, but at one time or another members of the lower, middle, and upper classes, as well as leaders of labor, industry, and agriculture, have turned to the armed forces for help in the solution of political and economic problems that they could not solve by themselves. The military once responded cautiously, acting like the reluctant partner in an unsought courtship, but when officers carried out their first coup on September 6, 1930, they accepted new responsibilities, thereafter becoming a self-proclaimed "guardian of the constitution" that considered itself above civilian law. As if to make their point, they have deposed six constitutional presidents since 1930—four of them after 1955—as well as six of their own de facto ones; and they have supplied the nation with presidents during eighteen of the past forty years.

Professionalism the Argentine Way

Military officers were not supposed to become politicians. The oligarchs who created the nation's modern armed forces wanted a professional military able to defend the country while leaving the affairs of state to them. That is why a president like Domingo Faustino Sarmiento, intent on "civilizing" the country, founded its first military college in 1870 and a naval academy soon thereafter. At the turn of the century a war college was added and a German colonel appointed its acting director. Professionalization requires expertise, institutional autonomy, internal control, and the creation of a sense of corporate identity. Formal rules must prevail over informal ones, while quality of performance and seniority serve as the basis for promotion. It was to achieve these ends that German instructors were hired, compulsory military service for twenty-year-old males made law, and statutes developed to regulate military careers, from recruitment through promotion and retirement. It seemed to work at first, and officers soon developed a real sense of professional purpose, performing initially as loyal servants of civilian authorities.[4]

While the army was taking its instruction from the then powerful Germans, the navy emulated the British, then ruler of the Atlantic. Argentina's first admirals purchased English ships and copied British organization. Considering themselves more sophisticated technically and more worldly than army generals, they recruited the sons of wealthy Anglophiles to their service. Their elitism has declined some with time, but they retain a very separate identity and still enjoy a rivalry with the larger army.[5]

Professionalization did not keep soldiers out of politics very long, however. The Radical party, excluded from office by ruling oligarchs at the turn of the century, recruited individual officers and soldiers to participate in the several unsuccessful insurrections that they staged to drive the oligarchs from office. Later in 1916, when the Radicals finally were allowed to govern, President Hipólito Yrigoyen repaid his rebellious military allies with reimbursements of the salaries they had lost when forced into retirement as punishment for having cast their lot with the Radicals. When charged with politicizing the military with such payoffs, Yrigoyen defended his right to do so, claiming that he was doing little more than rewarding officers who had understood that their "primordial obligations to country and constitution [were] far superior to all military regulations."[6] When officers removed Yrigoyen a decade later they would make the same claim, to his dismay and everlasting regret.

What unity there was within the services disappeared in the 1920s as officers disagreed over the propriety of the Radicals playing politics with them. Yrigoyen frequently sent the army to intervene in provinces and remove opposition officials, ostensibly to eradicate corruption, and many officers resented being used as if they were members of the president's political fraternity. At the same time, some among them devoted their energies to political debate within secret lodges formed by officers who were concerned about defining the military's role in society in more activist ways. It was from such lodges that a new generation sprung to the aid of oligarchs who had grown petrified by the Radicals' ineptness in dealing with the depression that struck Argentina in 1929. Led by retired General José Uriburu, they plotted for three months in mid-1930, some of them inspired by Uriburu's proposal to replace constitutional politics with fascism. The coup came on September 6, 1930, but Uriburu lasted only a short time, his fanatical nationalism and dreams of corporatism being too much for a oligarchy that felt more comfortable with their old constitutional charade.

The coup set a precedent that would be emulated many times afterward. By stepping in and taking it upon themselves to "organize" the nation's affairs, the armed forces became a legitimate participant in the nation's politics, one that every interest would thereafter consider a potential ally. They had in effect become the *partido militar,* a political organization with commitments that obligated future generations of officers to assume responsibility for the nation's governance whether in office or not.[7]

Officers opposed to Uriburu's extremist politics replaced him with more moderate General Agustín P. Justo, whom the oligarchy then elected president in a rigged contest. But divisions among officers over the country's direction persisted. At one extreme were so-called legalists, who preferred constitutional government. Their convictions were strong enough to cause them to launch unsuccessful coups against Justo in 1932 and 1934. They were opposed by authoritarian "corporatists," who had backed Uriburu only to lose out to Justo. Most officers positioned themselves between these two extremes, however, content either to help the oligarchy defend its fraudulent democracy or to stay out of politics altogether.[8] Political division within the military did not end in the 1930s, but has persisted to this day. Legalists supportive of constitutional democracy have reappeared in every generation, as have authoritarians. This is why a military that seems entirely fascist in its objectives can be heard to praise the virtues of democracy. Their chameleonlike political behavior reflects honest differences among them, as well as the preference of many for leaving the nation's supervision to civilians, fearful that their involvement in politics will breed internecine conflicts that will undermine their operating as a professional organization.

Until 1943 the oligarchy was served well by the armed forces, but the marriage was doomed to failure by the incompatibility of the military's ambitions for the country's economic modernization and the oligarchs' inertia. In the 1930s the officer corps doubled in size and so did their ambitions. Secret lodges thrived during World War II, as soldiers debated diplomatic posture and economic strategy just as civilians were doing. When the war began seventeen of thirty-four general officers in the army had undergone training in Germany, making most of them pro-Axis in sentiment and insistent on a policy of neutrality in the face of British and U.S. pressure on the civilian oligarchy to declare war against the Germans.[9] Discontent with the oligarchy's flirtations with the Allies grew within some lodges, as did a feeling of descent into helplessness in the face of war-induced economic isolation. Nationalistic officers wanted a strong Argentina and became convinced that the armed forces would have to take it upon themselves to change the nation's direction. Never in complete agreement over what direction to take once in charge, they put the lessons they had learned in 1930 to work, organizing a coup to evict the oligarchs in June 1943.

Two competing military factions joined in the conspiracy, one liberally inclined and the other corporatist. While liberals dominated the coup's original leadership, they were never completely in charge afterward. Both factions found places in the new cabinet and contested for influence over the nation's course. Two issues, one domestic and the other foreign, divided them. The former involved a choice between holding free elections or creating a "permanent" authoritarian government of some kind, and the latter between staying neutral or declaring war on the Axis powers. There was no easy way out of the dilemma, and President Ramírez vaccillated as long as possible, finally breaking relations with Germany in February 1944 and announcing elections for later that year. But the triumph of the pro-Allies liberals was only temporary, for while they did get the election they wanted, it was won not by a liberal but by nationalist Juan Perón.[10] What really disturbed Perón's rivals within the armed forces was his defeating them at their own game by mobilizing enough popular support to win a free election, something it was thought the nationalists, with their disdain for democracy, could never do. They tried to block Perón's ascent, as we learned in the previous chapter, but showed themselves most inept in doing so, effectively giving up when they released him from prison and turned him back to his *descamisados* on October 17, 1945.

Why rival officers did not just leave Perón in jail and put down the demonstrations violently is not self-evident. No doubt disagreements among service commanders over his imprisonment weakened their ability to stand firm. Moreover, he had many allies within the government who argued against taking on the workers directly in what was sure to be a bloody confrontation with lasting effects on the military's political legitimacy. Officers fear the masses and have never welcomed a war with them. They want to be respected for their leadership as well as their power and were desperate in 1945 to avoid contributing to the alienation and radicalization of the working class. In the end Perón gave them a way out, one that was preferable to continuous conflict between military authorities and the masses, even if risky.[11]

He glorified the armed forces, giving them a prominent position in the manufacture of weapons and in the creation of a steel industry. But the country's soldiers were never at home with his personalistic politics and conspiratorial ways; nor did they warm to the demagogic power accumulated by Evita, becoming most offended when Perón suggested her for the vice presidency in 1951. That same year his opponents in the army, with substantial support from the navy and air force, attempted a coup against him but lost when most of the army remained loyal. He punished the conspirators with imprisonment, but that did not deter more plotting against him, much of it picking up momentum during his battle with the Catholic church over the legalization of divorce in 1954. In June 1955 another coup was attempted, only to fail, but three months later the military succeeded, driving Perón into exile without his asking the masses to go to the streets to defend him.

Anti-Peronist Crusades

Perón's overthrow put the armed forces deeper into politics than ever before, increasing among them the conviction that they were all that stood between the nation and its self-destruction. One does not remove the leader of the country's most popular party and turn its governance over to the minority easily, even less so in an Argentina where Peronists believe that they alone are the nation's only legitimate rulers. Nor was it realistic to expect that his flight would spell the end of Peronism as a cause or political force. Yet that is precisely what General Pedro Aramburu and his cohorts set out to accomplish once they were firmly established by the end of 1955. But doing it proved more difficult than they had anticipated, and when a CGT convention was finally held in 1957 its members elected a new generation of leaders loyal to Perón, leaving the military where it had begun.

The Peronists' stubborn resistance to dismemberment left the armed forces with another political dilemma from which there was no easy escape. They wanted to create a civilian government able to direct the nation, one that was neither Peronist nor too feeble to deal with the Peronist opposition. When they began planning for the restoration of constitutional government they found themselves with just three options, none of which was satisfactory. They could hold free elections and accept a likely Peronist victory. Or they could hold elections and exclude them from participating, allowing the creation of a weak, minority government to whose destruction the Peronists would undoubtedly commit themselves. Or, finally, they could govern by themselves, something they were not yet convinced they could do satisfactorily. Not surprisingly they chose the second option, knowing full well that they were inviting Peronists to reject the entire constitutional process by excluding them. Claims that the Peronists' undemocratic behavior necessitated their exclusion were convincing to officers and the heads of other parties who wanted the government for themselves, but the working class would have none of it, declaring that any government so created would be illegitimate and the object of protests.

The script was written in 1958 and the charade acted out during the next eight years. Arturo Frondizi, the Radical party's candidate, won the presidential election that year, helped out by making an agreement with Perón that brought him votes in exchange for his promise to legalize a Peronist party during his tenure. But the CGT soon turned against Frondizi, depriving him of anything resembling majority support. He legalized its party nevertheless, only to be defeated by it in gubernatorial elections in 1962 and then deposed by the military for having permitted a Peronist triumph.

What to do next touched off a bitter conflict between factions within the armed forces that ended only after blood was shed by both sides. Army Commander Juan Carlos Onganía led one group, called the Azules, most of whom came from the cavalry and claimed the restoration of constitutional government as their cause. In rebellion against them stood anticonstitutionalist Colorados, who drew on the infantry, the engineer corps, and the navy for their support. Each wanted to decide what the armed forces' politics would be over the next few years.

For nearly six months they maneuvered against one another, eventually moving troops into positions and engaging in brief battles on a few military bases. With the critical support of the air force the Azules finally gained the upper hand, but not before retired General Benjamín Menéndez, a leader in the 1951 coup attempt against Perón, had led a last Colorado charge.[12] Colorado marines sent by the navy took over much of the city of La Plata just to the south of Buenos Aires as well as portions of the port in the capital. Simultaneously sailors on the Punta Indio and Puerto Belgrano bases announced their rebellion against Azule authorities. Azule armored units struck back, subduing Punta Indio but only after absorbing blows from naval air attacks. The Colorados gave up finally, and the Azules went ahead with their plan for elections in 1963. They also devoted themselves to unifying the armed forces once the dust had settled.[13]

The Azules prohibited Peronist candidates once again when elections were held in 1963, this time giving the victory to Radical Arturo Illia with only 25 percent of the popular vote. For the next three years the CGT harassed Illia's administration, gradually discrediting its authority and provoking another coup in 1966. Ironically the same officers who had fought within the armed forces to assure that constitutional government and military professionalism were restored led the coup against Illia in 1966, General Juan Carlos Onganía himself becoming president afterward. Illia's brief tenure had actually given Onganía the time he needed to unite the military in preparation for its trying to govern the country by itself. Military officers cannot run the country if they are at odds with each other. But once united by common convictions and purpose their chances of success are vastly improved, or so they believed when they set out to remake Argentina in their own image on June 28, 1966.[14]

Why Bureaucratic Authoritarianism?

The creation of military regimes in Brazil in 1964 and Argentina in 1966 devoted to ruling indefinitely was unprecedented and demands some explanation. Unfortunately, scholars have yet to agree on exactly what caused this strange departure from past behavior.[15] The most popular account views it as a political consequence of incomplete industrialization and class conflict in highly dependent countries. For two decades they had been modernizing their economies using a strategy of import substitution industrialization. But early in the 1960s the momentum generated by the creation of consumer goods industries had faded, putting pressures on authorities faced with rising expectations of a working class that had grown powerful with industrialization. Conflicts over too few goods grew, and civilian governments tried to patch them over with pacification measures that proved inflationary and economically destabilizing. Eventually it became obvious that in order to produce more and import less, industrialization had to be "deepened" with the addition of basic industries. That could be accomplished, however, only with the participation of multinational corporations, who were reluctant to invest in countries wracked by social conflicts that their leaders seemed too weak politically to resolve. Something more powerful was needed and bureaucratic authoritarianism was one source of such power. Advised by civilian and military technocrats devoted to attracting new capital from at home and abroad, officers took over and did as they were told, making it clear that they would govern their countries until they were satisfied that they had changed society enough to guarantee transition to orderly and highly disciplined civilian rule.[16]

There is a certain plausibility to such a story, at least in the Argentine case, since it describes the obvious conflicts generated by populism and insufficient and inconsistent economic growth. The efforts of the Onganía government to attract foreign investment after it took over lends further credibility to it. But one risks oversimplification by looking only at economic causes of such political change. Politics is conditioned and constrained by economic realities, but it is seldom caused by them alone. The officers who evicted Illia in 1966 had more on their mind than just economic growth. Equally influential was the political impasse into which they had put the country in 1955 and the frustration it had bred among them and much of the nation's upper and middle classes. The "Peronist problem" was very real to them, especially after watching the CGT use its *plan de lucha* to harass the Illia government, making it seem helpless before the country's fundamental political problem. Another solution had to be tried and governing by themselves until they had de-Peronized the nation was all that was left.[17]

If they needed grand ideas to help them justify their new crusade, Onganía and his colleagues found it in the national security doctrine that had been maturing in the region's war colleges during the 1950s and 1960s. The Brazilians had advanced it the furthest, having taken their inspiration from President Truman's anticommunist containment strategy and the counterinsurgency doctrines advanced by the French in their efforts to put down rebellion in Algeria. An added incentive came from Fidel Castro's triumph in Cuba in 1959 and the threat that Castro-inspired insurgents posed to militaries all over the hemisphere. To avert a similar fate Brazilian officers concentrated their energies on designing a war plan aimed at defeating the radical left in their midst.

The result, as prepared and taught at its war college, became the national security doctrine.[18]

Onganía appreciated the homework that the Brazilians had done for him. In early August 1964 he warned during a visit to the U.S. Military Academy at West Point that it had become the mission of Latin America's militaries to protect their countries against "exotic ideologies" that could upset authority in their republican systems. Back in Argentina the general's warnings were taken more seriously than they were at West Point, and it was not long before conservative magazines were predicting that he was on his way to becoming "an Argentine de Gaulle."[19]

The doctrine was an approach to politics that specialized in the identification of man's enemies. Marx was one of them, and Freud, the destroyer of families, another. Neither belonged in the loyal, patriotic society that the military wanted. But even they were not the source of the problem, just manifestations of it. More fundamental were flaws in human nature that had allowed excessive passion and aggression to go uncontrolled by reason. According to one Brazilian military theorist,

> . . . The general and growing insecurity in which distressed mankind is struggling today is the venomous opium that gives rise to and feeds these awful visions, able meanwhile to become a monstrous reality. The insecurity of citizens within the nation and the insecurity of the State facing other States, the omnipresent vision of war—civil war or subversive war or international war—dominate the world of our times and explain the neurotic distress with which panic-stricken crowds and the helpless persons, the disillusion and afflicted peoples, and finally humankind rises up and complains and struggles, ready for slavery if some lords or tyrants offer them on a dish of lentils a little security and peace.[20]

To General Golbery, the author of this statement (and advisor to Brazilian military presidents after 1964), people were consumed by a "venomous opium," reality was "monstrous," and crowds were "panic-striken," and "helpless and disillusioned" by "war." When confronted with social tension people became "neurotic victims" of it, always yielding to aggressors who threatened their safety or promised to feed them. People were weak and vulnerable and, therefore, had to be protected by those stronger than themselves, the best of them being military officers educated in these "truths" at war colleges and sworn to the nation's protection against itself. That soldiers might appear to be as uncivilized as society's worst enemies when they were at war with them did not concern Golbery, convinced as he was that the repression they practiced was more than justified by the ends that they pursued.

The Christian faith also compelled the military to action. To them the newer theologies of liberation, then popular at the grass roots all over Latin America, betrayed the beliefs of traditional Catholicism, subverting hierarchical authority in the church as well as in society. Without his own armies to do battle with betrayers of the faith, the Pope needed all the help that he could get from secular militaries, they rationalized, convinced that their defense of a medieval Christianity moralized their effort. Communism was the enemy of Christianity and capitalism, so those who criticized either were taken to be communist and deserving destruction. It was an old refrain, but to military officers who had watched Fidel Castro put their Cuban colleagues to the firing squad in 1959 and then pronounce himself a communist, it was a very persuasive one, especially in Argentina and Brazil. But even more important, it served as a convenient rationalization for a new kind of military intervention, one that sought to demobilize organized labor and the proponents of radical reform simultaneously. Proletarian resistance to authority had to be ended, as did all other sources of conflict, and the doctrine told everyone why their survival as nations depended on its being done.[21]

An Authoritarian Experiment

The Argentine military is wedded to political simplicity, so when it took over in 1966 it announced that it was going back to basics, telling the nation,

> The Armed Forces, interpreting the highest common interest, assumes the responsibility, not to be relinquished, of guaranteeing national unity and making general welfare possible, incorporating into the country the modern elements of culture, science, and technology. By so doing, they make a substantial change that raises the country to the place that it deserves, given the intelligence and human values of its inhabitants and the wealth with which Providence has endowed its territory.[22]

"Responsibility, not to be relinquished" was the key phrase, a reminder to everyone that the military would thereafter remain the judge and jury in national politics, whether in office or not. Onganía and his colleagues were as convinced as General Uriburu had been in 1930 that "only the armed forces, with their code of honor, patriotism, and superior sense of organization and discipline, could provide the leadership necessary to bring about a national revitalization."[23] Politics, as traditionally practiced in the country, was no longer affordable. Argentina had known enough of opportunism, disorder, demagoguery, and immorality. To eliminate such vices Onganía offered two solutions, one visionary and the other quite concrete. The vision was of a new social order, more coherent and socially integrated than before, and one in which something called "spiritual unity" replaced egoism as the principal determinant of human conduct, establishing a community ethic to replace individual ones. At its worst, it reflected a pathetic craving for the conversion of Argentina into the homogeneous and unified society that it never had been.[24]

This vision also had a longitudinal dimension, one that viewed the world's salvation as a progression that went through at least three separate stages. Having learned in the war college how economic, social, and political forces were related, officers knew that each had to be changed in order to affect the other. Onganía wanted to begin with the economy, then turn to the social and political structures to complete the nation's transformation. Somehow, once basic economic problems were solved, conversion of the populace to a new community ethic that bred consensus and harmony would follow, yielding conflict-free politics. It was as if officers had read texts about the coherence of a British or German society and thought that it could be replicated through their autocratic direction, ignoring for the time being that their authoritarianism would breed its own antithesis of opposition and protest.[25]

Onganía's concrete objectives were of a more familiar kind. He closed the legislature, outlawed all political parties, and took over the General Confederation of Labor, cutting off all channels of protest until his economic program was completed. Then he delegated immense authority to Economics Minister Adalbert Krieger Vasena, an internationally respected economist who had served in previous military governments. Krieger Vasena contended that the Argentine economy was plagued by incredible inefficiencies in the private as well as the public sector, most of them induced by excessive subsidization, overextended welfare programs, and an undisciplined working class. Accordingly, he announced a series of policies aimed at reducing the public sector deficit, raising taxes, cutting import tariffs, establishing wage controls and voluntary price controls, and allowing foreign investors easier access. And before long it seemed to take effect: inflation fell to its lowest level in three decades; investment rose; and the protests of organized labor were successfully repressed. Moreover, by enticing some union leaders into cooperating with the government while repressing others it seemed as if Onganía and his advisors had at last outmaneuvered their toughest opponent.[26]

But working-class docility was only temporary, and in May 1969 the government was wracked by an outburst of public protests, later known as the Cordobazo. They began slowly, escalating as violence increased on both sides, starting on May 15 when confrontations between university students and police during a protest against increases in cafeteria prices in the northern province of Corrientes resulted in one student's death. Two days later another student was killed when sympathetic students in Rosario also protested, and then one more on May 21, the latter only fifteen years of age. Indignation spread, but it was only when students in the interior city of Córdoba organized mass demonstrations with workers in the auto industry, themselves frustrated by Onganía's repression of organized labor, that it turned into a major assault on the president's authority. On May 29 workers left their factories to march on the city, challenging police as they did, putting up barricades, burning automobiles, foreign-owned businesses, and anything else they could find, defying authorities as long as they could. Finally the army was sent in, killing 12 persons in two days and injuring at least 100 while taking hundreds prisoner, including prominent labor leaders, whom it sentenced in military tribunals. In the end the army won, as the protestors knew it would, but peace had been broken and with it confidence in Onganía's reconstruction of a new nation. He tried to pass the blame to others, even dismissing the highly successful Krieger Vasena, but the damage done was irreparable. He had done the one thing that no authoritarian military president can afford to do in Argentina: he had allowed his people to demonstrate his failure to subdue them as he had promised to do.[27]

It may seem strange that a government as strong as Onganía's, one that had successfully put down the Córdoba riots, would allow the event to induce self-doubt. But it happens often among officers, and no amount of chest beating seems sufficient to overcome their fundamental political insecurity. They know how difficult subduing a society of which they are a contributing member really is. Too many forces have accumulated too much power and skill in wielding it to yield easily to their would-be oppressors. The working class is among them. Because their conformity with government policy is so essential to its success, no government can endure working-class defiance for very long. Officers were aware of all this, having witnessed Perón's mobilization of the working class and General Aramburu's failure to "de-Peronize" it after his expulsion. General Onganía and his colleagues had also watched the intensely partisan CGT vengefully devour the Radical party governments created in 1958 and 1963 in elections from which Peronist candidates had been excluded. When they took over in 1966 the armed forces had no "solution" to the problem, aware as they were that repression alone could not keep as powerful an organization as the CGT under their control. They chose to divide and conquer, meeting labor protests head on and ruthlessly suppressing them while at the same time inviting selected unions to arrangements of mutual accommodation, allowing their leadership to stay in place as long as they controlled their urge to protest unpopular policies. It was always touch and go, and disagreements among officers over Onganía's tactics were present from the day be began. The Cordobazo proved to be too much for his critics within the army, and his refusal to listen to them only hastened his demise. Arrogant to the end, he hung on for another year until the plotters could marshal enough support within the junta to depose him in May 1970.

A Fundamental Political Problem

It is not just the occasional unanticipated crisis that does military authoritarianism in, but also the inability of military officers to create political institutions that can take over from their autocratic ones, themselves insufficient to subdue a society as energetic and experienced in political conflict as Argentina's. Argentine officers are not comfortable with political engineering. Nor are they very knowledgeable about their own society. They know some things about their people, but by reason of their profession and its self-imposed isolation, their understanding of how Argentina works is quite superficial. They seldom experience its diversity or exchange ideas with a very wide range of civilians. Their own world is a rather basic one, composed of goods and evils, orders and obedience. That is why they are compelled to abdicate the economy's management to civilians whom they do not really trust. Their collusion with technocrats is never as intimate as their critics presume but is, like so many things in military governance, a marriage of convenience between two groups that need each other to advance their respective interests.[28]

Military governments need more than ideas and advisors to become successful, however. They also require public support. This may sound strange given their power and willingness to apply it repressively. But it is one thing to stage a coup and close down political parties and labor unions and quite another to sustain the reconstruction of a nation's politics and economy using force alone. Everyone must play a part, most particularly the members of the middle and upper classes who manage and finance the nation's most powerful public and private institutions. But in winning and retaining their allegiance military officers are rather inept, if only because an inferiority complex that makes their working with competent civilians so threatening to them. Although they appear to despise their subjects, they want desperately to win their recognition and approval. However, they have no clear idea about how to do it. With the exception of daring stunts like the Malvinas invasion, they are forced by their habits to rely primarily on the public's appreciation for their repression of conflict. It is as if they expect the public to assess their performance much as their military superiors did when they were junior officers, winning approval by defeating "enemies" in a disciplined and polished manner.

What they do not understand is that the people who appear to appreciate them when they put an end to lawlessness are never certain that the military's kind of authoritarianism is the type they really prefer. In fact, most of their civilian suitors always turn out to be very fickle allies whose desire for their own control over the state turns them eventually against their military rescuers. Support for military intervention is usually motivated by rather narrow, short-term self-interests rather than philosophical convictions. Rampant inflation, working-class protest, terrorism, or a bad business climate frighten them and alienate them from weak civilian-run governments, prompting their acceptance of military intervention as a necessary evil in times of crisis. This gives the military a certain legitimacy, but it is of a highly instrumental kind that lasts only until order is restored or the military proves itself incapable of solving fundamental economic problems. In either case, demands for the restoration of civilian government will be heard within a few years of the coup as career politicians, after a breather, become eager to get back to work serving their patronage-hungry constituents. Officers may ignore them at first, but public disaffection with their authoritarian ways always grows. Within a time they will disagree over how to respond to such discontent, feeding impressions of their losing control over each other, which in turn foster hopes that added pressure will cause them to give up their enterprise rather than risk serious conflicts between the three services. There is no easy solution to the problem they face: holding firm might work for a time, but it will only reinforce the public's perception of a regime in serious trouble because it fears its authority is dissipating rapidly. Ideally, they might find a way out by finishing the creation of new political institutions to replace their autocratic ones, establishing a government that allows for enough civilian involvement to placate or coopt their critics. But they seem incapable of such creativity.

Onganía's regime was brought down by all of these things, leading one to conclude in 1973 that Argentina was not amenable to being reformed by its military. Nor was the military capable of progressing beyond the first of its three stages of reconstruction. But the most obvious things in life are not always the most influential, especially where compulsion to ignore them runs deep. So it was when General

Jorge Videla and his colleagues decided to give authoritarianism another try in 1976, confident that then, more than ever before, Argentines would appreciate what the armed forces could do for them.

Going to War

Exhibiting a somber formality characteristic of officers when they take on the chore of ruling the nation, the junta that was created on March 24, 1976, pronounced constitutional government a failure. Argentines needed discipline not liberty and now they would have it. As officers saw it, politicians had become too partisan, labor leaders too selfish and corrupt, businessmen too slovenly and unproductive, and themselves tired of trying to set things straight by meddling in elections and threatening coups for nearly two decades with little success. Economic debauchery had reached its limits and the time had come to restore discipline using the laws of supply and demand as well as political repression. Much like Puritans intent on punishing people for their sins, they demanded that the evils of populism be replaced by the cold rationality of the marketplace. It all seemed rather utopian at the time, but that did not reduce its appeal to many Argentines who were themselves exhausted by political stalemates and economic crises. For them it was time to take on the nation's "Italianized" way of life and purge it of its licentious, populist ways.[29]

General Jorge Videla seemed the right man for the job, having risen up the hierarchy as a student and teacher of the army's national security ideology. When the military evicted the oligarchy back in 1943 Videla was in his final year at the Colegio Militar, nineteen years of age. He started his career as an infantry second lieutenant in 1944, ending his first decade of service in 1954 as an instructor in the Colegio. Then he went on to study in the Escuela Superior de Guerra, Argentina's war college. In 1956, not long after Perón's overthrow, he began his "international" education, serving as aide to the chief of Argentina's first delegation to the Inter-American Defense Council in Washington, D.C., returning home in 1959 to teach military intelligence courses until 1961, when he took over as head of cadets at the Colegio Militar. Any officer who aspires to lead the army must become a military politician operating within the Defense Ministry's hierarchy, and in 1962 Videla moved into the army's command, where he observed the conflict between Colorados and Azules that erupted that year. In 1964 he went abroad again, this time to study counterinsurgency tactics under U.S. instructors at their school in the Panama Canal Zone, then in its heyday as part of the U.S. effort to help Latin American armies prevent more Castros.

The following year he joined with colleagues to teach strategy in the Centro de Altos Estudios, an organization for advanced study devoted to preparing colonels for their responsibilities as the nation's guardians at home and abroad. It was no coincidence that Videla later drew much of his presidential staff from colleagues and students he had known at the Centro. But that would come later; in 1973 he was given the highest honor for the consummate "professional" when he was appointed head of the Colegio Militar. From there he went on to become the army's commander-in-chief in 1975, and then president after the coup a year later. No officer plots a career intended to end in the presidency, but had one been designed for an officer planning to lead a war against terrorism, it would have looked like Videla's.[30]

He went to work right away, unleashing the three services' intelligence and counterinsurgency units to make war on the Montoneros and the ERP guerrillas, who were waging their own war against the most powerful members of the national establishment. It went quietly and methodically, with no boasting about arrests or killings. Videla was a professional and not a politician, one who had a job to do and did it brutally and efficiently without concern for what any but his fellow officers thought about it. For him the terrorist was the lowest form of life, a mixture of delinquent, mentally insane, and Marxist mercenary. To reward terrorism by neglecting to combat it was tantamount to treason.[31] He did not ask civilians whether they agreed, confident that their fright and passivity was endorsement enough if any were needed. Most people pretended not to notice what he was doing, going about their lives assuming that it would all be over quickly. But many others, most of whom had never committed acts of terrorism, lived in fear, worried that they too might be taken away from their homes in one of the government's infamous, unmarked, gray Ford Falcons, never to be seen again. The intelligence arms of the three services and the police took several "suspects" daily to the 280 prisons that they had secretly created, most of them on military bases in or near the nation's largest cities, where they tortured and killed them and destroyed records of their having been arrested. That the Nazis had done such things in Germany everyone knew, but Argentina was not Germany, nor was its military "Germanic" in character any longer. That is why it all seemed so unbelievable at first; but as disappearances and deaths accumulated, it became obvious that the country was being raped by its own kind.

A decade later most Argentines would deny having known at the time how far the military was going with its "war," but its deeds were never entirely hidden from public view. Though it was not until investigations completed in 1984 revealed how many lives were actually taken that the severity of the repression was documented, people knew that some among them were disappearing, perhaps for good. Many in fact, especially in the business community, were active supporters of the military's crackdown, ostracizing those among them who objected to cleansing the country of its youthful "undesirables." And very few in the nation's political parties or its most prominent institutions spoke out against the barbarity, resigning themselves to living with it for the time being, watching silently as those who did protest, like *Buenos Aires Herald* editor Robert Cox, were chased into exile. As a result, they now must come to terms with their own consciences, coping in individual ways with the moral scar that their military's crimes and their tolerance of them have left, knowing that no number of show trials will ever remove it entirely.[32]

An Experiment in Economic Liberty

There is something paradoxical about authoritarians becoming the advocates of economic liberty, but it never bothered them. As they saw it politics and economics each had their own logics and power structures, so there was no need to connect them as liberalism had once done, making freedom in each dependent on its existence in the other. While Videla's policemen were secretly pulling up to houses and kidnapping whomever they pleased, wealthy businessman José Martínez de Hoz, a collaborator with previous military governments, worked on the liberation of the nation's troubled economy. He had persuaded the junta that what Argentina needed was a massive dose of economic liberalism that aimed at transforming its highly subsidized and overregulated enterprises into ones that lived or died by the dictates of supply and demand in national and international marketplaces. Like Krieger Vasena during the Onganía years, Martínez de Hoz was convinced that Argentina languished because of the inefficiency of enterprises that relied far too much on a protected national market for their survival. With production for the domestic market reaching its natural limits, real growth in the future would have to come from exports. And because commodity exports were not, by themselves, sufficient to sustain rapid growth, industry would have to do the job. But that would not come easily for, in order to compete with Third World industrial product exporters like Taiwan, Korea, and Brazil, Argentina would have to reduce the prices of its industrial products substantially by cutting labor costs and achieving higher industrial efficiency. And the only way to do that was to force domestic firms to compete with lower-priced imports by reducing tariffs even if it led to the failure of local industries that could not compete.

Martínez de Hoz did not write the final chapter in Argentine economic history during the next five years, but he did produce one of the country's most controversial ones. He was well known inside and outside the country, born into a wealthy old family with substantial interests in land and industry. He was the modern oligarch: articulate, well acquainted with business leaders in Europe and the United States, and always available to assist any Argentine government that would entrust the economy to him and his sophisticated colleagues. He had served briefly as economics minister in 1962 in a military government, had supported the efforts of Krieger Vasena during the Onganía years, and had made his proposals known to military officers before the 1976 coup. His appointment as Economics Minister was never automatic, however; none of them are. Generals are not closely acquainted with most civilian economists. When they create a government they often screen candidates for positions in it, listening to their proposals and then deliberating among themselves before announcing their choices. Martínez de Hoz was especially appealing in 1976 because of his connections with bankers in New York and London at a time when the country was being overwhelmed by its foreign debt. Videla also hoped that this wealthy entrepreneur would persuade Argentina's rich to bring their money home after three years of capital flight under the Peronists. Still, the new minister's internationalist economics, with its emphasis on free trade and receptiveness to foreign investment, frightened some officers, many of them reluctant to abandon their nationalism for what seemed a risky reentry into the world economy on foreigners' terms. Their distrust of Martínez de Hoz put many obstacles in his path later on, most of them coming when he tried to reduce the size of the public sector and its many military-directed enterprises.[33]

It is popular in Argentina today to believe that it was greed more than economic philosophy that motivated Martínez de Hoz. It is not easy to separate the two ever, and even harder when the philosophy espoused favors the minister's social class more than it does the others. But to stress personal motives is to ignore the economic ideas on which his programs were founded, ideas then popular in Chile and Uruguay as well as Argentina, inspired by monetarists in the United States and their students who had returned home to their respective Latin American countries in the 1960s and 1970s to advocate the restoration of market economics to countries where populism had produced an undisciplined work force, a bloated public sector, and a class of industrialists who survived primarily because they were protected against foreign competition. This economy of protection and speculation, they insisted, had to be transformed into one of production. As they saw it, the logic of their analysis was quite compelling.[34]

Businessmen were totally unprepared for what followed. Com-

4.1 Phases of Economic Policy, 1976–81

Phase 1	Orthodox stabilization (April 1976–February 1977)
Phase 2	Unorthodox "price truce" (March–August 1977)
Phase 3	Credit squeeze (September 1977–November 1978)
Phase 4	Application of "convergence" (December 1978–February 1981)

plaints against their inefficiencies had been made before but seldom had they been punished for them, and they had no reason to expect that their nationalistic military would allow it to happen this time. But the new minister was determined to break the cycle by making local manufacturers compete in an open market that included cheaper imported goods. Well-financed, capital-intensive industries could adapt to the challenge, but for the vast majority who had survived through protection, tariff reduction brought the threat of disaster. It was not just a matter of large firms versus small ones or foreign versus domestic, for many large foreign enterprises had come into the Argentine market in order to get under the country's tariff barriers, and once in place they were no more eager for liberalization than anyone else.[35]

The plan was composed of three essentials: first, tariff reductions to invite competition from imported products, something which would be achieved gradually over three or four years, forcing reductions in costs and less inflation along the way; second, the freeing of capital markets previously controlled and subsidized by government, allowing supply and demand to determine interest rates again; and third, reductions in the public sector deficit, which had reached 16 percent of the gross domestic product, by cutting wages, increasing taxes, and selling hundreds of public enterprises.[36] (See Table 4.1.)

But plans, no matter how well designed, cannot be implemented while everything else is "held constant." Argentina was caught in a crisis in 1976, with the rate of inflation rising to almost 600 percent annually and foreign debts in need of immediate renegotiation. Martínez de Hoz was forced to adopt emergency measures as well as long-term ones, beginning immediately with a set of orthodox stabilization policies. They were accompanied with a relaxation of price, financial, and marketing regulation and improved export incentives, while wages were controlled, causing a sharp decline in real wages. In 1976 alone the salaries of public employees dropped from 16.2 percent of the national product to 9.8 percent, helping to reduce total public spending by 6 percent.[37] A renegotiation of the foreign debt followed agreements with the International Monetary Fund on short-term financing, and thanks to a bumper wheat crop, the trade balance improved soon thereafter. At the same time tariff reductions were begun, albeit slowly, but enough to induce substantial competition from imports by the end of 1977. On balance conditions improved in 1977, exports and foreign exchange reserves rising, gross domestic savings increasing by one-fourth, and the government deficit cut almost in half.

Inflation forced him to set aside the war against regulation for a brief period in order to call for a "price truce" starting in March 1977 that asked the country's 800 largest corporations to freeze prices for 120 days in the hope of breaking the dynamism of inflation long enough to cause people to alter expectations and change their price-setting behavior. Then in June 1977 the government announced a major financial reform aimed at attracting deposits into the banking system. For almost three decades interest rates had been administered and kept negative, denying the financial system an important role in the transfer of resources in the country since depositors, facing high inflation and negative interest rates, invested only in very short-term assets. He decontrolled interest rates and removed restrictions on the creation of new financial institutions, causing lending rates to become positive eventually, which in turn caused a rapid expansion in banking. Businessmen borrowed heavily, taking their chances on interest rates not rising significantly more and on business improving enough to make their borrowing profitable, and short-term foreign depositors took advantage of the removal of restrictions on running money in and out of Argentina. For a while it looked as if the government had built a new financial system almost overnight.

Authorities made what would become a fateful decision in December 1978. Frustrated by inflation's resistance to treatment, they decided to go after it using foreign exchange policy. It was something like returning to the gold standard without gold in which the government would set exchange rates, declaring devaluations at scheduled intervals, but doing so at a rate that overvalued the peso enough to make imported goods less expensive than domestic ones. What this would do, it was hoped, was induce slower price increases at home under the pressure of competition from imports, bringing the rate of inflation down as it did. To no one's surprise the peso was soon overvalued by as much as 50 percent, and by 1980 visitors to Buenos Aires were finding it one of the most expensive cities anywhere while middle- and upper-class Argentines were buying cheap dollars and using them to travel all over the world, bringing home with them the latest in consumer electronics and designer clothes. Meanwhile, after almost going to war with Chile over islands in the Beagle Channel claimed by both countries, the military also went shopping, adding expensive items to its weapons arsenal. Argentines simply went on a buying spree that turned their $2 billion current account surplus in 1978 into a $5.7 billion deficit by 1980. Yet even that seemed manageable at the time since high interest rates were attracting enough dollars to the country to finance the negative commercial balance.[38]

In capitalist systems economists try to induce desired behavior using the incentives and regulations allowed them by law and tradition. They make assumptions about profit motives and try to design policies that take advantage of them while achieving societal objectives. So it was when Martínez de Hoz went to work on the economy. He wanted desperately to force Argentine entrepreneurs to adapt their expectations to the discipline imposed by greater competition, ending their reliance on government subsidization of their operations. It was an audacious effort that required time to work and enough incremental success to build confidence in its permanence. But suspicious Argentines had heard it all before and were as skeptical of his ability to work miracles as they had been of his predecessors. Their perspective is short term and quite rational, educated on generations of policy failures that teach one always to be prepared for the worst. They waited and watched in 1978 and 1979, and sure enough, things did not turn out as they were supposed to. For one thing, bankers quickly got carried away with their new freedom, overextending themselves by taking in far more deposits than they could service adequately. That they did so was due in part to the incomplete nature of the new financial reforms. While interest rates were freed, the government's 100 percent guarantee of deposits was not ended, prompting new and old commercial banks to bid aggressively for deposits and accumulate an abundance of risky portfolios. When some very large banks suddenly collapsed in 1980, the government was forced to bail them out, along with some of the large manufacturers that were also technically bankrupt. By June they had seized 13 percent of the deposits in private banks. But the bailout led to rapid monetary expansion and new pressures on prices.[39]

The overvalued exchange rate made things even worse. Here the issue of public confidence is critical since the more the currency is overvalued the more people expect its devaluation and act accordingly. Only the fool neglects to protect himself by purchasing as many dollars as possible before the inevitable devaluation makes dollars even more expensive. And Argentines are not fools: while Martínez de Hoz assured the public that he would not abandon his system of incremental devaluations no matter how much capital fled the country, everyone ran for cover, buying scarce dollars at ever higher prices on the black market. At the same time conditions went sour for business. They had

borrowed heavily after the financial reforms, and private sector indebtedness had tripled during 1979 and 1980, but high and variable interest
rates and a recession that began in 1980 caught many of them overextended, inducing record bankruptcies and a financial crisis.[40]

As disappointing as all of this was, few things frustrated Martínez
de Hoz more than the resistance of the public sector to surgery. At first
substantial progress was made. Tariff reduction and the liberation of
capital markets reduced the influence of the state over private business
substantially, and his freezing public-employee salaries brought down
the deficit as a percent of the national product from 16 to 5.6 percent in
only two years. Moreover, he managed to replace Central Bank financing of the deficit by making government securities attractive in the open
market. But that only scratched the surface. More important in the long
haul was the sale of public enterprises, a campaign designed to reduce
substantially the government's operation of deficit-ridden ventures. But
little progress was made, the government selling off only its smallest
firms. The larger, less efficient ones were no more attractive to the
private sector than they were to the people who wanted to sell them. Nor
was the military enthusiastic about reducing the size of the government
since they enjoyed their role in its expansion and management.[41]

Argentines will always debate, as will economists elsewhere,
whether or not trade liberalization was the primary cause of the government's failure. That it affected the performance of industry is undeniable: the output of import competing firms fell by 9 percent and the size
of the industrial workforce dropped by 20 percent.[42] But regardless of
such "achievements," it was doomed to failure by the mismanagement
of the rest of the program. Budget cuts were blocked by military officers
trying to prepare for war against Chile, and overvalued exchange rates
made it impossible to keep dollars in the country. And when price
controls were abandoned, foreign exchange made available, and labor
subdued, businessmen who wanted to take advantage of such incentives often found themselves stymied by variations in relative prices and
interest rates and uncertainties about how long the government could
sustain its overvalued exchange rate in the face of foreign debt pressures. Bankruptcies rose almost fivefold between 1976 and 1980, reaching the equivalent of about $1 billion in liabilities (roughly equivalent to
3 percent of total sector liabilities), too much to sustain confidence in
the government's program. Nor did their borrowing abroad do the country that much good in the long run. Of the $35 billion that was lent
Argentina between 1976 and 1983, little if any was used to finance
additional investment. Thus it was that officials who were determined to
stabilize market behaviors actually touched off new instabilities and

prompted waves of speculation. Their whipping of the wild stallion, it seems, just made it buck more after a temporary pause.[43]

They, like the Chileans and Uruguayans who tried to remake their economies in much the same way in the late 1970s, were the victims of a very superficial understanding of the reasons for the success of Japan, Korea, and Taiwan, whose industrial export growth they had hoped to replicate. Their elitism caused them to place emphasis on firm government leadership and good relations with "good" industries, but those were only two parts of the Oriental success story. Even more important were their exceptionally high rates of capital formation, a high degree of labor discipline, and an unswerving entrepreneurial dedication to quality control and to the aggressive pursuit of export markets, all of which are usually missing in the Latin American economies. Once again, it seemed, the neoclassical economist's frustration with the status quo and his own inability to make basic changes in the private sector caused him to try another short-cut approach, which, by its partiality, was doomed to fail from the beginning.[44]

When General Roberto Viola succeeded Videla as scheduled at the end of March in 1981, he was greeted with the complaints of indebted Argentine businessmen, who demanded the dismissal of Martínez de Hoz and his team, and to the latter's surprise, Viola accommodated them. The new economics cabinet included a potpourri of people, many of them spokesmen for the industrial and agricultural interest groups that had criticized Martínez de Hoz's policies. Viola wanted to placate entrepreneurs, but thanks to a world recession that struck in 1981, conditions became worse rather than better, the GDP falling by 6 percent that year (and manufacturing by 14 percent) (see Table 4.2). Recognizing that the overvalued exchange rate was inflicting serious damage on the country's productive base and leading to unsustainable losses of foreign exchange, Viola announced a series of large devaluations during his first six months, suspended the tariff reduction program, reintroduced export taxes and import licensing, and reduced public expenditures, the net result of which was to push several overextended producers into bankruptcy. But the situation only became worse in 1982, and fearing great damage to a business community that was deeply in debt and a banking system equally in trouble, authorities engineered a sweeping liquidation of domestic indebtedness via mandatory refinancing at highly negative real interest rates, the cost of which was a renewed acceleration of inflation and the flight of savers from banks. Worse yet, the foreign debt skyrocketed thanks to the military's encouragement of heavy borrowing by public enterprises in 1980 and 1981 in order to protect the overvalued peso. As a result, the debt, which had been $8 billion in 1975, grew to $27 billion in 1980, and shot up to $45 billion by the time the military left office at the end of 1983. Clearly, the armed forces had failed dismally, and as if to help their successors appreciate that fact, they left an economy that was in disastrous shape and getting worse.[45]

4.2   Economic Performance, 1976–83 (annual percentage change)

Year	Total Investment	GDP Growth	Wholesale Price Index
1976	6.4	−0.5	498.7
1977	19.4	6.4	149.0
1978	−15.2	−3.4	149.4
1979	7.9	6.7	149.3
1980	7.2	0.7	75.4
1981	−23.1	−6.2	109.6
1982	−15.3	−5.1	256.2
1983	−8.4	3.1	360.9

Source: Clarín, economic supp., January 13, 1985, p. 11.

A Verdict on Military Dictatorship

Political failure has become a way of life for the Argentine armed forces. The Videla–Viola–Galtieri debacle is only the latest example. In 1930 Uriburu was forced by Justo to give up his corporatist adventure before it had really begun; Aramburu gave way to Frondizi in 1958, a politician whom he did not trust; Illia was never the first choice of the Azules, who supervised the election in 1963; and the last thing that Onganía wanted in 1966 was to see his "revolution" ended by Juan Perón's election seven years later.

Their failure, it seems, is inherent in their assignment and the public's ambivalence toward it. They always begin by achieving their most immediate objectives only to give up before they reach their ultimate ones. Taking over in times of crisis, they assert their authority, closing political parties and legislatures and intervening labor unions. Then they go to work on the economy, more often than not imposing austerity to deal with high inflation and other disorders, determined to maintain the integrity of the capitalist economy and promote its development with a combination of incentives to the private sector and investments by the public one. Within two years substantial progress is made and the military's triumph celebrated, especially in the international business community. But such achievements are always short-lived. Other economic problems arise, disclosing the superficiality of the initial recovery.

The controversiality of military policies invites dissent and opposition from the bourgeoisie as well as the proletariat. They need the cooperation of entrepreneurs to achieve economic recovery, but their curative programs frequently alienate large sectors of the business community, as Martínez de Hoz did when he liberalized trade in the late 1970s. Entrepreneurs are hurt by such measures, and the government's subjugation of labor is seldom enough to compensate them for the economic losses they incur. They may not complain much at first, but as adversities accumulate, some businessmen will attack military policies as counterproductive, gradually escalating their protests into the kind of assault on authorities that causes everyone to wonder whether they will force major revisions in policy. And when that happens, no promises to hold firm to its original plan seem enough to prevent public losses of confidence and the counterproductive compensatory entrepreneurial behaviors that undermine policy.

Onganía and Videla had also dreamed of launching a new form of politics in which civilians would be allowed to participate again only after they developed a common purpose and desire to obey authority. It was as if they wanted them to submerge their class differences and competing interests because they were ordered to do so. People were supposed to trade their compulsion to compete for devotion to their community. Communists ask people to do much the same thing, but they have an ideology that sets everyone's priorities for them and an organization that regulates down to the grass roots. The Argentine armed forces, on the other hand, could do no better than articulate a few vague notions about disciplined behavior and paternal authority without showing people how to translate either into effective political practice. They are not equipped by training or experience to build new political institutions and channel behavior through them. When they dare try they never progress beyond the reorganization of the executive branch, which is the only part of the government which they know much about.

A well-ingrained habit of dissension and rivalry between the three services and among army commanders also debilitates juntas when they try to lead the nation in a new direction. Conflicts among officers can be hidden from public view for a time, but they always reappear when presidential succession becomes an issue. Actually, the problem really starts with the appointment of the first president. Officers disagree less over the choice than over how much authority to give him, some preferring to let him rule as a dictator while others, fearful of losing control over their presidential colleague, demand that authority be kept collegial, reserving substantial power for the three service commanders who form the junta. The arrangement is never very neat, no matter how hard the junta works to appear united behind the president. It grows worse when commands are rotated all the way up to the junta. New service commanders do not necessarily come from the same factions as those who originally appointed the president, and they often put new pressures on the president, which, when ignored, can escalate into agitation for his replacement. Nothing is automatic, neither continuity nor disruption; rather, the military junta and its president engage in a politics of their own, sometimes in very self-destructive ways. When officers removed Onganía in 1970 after waging a battle with him over policy, the military lost what unity it had enjoyed, leaving the new president General Roberto Levingston without a solid base of support to sustain his command. Less than a year later General Alejandro Lanusse replaced him and led the way back to elections. Similarly, controversy between the navy and army over the choice of General Roberto Viola to succeed Videla in 1981 weakened his presidency and led to General Leopoldo Galtieri's replacing him, in what would mark the beginning of the end of military rule once again. Over and over the armed forces became their own worst enemy.

Their task is not made any easier, of course, by how little confidence the public has in their ability to change things. People expect juntas to impose order on society and to repair the economy, but not to make any real progress toward political reform. They do not believe that generals have it in them intellectually or organizationally to create new institutions in which civilians can participate politically. Unlike in Brazil, where civilian politicians long ago resigned themselves to working with officers toward the design of new political rules that accommodate military preferences, the Argentines are confident that they do not have to accommodate them. They know that officers cannot succeed on their own or find many civilian politicians to assist them. When General Alejandro Lanusse called elections in 1973, for example, he hoped to form a new political movement, joining conservatives and moderates behind his candidacy or that of another officer, but it fizzled well before taking off for lack of politician support. Argentines neither want to elect military presidents nor trust their ability to do anything more creative politically than abdicate their authority when exhaustion and dissension predictably set in.

The Future: Soldiers or State Capitalists?

The armed forces are not significantly different today from what they were thirty or forty years ago. New generations of officers have risen up through the hierarchy and retired in the interim, but they all represent

4.3 Argentine Military Personnel

Branch	Total Personnel	Conscripts
Army	130,000	80,000
Navy	37,000	18,000
Naval Air	3,000	0
Marine Corps	6,000	0
Air Force	20,000	10,000
Total	196,000	108,000

Source: Adrian English, *Armed Forces of Latin America* (London: Jane's, 1984), pp. 17–68.

the same traditions and organizations. If anything, they are more numerous and better equipped than ever. Total forces number 196,000, the army accounting for 70 percent of them (see Table 4.3). One estimate of defense expenditures as a percentage of the gross national product put it at 8.1 percent in 1982, by far the largest in Latin America (Cuba being second at 5.1 percent).[46] No doubt some of this was due to war expenditures, but the military budget had grown substantially before the Malvinas, induced by fear of war with Chile in 1968 and pushed by Videla throughout his administration. Per capita defense expenditures rose to $56 in the late 1970s, placing Argentina behind just Cuba and Chile in the Latin American expenditure rankings.[47]

They lost substantial material in the war over the Malvinas, the most costly being the Cruiser *Belgrano,* the submarine *Santa Fe,* and several aircraft. But they were far from decimated. Moreover, since the war's conclusion they have begun to rearm, ordering twenty-four secondhand Skyhawk fighters from Israel, four Super Etendards from France, and twelve Embraer Xavante light-strike aircraft. They also added two Meko Type 360 destroyers and two Meko 140 light frigates manufactured in West Germany. If anything, the war has induced officers to demand better weapons, putting pressure on presidents to spend large portions of their scarce resources to keep them happy.[48]

The social origins of officers vary as widely today as they did forty years ago. Some of them, with names like Alvear, Lanusse, and Alvarado, come from upper-class families tied to the land. But many more are like Perón and Galtieri, the offspring of middle- and lower-middle-class families. Like their peers in other countries they are attracted to the armed forces by their friends, relatives, and hopes for professional advancement. Officers recruit their sons in great abundance, an estimated 40 percent of the cadets coming from military families in recent years. That is not unusual, of course; the proportion is about the same in Brazil, a little higher in France, and nearly 65 percent in Spain.[49] Such origins contribute to the castelike character of military services all over the world. Most Argentine officers begin training in secondary school at age fifteen, learning to understand the adult world in military terms and living in it according to military rules. Education in other military institutions at home and abroad follows, all the way to the war college if they advance that far. They always operate with great formality, whatever their rank, and are heavily criticized for what appears to be excessive pomposity by civilians of all classes. Some aspire to rise socially in society at large, but few are admitted by the upper classes into their social circles. Naturally, such exclusion only reinforces the officer's sense of being unappreciated, manifesting itself in an obvious defensiveness in most of his dealings with civilians.

What the military has become since the turn of the century is less a group tied by blood to the nation's wealthiest citizens than a castelike organization whose leaders are as interested in protecting their own power and privileges as they are in defending one social class from another. They have always taken the nation's military defense seriously, their recent behavior notwithstanding. They consider themselves modern soldiers, sailors, and aviators whose preparation for battle is one of their prime responsibilities. But that does not reduce the conviction of some officers that they are the only persons in Argentina who are institutionally capable of preventing its self-destruction through political conflict and armed violence.

Something more is involved as well. Directing a government is not alien to them primarily because they are so deeply involved in the government when civilians are in the presidential palace. Few militaries anywhere in the world operate as many industries and utilities as Argentine officers do. Their ventures began in the 1920s, expanded after World War II as part of Perón's development plan, and have continued to grow ever since. In 1943 the military junta authorized the establishment of the General Directorate of Military Factories (Dirección General de Fabricaciones Militares), a board that resembles an interlocking directorate of a large conglomerate. Its factories not only supply small arms, armored vehicles, and light aircraft to the Argentine armed forces and other militaries in the Third World, but they also produce lumber, petrochemicals, iron and steel, and equipment for other public enterprises, such as the railways and the national oil company. For example, they provide 80 percent of the nitric acid, 40 percent of the ether, and 38 percent of the sulfuric acid consumed nationally. Together Fabricaciones' enterprises produce $2.2 billion in goods currently, or about 2.5 percent of the national product. And with them comes substantial political power within the public sector as well as an interdependence between the military and private enterprises that supply one another. That is why it is not at all unusual to find retired officers employed by firms who know where their business comes from, just as in the United States.[50]

The military's economic power creates all sorts of problems for anyone who wants to set policy in Argentina, as every president has discovered. Officers who make their careers running government corporations as well as their service enterprises are among the first to block intrusions into their domains, no matter how necessary administrative reform and fiscal austerity may be. In the end little gets changed and everyone blames someone else for the failure, the military complaining of the power of public employee unions in nonmilitary enterprises, economists pointing to sabotage by subsidized industries in the private sector, and military presidents blaming the indiscipline of the entire society. But the fact remains that no obstacle is larger than that of the military's protection of its own territory.

It is this deep penetration of the public sector as well as its anticommunism that guarantees the military's political involvement for some time to come. Displeasure with particular politicians comes and goes, attitudes toward Peronism differ among officers, as do opinions of democratic politics, but military management of large parts of the public sector is permanent as Raul Alfonsín discovered when he and his fellow Radicals took over from the armed forces in 1983.

Notes

1. *New York Times*, April 27, 1985, p. 3. Although a coup was not imminent and Alfonsín, no doubt, was using the threat of one to mobilize support for a government that was in danger of losing its popularity, the fact that he would resort to such warnings after pretending for two years that he had the armed forces under control is an indication of how real the possibility has become once again.

2. Torcuarto S. Di Tella, "Reflections on the Argentine Crisis: Are We at the End of an Epoch?" Occasional Paper Series, no. 3 (Washington, D.C.: American Enterprise Institute, January 1982), pp. 10–11.

3. Alain Rouquie, "Hegemonía militar, estado y dominación social," in *Argentina Hoy*, ed. Alain Rouquie (Mexico City: Siglo XXI, 1982), pp. 26–27.

4. Robert Potash, "The Impact of Professionalism on the 20th Century Argentine Military," University of Massachusetts Program in Latin American Studies Occasional Paper, no. 3, 1977. Also see Alain Rouquie, *Poder militar y sociedad política en la Argentina, Vol. I, hasta 1943* (Buenos Aires: EMECE, 1978), pp. 89–100.

5. Rouquie, *Poder militar y sociedad política*, pp. 101–104.

6. Robert Potash, *The Army and Politics in Argentina: 1928 to 1945* (Stanford: Stanford University Press, 1969), p. 11.

7. On the 1930 coup and Uriburu's rise and fall, see ibid., ch. 2.

8. Ruben M. Perina, *Onganía, Levingston, Lanusse: Los militares en la política argentina* (Buenos Aires: Belgrano, 1983), pp. 48–49.

9. Adrian J. English, *Armed Forces of Latin America* (London: Jane's, 1984), p. 65.

10. Perina, *Onganía, Levingston, Lanusse*, pp. 50–53. Also Potash, *The Army and Politics in Argentina 1945–1962*, ch. 1.

11. On Perón's tactics and his rivals' concessions to him in late 1945, see Felix Luna, *El 45* (Buenos Aires: Sudamericana, 1971).

12. Benjamín Menéndez was also the father of Major General Mario Benjamín Menéndez, the officer whom President Galtieri appointed as governor of the Malvinas Islands after the invasion in 1962 and, therefore, the person who surrendered to the British much as his father had done to the Azules twenty years before.

13. The Azul-Colorado conflict is summarized in Luis Gregorich, *La republica perdida* (Buenos Aires: Sudamericana-Planeta, 1983), pp. 118–119; and Alain Rouquie, *Poder militar y sociedad política en la Argentina*, Vol. II (Buenos Aires: EMECE, 1982), pp. 359–361.

14. Guillermo O'Donnell, *El estado burocrático autoritario* (Buenos Aires: Belgrano, 1982), pp. 85–87.

15. For a discussion of the dispute among scholars over the causes of bureaucratic authoritarianism, see Michael Wallerstein, "The Collapse of Democracy in Brazil," *Latin American Research Review* 15, no. 3 (1980): 3–43.

16. The inventor of this explanation was Argentine political scientist Guillermo O'Donnell, who elaborates on it in several works, beginning with *Modernization and Bureaucratic-Authoritarianism: Studies in South American Politics* (Berkeley: Institute of International Studies, University of California, 1973). Also see David Collier, ed., *The New Authoritarianism in Latin America* (Princeton: Princeton University Press, 1979).

17. In his more recent study of the Onganía regime O'Donnell confirms the variety of motives that led to the coup. See O'Donnell, *El estado burocrático autoritario*.

18. Alfred Stepan, *The Military in Politics: Changing Patterns in Brazil* (Princeton: Princeton University Press, 1971).

19. Gregorich, *La república perdida*, p. 143.

20. General Golbery do Couto e Silva, *Geopolítica do Brasil* (Rio: José Olympio, 1967), p. 9, quoted in José Comblin, *The Church and the National Security State* (Maryknoll, N.Y.: Orbis, 1979), p. 90.

21. On the debates within the army that preceded the coup, see O'Donnell, *El estado burocrático authoritario*, pp. 85–103.

22. Quoted in Comblin, *The Church and the National Security State*, p. 76.

23. Wayne Smith, "The Return of Peronism" in Frederick C. Turner and Jose E. Miguens, *Peron and the Reshaping of Argentina*, (Pittsburgh: University of Pittsburgh Press, 1983), p. 98.

24. O'Donnell, *El estado burocrático autoritario*, p. 95.

25. On the "stage theory," see Gary W. Wynia, *Argentina in the Postwar Era: Politics and Economic Policy-Making in a Divided Society* (Albuquerque: University of New Mexico Press, 1978), pp. 172–176.

26. Wynia, *Argentina in the Postwar Era*, ch. 6; O'Donnell, *El estado burocrático autoritario*, ch. 4–5.

27. Daniel Villar, *El Cordobazo* (Buenos Aires: La Historia Popular, 1971).

28. Felix Luna, *Golpes militares y salidas electorales* (Buenos Aires: Sudamericana, 1983), ch. 12.

29. The military's thinking and the documents it issued to explain itself are presented

in Marcelo Cavarozzi, *Autoritarismo y democracia: (1955–1983)* (Buenos Aires: Centro Editor de America Latina, 1983).

30. Gustavo Druetta, "Guerra, política y sociedad en la ideología de la corporación militar argentina," *Critica y utopia* 10/11 (1983): 127–128.

31. Ibid., p. 131.

32. This interpretation of events draws heavily on the findings of the Sabato Commission, which President Raul Alfonsín appointed to investigate the disappearances and which reported its findings to him in October 1984.

33. Jorge Schvarzer, *Martínez de Hoz: La lógica política de la política económica* (Buenos Aires: Centro de Investigaciones Sociales Sobre el Estado y la Administración, 1983), p. 34.

34. Marcelo Cavarozzi, "Argentina at the Crossroads: Pathways and Obstacles to Democratization at the Present Political Conjuncture," Woodrow Wilson Latin America Center Working Paper, no. 115, 1982, p. 3.

35. The implications of tariff policy are examined in Adolfo Canitrot, *Teoría y práctica del liberalismo y apertura economica en la Argentina: 1976–1981,* vol. 3, no. 10 (Buenos Aires: CEDES, 1980).

36. Ibid.

37. Schvarzer, *Martínez de Hoz,* p. 37.

38. This summary relies heavily on Guido Di Tella, "La Argentina económica," *Criterio* (Navidad 1982): 761.

39. Between January 1977 and June 1982, twenty-six banks and seventy-eight finance companies went bankrupt. For more detail see Ernesto V. Feldman, "La crisis financiera argentina: 1980–1982," *Desarrollo económico* 23, no. 91 (October–December 1983): 449–455. Also see Jan Peter Wogart, "Combining Price Stabilization with Trade and Financial Liberalization Policies: The Argentine Experience, 1976–1981," *Journal of Interamerican Studies and World Affairs* 25, no. 4 (November 1983): 468 ff.

40. *Latin American Regional Report: Southern Cone,* March 6, 1981, p. 6.

41. Canitrot, *Teoría y práctica del liberalismo y apertura economica en la Argentina: 1976–1981,* pp. 61–65.

42. Wogart, "Combining Price Stabilization with Trade and Financial Liberalization Policies," pp. 462–465.

43. Ibid.

44. William P. Glade, "Latin America: Options and Nonoptions in Contemporary Development Strategy," *American Enterprise Institute Foreign Policy and Defense Review* 5, no. 3 (Winter 1985): 13.

45. World Bank, "Economic Memorandum on Argentina," June 22, 1984, pp. 7–8.

46. English, *Armed Forces of Latin America,* pp. 68–72, 476.

47. International Institute for Strategic Studies, *The Military Balance 1983–1984* (London: IISS, 1983).

48. English, *Armed Forces of Latin America,* p. 468.

49. Rouquie, *Poder militar y sociedad política en la Argentina,* 2:327.

50. Ibid., pp. 321–325; and *The Economist,* February 16, 1985, p. 67.

5

The Radicals Rebound

The Radical party was not supposed to win the 1983 presidential election, but, thanks to Raul Alfonsín and the nation's fatigue, it did. Long a dissident in his own party, Alfonsín pulled the upset of his generation by defeating Peronist Italo Luder with 52 percent of the popular vote to Luder's 40 percent. A decade before the numbers had been reversed, with Perón winning in a landslide and Radical Ricardo Balbin receiving only 24 percent. But suddenly, after being relegated to what seemed permanent minority status, the Radicals were back, enjoying majority support for the first time since 1928.

Although Perón's death in 1974 certainly helped the Radicals, it was not the sole cause of the Peronists' defeat. The Peronists still had the CGT to draw upon, and union leaders worked hard to rally the masses for another battle, winning, in fact, a plurality of seats in the Senate and second place in the Chamber of Deputies. What Argentines rejected in 1983 was not the Peronist party per se, but the idea of another Peronist president. The memory of Isabel Perón's disaster in 1976 was fresh, as was fear of living through another cycle of Peronist and military rulers. Most people wanted a respite from militarism, and the unspectacular Alfonsín, known more for integrity than charisma, seemed to offer the best possibility for achieving it. He could not save the nation from its worst vices; no one could. But committed as he was to old-fashioned democratic government, he could become a vehicle for restoring badly needed civility to national life.

Alfonsín was more popular than the Radical party was in 1983, but he was very much a Radical, the new leader of one of the nation's oldest parties and, since World War II, its second largest. By attracting more voters than any Radical had done since 1928 and carrying several gubernatorial candidates on his coattails, he gave Radicalism new life, saving it, for the moment at least, from permanent residence among the anti-Peronist minority. But it was still *the* Radical party, a modest, closely knit community of democratic politicians who were convinced that they were morally superior to their rivals. They had suffered occasional persecution, repeated electoral defeats, and destructive divisions within their own ranks, but they were once again eager to demonstrate their love for old-fashioned constitutional government.

Radical Origins

The name "Radical" seems a misnomer today, for Alfonsín's platform resembled nothing more extreme than an Argentine version of European social democracy. But at its inception almost a century ago the party was radical, at least it seemed so to the oligarchs, who had no intention of sharing their control over the nation with others. Argentina pretended to operate as a constitutional democracy during the last half of the nineteenth century, but it never came close to being one for any but the 10 percent of the population that was allowed to vote. The people who founded the Radical party wanted this changed through political not social reform. Most of them came from the same class as those who ruled the country but were excluded from the inner circles of government and resented it. Desperate to make their way in, they tried every tactic imaginable, from petition to violent insurrection, but a quarter-century would pass before they were given what they wanted.

Argentine oligarchs were a powerful lot, who contested with each other for the nation's economic bounty while coexisting politically. They had fought among themselves for almost fifty years before coming to terms and creating a lasting political order in the 1850s. Thereafter their competition was confined to the marketplace, where land and labor were acquired and incredible wealth accumulated. It was never as neat as it seems in retrospect, for their enterprise was always a vulnerable one, dependent on markets and investors from abroad. Economic crises brought dissension within their ranks, as some among them used their power to advance themselves under the worst of conditions at the expense of colleagues who were less well positioned. Typical was the depression that struck in 1889, the result of one underway in Europe at the time. When its pain was felt, it was not the country's small and vulnerable proletariat that protested, but the merchants and less-favored cattlemen who watched as the ruling *porteño* elite and their British backers prospered while everyone else paid dearly for the crisis. It was in the midst of such discontent that the Radical party was born on September 1, 1889, when a few men calling themselves the Unión Cívica de la Juventud (Civic Union of Youth) organized a public protest to demand greater influence over the government's handling of such infirmities via honest elections and real representation. Two years later, on July 2, 1891, the movement's founders relabeled their creation the

Unión Cívica Radical, the name the party retains today. Highly moralistic in their rhetoric and unprecedented in their dedication to the accomplishment of a single objective—free elections—they called on the largely disenfranchised Argentine middle class to join them in their effort to force their way in. Revolutionary they were not, except in their belief in universal manhood suffrage. But their cause was a popular one in this rapidly urbanizing country of disenfranchised immigrants, and the Radicals milked it for all that it was worth.[1]

Their stubborn campaign is instructive for what it says about political rivalry and the measures that were required to dislodge incumbents at the time. It is also a reminder of how democrats had to sacrifice their principles in order to acquire political power. Three times the Radicals resorted to conspiracy and popular insurrection only to be defeated by authorities each time. But they continued just the same until the ruling oligarchs finally saw fit to let them in twenty-four years after their struggle had started.

Their quest began with a try at elections in 1892. Instead of selecting one of their own to lead the ticket, they nominated retired army general Bartolome Mitre, hoping to outfox the conservative incumbents by making it difficult for them to oppose the popular old general. But it was they who were tricked, as right under their noses the incumbents stole Mitre from them, persuading him to merge his ticket with theirs, leaving the Radicals out in the cold. The incident left them in confusion, some deciding to stay with Mitre in the hope of getting a foot in the door while most of their colleagues angrily boycotted the election in protest. Dividing and conquering oppositions is a favorite tactic of political elites everywhere, and in Argentina the Radicals would become its victims often in the years ahead.

Frustration grew and the Radicals' patience declined swiftly after their election debacle, leading some to resort to violence in 1893. With the aid of a few sympathetic military officers they tried to launch a revolt, only to be defeated rather easily. Undaunted, they resorted to force again in 1897 and 1904, only to meet the same dismal fate. Yet by taking on the oligarchy directly they won the support of many in the country's middle and lower classes who gradually accepted Radical cause as their own. No one was bothered by the apparent contradiction between their advocacy of democracy and their fomenting violent insurrections, for they knew that theirs was hardly the kind of liberal society in which the ruling class conceded reforms without putting up a fight.[2]

Yet, concessions did eventually come, two and one-half decades and three insurrections after the Radicals' quest had begun, when in 1912 conservative president Roque Saez Peña pushed passage of electoral reforms that guaranteed for the first time a secret ballot and universal manhood suffrage (women did not receive the right to vote until the Peronists put it in their constitution in 1949). Why a ruling elite gives ground politically to its democratic opponents is seldom apparent, and historians are of different opinions in Saez Peña's case. Concern about the mobilization of the immigrant proletariat by socialists in the labor movement may have convinced him that Radicals were preferable as the government's inevitable opponent. A working class loyal to moderate Radicals who were content with the economic status quo posed less of a threat than did a proletarian party inspired by visions of radical re-distributions of property. This explanation, though quite plausible, gives more credit for foresight and cunning to the old guard than they probably deserve. As likely was their conviction that they could dispose of the noisy Radicals by defeating them in an honest election. Conservatives believed that the Radicals' popularity was due more to clever exploitation of their victimization than it was to what they had to offer the nation as prospective rulers. It was not hard for them to imagine that when faced with a choice between Radicals and conservatives, most Argentines would stick with what they knew best. Incumbents, especially those who have ruled for more than a half-century, tend to make such assumptions until their unanticipated defeat forces them to think otherwise. Paternalists at heart, oligarchs believe that their people appreciate the direction they have given them and will reward them accordingly. No doubt that was the case in Argentina in 1916 when, to their surprise and regret, the incumbents watched as the Radicals triumphed easily in the presidential elections, leaving only the Senate for the conservatives to control.[3]

The Raul Alfonsín of 1916 was Hipólito Yrigoyen, the slayer of an opposition that was supposed to be impossible to defeat. Having been the party's leader for twenty years he was the natural candidate for president. He proclaimed a belief in democracy but since 1896 had ruled over the party like an autocrat intolerant of dissent. His politics was less that of the twentieth-century democrat than of a "nineteenth century caudillo in modern dress," as his biographers have often noted, a man who was dour and aloof, self-righteous and stubborn, and without many redeeming virtues other than his loyalty to those devoted to him.[4] He seldom spoke in public to anyone, preferring instead to deal in private with friends and foes alike, much like the clandestine conspirator whose followers waited in rapture for notice of his next move. It was the kind of behavior that would inevitably divide the party, but it also set a standard that his successors would try to imitate, making this party of democracy heavily dependent on the leadership of one or two strong persons.

The oligarchy had little to fear from Yrigoyen initially, for though he had taken their government from them, he had no intention of evicting them from the *pampas* as well. He understood his nation's export economy and what made the country prosper and was not about to upset it in any significant way. The Radicals wanted their piece of the pie, but that never required their baking a new one to get it. As nationalists they gave the government more control over the nation's resources, as when they created a government petroleum company, and they filled the bureaucracy with their constituents, but they imposed few regulations on an economy they accepted as the country's only legitimate means to development. They did not ignore the working class entirely, since much of Yrigoyen's support had come from it, setting higher standards for working conditions in factories, adopting an eight-hour workday, and putting limits on child employment. But their sense of social justice never included toleration of proletarian militancy. And if there had been any doubts about how far they would go to preserve the power structure of which they were now a small part, they were ended during the infamous Semana Trágica in 1919, when strikes provoked Yrigoyen's sending the police in to pound on the culprits and bring them into line.[5]

The Radicals wanted to become the nation's permanent majority party, and they appeared to be on their way to doing so in the 1920s. It was a good time for the country economically; the oligarchy and the middle class prospered, and the Radicals, with their strident nationalism and neutralism during and after World War I, gave Argentines a new pride in their embryonic nationhood. But they never quite made it, becoming victims of their own internal divisions, Yrigoyen's obstinacy and feebleness of mind, and the oligarchy's refusal to trust the Radicals' leading the country from a crisis in which the wealthy had the most to lose.

That someone like Yrigoyen would sow the seeds of division within his own party was predictable. It began with the choice of his successor to the presidency in 1922. Marcelo de T. Alvear was Yrigoyen's candidate, but he brushed away his mentor immediately after his election, accepting leadership of the "antipersonalists" in the party, who, as their name suggests, had grown weary of the party's domination by Yrigoyen. They were more urbane than Yrigoyen's crowd and wanted a president that fit more into the twentieth than the nineteenth century. That is why they backed the more pragmatic and less populist Alvear, a man who was never embarrassed by his upper-class origins and one whose presidency more resembled that of a constitutional monarch than a middle-class politician.[6] There was little that Yrigoyen could do to rein in Alvear during his presidency, so he waited and struck back by running for the presidency again in 1928. A battle for the nomination ensued with the seventy-six-year-old Yrigoyen the easy victor; frustrated, the antipersonalists defected to opposition, supporting Yrigoyen's conservative opponent at the polls, but it was hardly enough to halt the old patriarch's populist campaign, which collected him 57 percent of the vote.

It was all downhill thereafter, however. To begin with, Yrigoyen's crusade for personal vindication alienated what few friends he had among the oligarchy, people who had worked with the Radicals and kept members of their own class at bay during the 1920s. Then, after one of the most prosperous years ever in 1928, the depression struck, catching by surprise the reclusive old president, who showed little inclination to do anything about his collapsing economy or for its victims. Policy decisions had to be made but few were, and the longer he waited the more the public turned away from him, becoming easy prey for an opposition that warned of disaster. In consort, oligarchs and antipersonalist Radicals persuaded fascist-admiring José Uriburu to end it all with a coup on September 6, 1930, terminating the country's fourteen-year experiment in constitutional democracy.

Yrigoyen died three years later, a rejected man. But that has not prevented his successors in the Radical party from elevating him to heroic stature in their memories, much as the Peronists do with Juan and Evita, though most Radicals would deny being party to such myth making. To them he is the founding father whose dedication to the fight against rich authoritarians became a fundamental Radical objective. No party meeting begins anymore without paying homage to the "spirit and purpose" given Radicalism by Yrigoyen and his cohorts. It is symptomatic of a sentimentalism that the politically liberal Radicals do not really want to shake.

But whatever the use of legend, the impact of Yrigoyen is undeniable, as even his opponents noted at his death:

> Few men have exercised as vast an influence in our political, economic and spiritual life in the last fifty years. His achievements are as memorable as the great epidemics. . . . The old curse of superstitious caudillismo is a fatality of our Indo-Hispanic inheritance. It reproduces and will continue to reproduce itself for many years in notable ways. But it will never again repeat in a form as complex, grand, and perfect.[7]

One can only speculate about what would have become of Radicalism had Yrigoyen not divided it when he returned to the presidency in 1928 and then mismanaged the nation's greatest economic crisis. He might have chosen a younger and wiser successor, who could have taken the party and the country through the depression without provoking a coup. Alternatively, however, the antipersonalists might have prevailed, making the party more conservative and less popular with its lower-middle- and working-class membership and losing its majority in the process. But most likely Radicalism was doomed by the country's power structure and by the oligarchy's unwillingness to trust any party but its own to protect its interests in a time of such obvious crisis. Whatever might have been the case, the depression quite definitely brought the destruction of the Radical experiment in democratic government and the disappearance of the Radical majority. For the next half-century it would seem that the party's chance had come and forever gone.

Radicals in Opposition

With Yrigoyen in jail after the coup and his party seemingly broken, the oligarchy traded fascist Uriburu for the less ambitious General José Uriburu in the hope of gaining some legitimacy for the new order. As a popularity test, gubernatorial elections were called in Buenos Aires province not long after the coup, with the oligarchy hoping that a new realism would drive most people to lend their support to the regime. But these hopes were to be disappointed. Just as they had done back in 1916, the Radicals rallied the opponents of authoritarianism and roundly defeated the government's candidates, making a mockery of its claim of legitimacy. Getting the message, Uriburu and his upper-class backers decided to give up their quest for popularity and get on with engineering the nation's economic recovery. With the collaboration of several antipersonalist Radicals who preferred power over principle, they rigged subsequent elections, allowing other parties only some seats in what became a rubber-stamp legislature.[8]

Their subjugation left the rest of the Radicals with old but familiar choices. They could abstain from participating in the new political charade and protest democracy's abuse by authorities, as they had done before 1916, or they could accept the military-backed conservative government as a necessary fact of life and play the role of loyal but subservient opponent that it demanded of them. Not surprisingly, they chose abstention, hammering away at the government's unpopularity in hopes of forcing its retreat. In 1931 they were joined by Alvear, who chose to abandon his antipersonalist followers, realizing that with Yrigoyen jailed he had a chance to retake control over the largest wing of the party. His return was not celebrated, but he was rewarded with the leadership post, nevertheless.

Radical protests had little effect on the ruling Concordancia alliance of conservatives and antipersonalists who devoted their authority to keeping everyone in line while they dealt with the troubled economy. But they were never comfortable with popular opposition and persisted in their attempts to coopt Radicals into the regime. In 1935 they promised Alvear that they would hold free elections in the early 1940s if he would lend his blessing to elections in 1937, offering his own candidacy in a contest that everyone knew would be rigged for the Concordancia candidate. Always ambitious and now tired of exclusion, Alvear went for the bait, trying as best he could to lead his party back to the polls. To complete the show, the government chose as its candidate Roberto Ortiz, himself a Radical who had signed up with the Concordancia in 1931 along with other antipersonalists. His service as Justo's finance minister between 1935 and 1937 had proved his reliability and loyalty. In the tightly controlled presidential election, he was rewarded with 54 percent of the vote, with only 40 percent allowed to go to Alvear. The episode left the Radical party more divided than ever. Many of its younger members left the party to protest Alvear's opportunism and to demand the formation of a new Radical party that would be truer to Yrigoyen's original commitment to popular democratic government.[9]

The nation's political farce did give authorities some latitude for dealing with its economic recovery. But the politics practiced inflicted permanent damage on the country, making a mockery of the oligarchy's pretense to civility and reinforcing already rampant cynicism about the purposes that democratic institutions really served. By turning the clock back and abusing the Radicals into colluding in the maintenance of a fraudulent political process after 1937, they halted progress toward the integration of the middle class and the masses into the national power structure. What they achieved instead was the division of society into a politically alienated mass and a ruling class whose paternalism never extended very deeply below its own ranks. It could not help but invite a challenge from below that would be as belligerent as it was desperate. That it would turn out to be so unrevolutionary when it came a decade later was due more to Perón's sharing their fear of the Marxist left than it was to anything they had done to make accommodation easier through their actions in the 1930s.

The 1930s was not a total loss for the Radical party, however. When Alvear agreed to participate in the 1937 elections youthful protestors in the party formed the Fuerza de Orientación Radical de la Joven Argentina (FORJA), an idea factory that advocated a more militant nationalism and greater state involvement in the country's industrialization, starting with the nationalization of all natural resources and public utilities and the breaking up of all foreign oligopolies. They were frustrated not just with the oligarchy and its abuses of authority and party leaders and their self-defeating opportunism, but also with the nation's rush to restore its reliance on Britain for trade and capital as revealed in the humiliating concessions that Britain extracted from Argentina in the Roca-Runciman agreement in 1933. The FORJA people convinced themselves that Argentina's malaise stemmed from foreign exploitation of its immense wealth and that its progress would come only after its dependence on foreigners was ended. It was a popular argument and remains so today. Argentines rely on their nationalism to explain a great deal to themselves, and the more difficult conditions are for them, the more appealing the notion of foreign exploitation becomes. The young Radicals thought they had an issue that would rejuvenate their party, but they were ignored by Alvear and his aged colleagues. Instead it was young military officers who found such ideas attractive and incorporated them into their own agendas after they removed the oligarchs in 1943. Not surprisingly, several from the FORJA crowd turned up in the Peronist party when it was organized two years later.[10]

Alvear died in 1942 at the age of seventy-three, leaving the Radicals without a dominant personality to lead them for the first time since their creation. Moreover, it marked the end of nearly a half-century in which this party of democracy had been run by just two persons, Yrigoyen and Alvear. It survived them thanks to its solid infrastructure of grass-roots committees and provincial organizations and Alvear's cronies retaining substantial control at the top. It was also sustained by its participation in congressional elections after 1937, for despite being outfoxed in the presidential contest, they were allowed to add seats in Congress, winning a majority of those contested in 1940. To his credit Ortiz refrained from tampering with Congress while he was president, giving the Radicals a sense of rising up once again, albeit slowly and under the watchful eye of authorities who were not yet ready to turn the entire government over to them.

The Radicals' resurrection took a turn for the worse after 1940, though the fault was not theirs this time. Illness forced Ortiz to relinquish the presidency to his vice president, the very conservative Ramón Castillo, who had never shared his faith in tutelary democracy. Later when the time came to announce candidates for elections in 1944, he made it known that his choice was a fellow conservative, the reactionary provincial oligarch Robustiano Patrón Costas, whom Castillo intended to assure election using all of the authority he had. Bitterly disappointed, the Radicals had little choice but to look for help elsewhere, as conservatives had done when discontent with Yrigoyen peaked in 1930, military intervention being the obvious choice to rid the nation of Castillo and start over. There is no evidence that they conspired with officers to stage a coup, but they did not have to since nationalists within the military were already prepared to take matters into their own hands. When they did no complaints were heard from Radical circles; instead they set their sights immediately on preparing for what the Radicals hoped would be the restoration of constitutional democracy and an easy victory for them in new elections.

Thanks to the oligarchy's monopolization of power and the repression of movements on the extreme left (moderate socialists were allowed to function and occupy seats in Congress), no other popular party had developed the support needed to defeat the Radicals. That is why when elections were called by the military for early in 1946, the Radicals were convinced that victory would come easily, so much so that they refused help from army officers who offered to write the election rules to favor them. And when Juan Perón, still unsure of his base in mid-1945, proposed to join forces with them, with him leading the ticket, they refused outright. Not until the outpouring of working-class support for Perón on October 17 did they begin to comprehend how popular their real competitor had become, and in last-minute desperation they turned to conservatives and socialists for help, creating an electoral alliance aimed at stopping the Peronist surge. But they were too late. After fifteen years on the outside looking in, the Radicals would spend twelve more watching while Perón stole the agenda of their most progressive members and blocked their access to power even more effectively than the oligarchy had.[11]

A New Era: Two Radicals Instead of One

A casual glance at events between Perón's election in 1946 and Raul Alfonsín's in 1983 reveals why the Radicals were so euphoric about Alfonsín's triumph. Winners always celebrate victory, to be sure, but 1983 was very special, being the first time ever that a Radical had defeated a Peronist in a free presidential election. Getting there had not been easy. The quest began in 1955, when the military sent Perón into exile and promised to restore constitutional democracy to the country. The Radicals endorsed the coup and played an active part in the military's preparation of the new rules of electoral competition. Aramburu was determined to destroy the Peronist movement by purging labor of its leadership and banning all other Peronist organizations, freeing the rank and file to express their preferences through another party, such as the Radicals. Convinced that Perón had stolen the working class from them, Radicals found it hard to question Aramburu's motives or to do anything but praise his objectives. At last they would have their chance to woo the Argentine masses back to the party most of their parents had supported in 1928. Or so they wanted to believe when elections were called for 1958.

But life is not that simple in Argentina, and wishing an end to Peronism did little to eliminate it. Well before election day it was obvious that a working class that had watched under duress while the Radicals collaborated with the military in the elimination of the Peronist party was not about to thank them for their liberation by voting Radical. Whoever won in 1958 would do so with the knowledge that the nation's majority had effectively been excluded from their selection. Recognition of this fact confronted the Radicals with another in their long line of unwanted dilemmas. Should they ignore the Peronists and win an election which the working class boycotted to protest their party's exclusion, they would not secure anything resembling the popular legitimacy that they needed to govern a very divided nation. Yet if they appealed to the Peronists with promises to legalize their party after the election or similar concessions, they invited the wrath of the armed forces and, more likely than not, defeat by the Peronists once they participated again. There was no satisfactory solution and the Radicals knew it.

When they went to their convention in 1957 they had to make two choices: one of strategy to resolve the Peronist dilemma; and the other among prospective presidential candidates. The equation was not as complex as it seemed, however, thanks to the Radical habit of splitting into factions backing two candidates who favored opposite strategies. Almost before they had started their deliberations they had divided into two distinct Radical parties, one behind Arturo Frondizi, which called itself the Unión Cívica Radical Intransigente (UCRI), the other supporting Ricardo Balbín and his Unión Cívica Radical del Pueblo (UCRP). Balbín and Frondizi were once good friends who had collaborated in an assault on the party leadership after its defeat by the Peronists in 1946, turning their reformist Movimiento Intransigente Radical into the dominant force within the party. They were rewarded with Balbín's nomination for the presidency and Frondizi's for the vice presidency in the 1951 elections won by Perón. In 1958, Frondizi insisted that it was his turn to lead the ticket, but Balbín refused to allow it. So when Frondizi attracted enough delegates to win the nomination, Balbín boycotted the convention and organized one of his own with nearly half of the party in attendance a few weeks later.[12]

The two factions were separated as much by matters of strategy as they were by personalities. Balbín accepted the military's exclusion of the Peronists, convinced that it was justified by the Peronists' anti-democratic behavior. Until democracy was restored and its ethics practiced by everyone, allowing Peronist participation would be self-defeating for democrats. Frondizi, in contrast, believed that with or without Perón to lead it, the Peronist movement was there to stay, too large a part of the electorate to be excluded entirely. No president could rule for long over an alienated majority. He also knew that with Peronist support he would be unbeatable, so in January 1958, a few months before the election, he sent close friend Rogelio Frigerio to Caracas, where he negotiated an agreement with the exiled Perón in which Frondizi promised to legalize Peronist organizations after his inauguration in exchange for Perón's endorsement. It worked just as planned on election day: with substantial Peronist support Frondizi came out on top just short of a majority while Balbín received only 29 percent.[13]

Frondizi was full of surprises after his inauguration. A notorious nationalist prior to his nomination, he was forced by rising inflation and a balance-of-payments crisis to invite the help of the International Monetary Fund, which brought recommendations for tough austerity measures with its financial aid. But that was not all. As he prepared for the election Frondizi became convinced that something new was essential to launch the Argentine economy into more rapid growth after a decade of stagnation. Heavily influenced by confidant and businessman Frigerio, Frondizi concluded that populism had run its course, creating a large consumer goods industry whose imports of capital goods and basic supplies exhausted the nation's export earnings far too rapidly. Its only option was to build its own capital goods industry, displacing imports just as consumer goods industries had done a decade before. Argentina needed more iron, steel, and petrochemical industries, and Frondizi was determined to see them built even if it took multinational corporations to get the job done.[14]

It was a bit strange, the president who had sought an alliance with the Peronists selecting policies that were certain to alienate the working class and its nationalistic cheerleaders. But Frondizi had little choice in the matter once in office. The Argentine economy was in trouble, and it needed substantial new investment to re-ignite growth. Yet, that which is so obvious to the economist is seldom reasonable to the partisan who thinks that he is adversely affected by new policies. Frondizi was attacked from all sides during his four-year tenure, by a labor movement that felt itself betrayed, by rivals in the UCRP who accused him of abandoning the Radical platform, and by conservatives who resented a foreign policy of nonalignment whose most offensive gesture was Frondizi's welcoming Che Guevara on his visit home in August 1961. But Frondizi's real battle was always with the armed forces, who had lost what little trust they had in him when he made his pact with Perón.

In normal democracies political parties participate within a single political system, competing with other parties for control over the government. Not so in Argentina: after 1955 it had two political systems, one in which political parties competed for the right to direct the government; and a second one in which the Peronists and the military were locked in a battle that spilled onto everyone else. Frondizi was an obvious case in point. He had used the Peronists for political advantage and they him, but the conspiracy left him at the mercy of a suspicious military. No president before or since has suffered more rumors of coups, many of which ended in attempts that were abortive. The last straw was Frondizi's keeping a promise to allow the Peronists to participate in elections during his tenure. When he did so in 1962, they scored impressive victories in gubernatorial elections in the most populated provinces, something the armed forces were not yet ready to tolerate. Within a few days they moved in and Frondizi moved out, first to prison, where he was held until the ruling junta could sort things out.

When new elections were called for July 1963 and the Peronist party was again excluded, victory went to the UCRP. This time, however, Balbín stepped aside, allowing provincial physician Arturo Illia to head the ticket in an attempt to attract some of Balbín's enemies back into the Radical party. It was a strange election in many ways. Until just before the election it was not certain whether the military would allow the Peronists to participate or not. When they chose to exclude them, causing Peronists to promise abstention, they improved the chances of conservatives who backed the candidacy of retired General Pedro Aramburu. Though not the favorite of everyone in the armed forces, Aramburu seemed to offer Argentines the opportunity to select someone who stood a better chance than any Radical did of withstanding pressures from the armed forces. But with twenty-eight other presidential candidates to contest with, Illia won with just 25 percent of the vote. It was an auspicious beginning for the quiet, grandfatherly new president whose small plurality invited complaints of illegitimacy throughout his tenure.

Illia refused to act like a president who was supported by only a fourth of the electorate. Faithful to his belief in constitutional democracy almost to a fault, he governed the nation as if he had a real mandate, hoping that steady and unspectacular leadership would calm his people and teach them the virtues of political liberty. His economic policies were nationalist in spirit but hardly extreme, his respect for civil liberty consistently enforced, and his tolerance for the opposition greater than Argentines had ever known. Yet, neither such noble virtues nor bumper crops and a booming recovery proved enough to prevent the powerful forces in society from undermining this latest try at democracy.

The armed forces were the least prepared to tolerate democracy. They had fought among themselves during 1962 over its desirability in Argentina, and in 1963 the winners of the dispute proceeded to hold elections, hoping that a new party led by General Pedro Aramburu would triumph. But their gamble failed and they were left with Illia, another of the politicians for whom they had nothing but disdain. Soon after the new president's inauguration the officers who had defended constitutional government in 1962 were heard complaining privately that they had made a mistake, one that became even more obvious as they watched the new president attacked by the CGT and its *plan de lucha* that was aimed at immobilizing the Radical government. Illia tried to calm his union adversaries by raising their wages, something the Radicals also hoped would pacify the masses and even win a few to their side, but the protests were more political than economic and did not end until 1,400 factory "occupations" later when Illia had fallen.[15]

Illia did not help his relations with the armed forces when he committed himself to an open political process that allowed every party a chance to participate, including the Peronists. No doubt he was enticed by the thought of defeating the Peronists at the polls as much as he was by simple democratic principle. The temptation to do battle with the Peronists in honest elections comes naturally to democrats like the Radicals, who insist on believing that if the masses came to know them many would prefer their honesty and integrity to the corruption and bullying of their Peronist bosses. It did not seem to matter that Yrigoyen was remembered by the working class more for his repression of them than his paternalism or that to the masses the Radicals had become a minority party of shopkeepers, dentists, and schoolteachers rather than the populists that they pretended to be. But what else could the Radicals do? They wanted to govern and knew that they could not do it for very long if the majority remained Peronist.

The Radicals went into congressional elections in March 1965 hoping for a good showing and they got one, but the Peronists did even better, topping the UCRP's 28 percent with 30 percent of their own. Not all seats were up so Illia retained a plurality in Congress, but their entrance into the legislative process gave the Peronists another point of attack from which to harass the president. Unlike in 1962 the armed forces reacted calmly at first, letting the Peronists take their seats and allowing Illia to deal with them. But their passivity could not disguise further unhappiness with the situation that led to their planning Illia's removal a year later.

Still, the need for a military coup never seemed less obvious than in 1966. No single event or crisis provoked it. Nor was the economy in deep trouble. On the contrary, the national product had grown by almost 20 percent in two years and inflation had risen only from 24 to 29 percent, hardly anything to cause concern in Argentina. Moreover, people were enjoying more liberty than they had in decades, and despite CGT militancy, most were exercising it judiciously. So why a coup?

It pays to recall that militaries do not behave like machines that explode only when their engines become overheated. They have ideas about how their societies should be governed just as everyone else does. They also react to their own expectations for the country and the failure of incumbents to meet them. In 1966 the nation was not accomplishing as much as they thought it could, and it was easy to blame democratic politics and its waste of energy for the country's plight. Officers dreamed of a powerful Argentina that was prosperous at home and prominent abroad, and they were convinced that it would never be theirs as long as Radicals and Peronists were slugging it out, distracting citizens from their real duties to the nation. They, like so many Argentines, were prisoners of the country's glorious past and frustrated with its conflict-ridden present; it was easy to believe that greatness awaited them just around a corner which they could turn if only people with conviction and determination took charge and led them there. If they needed encouragement, the country's foreign and domestic bankers and industrialists offered it with their complaints about the nation's political retardation and promises of abundance once a politics-free investment climate was achieved. Moreover, they only had to look next door for the model they needed: the Brazilian armed forces had seized the initiative and were hard at work stabilizing their economy in the name of modernization, meeting little resistance from the politicians whom they had deposed. It seemed just the thing for officers who had grown weary of *planes de lucha* and procrastinating presidents.[16]

The 1966 coup was not, however, just the work of military officers and businessmen out to protect their respective interests. Labor leaders were just as eager to see Illia toppled as the military was. They did not conspire directly with them but did all they could to encourage a coup by undermining Illia's authority at every turn, quite aware of where their efforts would lead. Peronists have always been a bit schizophrenic about the armed forces, having been created by a military government only to be repressed by General Aramburu and his successors. But their persecution had never caused them to abandon hope of drawing the military back to their side, and there were always a few nationalistic colonels around who encouraged them to believe that it could be done. Trying for it was certainly tempting since a combination of the military and the masses guaranteed the Peronists a powerful state to direct. So as remote as the possibility seemed in 1966, the prize was too big to ignore when the time came to place a few bets.[17]

The fact that capital and labor would combine to destroy one of Argentina's more democratic regimes says much about the nature of Argentine politics and support for authoritarian means to achieve narrow partisan ends. It also says something about how little confidence Argentines have in democracy itself. Few people are willing to bet on democracy working whenever it is tried; instead, within a year of a government's election it becomes popular to predict its demise and leave its defense to those who run it. Conventional wisdom teaches that even if one does not work for its termination many others will, so little is gained from planning on its survival. Instead, one just watches from a distance while someone else puts the constitution into storage. That is how it seemed on June 30, 1966, when a few officers entered Illia's office and informed him that they had been ordered by their commander-in-chief to remove him. Not one to suffer insult lightly, he threw them out, insisting that he was the commander-in-chief and had given no such order. Taken by surprise they departed to consult, and then sent in the police to arrest the president and escort him from the Casa Rosada.[18]

The Rise of Raul Alfonsín

The Radicals spent the next decade and a half reassessing their role in politics, never accepting their irrelevance even though it appeared that they were doomed to permanent minority status. Their party was closed by the military in 1966, forcing them to cling to the friendships they had made during decades of politics. They took on the appearance of a kind of fraternal organization that was kept alive by the habits of small-town, petit bourgeois career politicians whose love of legality and fondness for each other prevented their disappearance as a political community. Radicals had always enjoyed a collegiality that was unusual in Argentine politics, sustained by their devotion to doing everything in committees, from plotting future political strategies to sharing the latest gossip.

In contrast to Peronists, who take their energy from mass demonstrations and demagogic rhetoric, Radicals can be downright boring in their endless meetings and consultations. It does not make for spectacular or even exciting governance, for nothing ever seems to get settled and presidents obligated to involve dozens of party stalwarts in their decisions give the appearance of never really deciding anything. It also makes them easy targets for opponents who demand instant solutions to every problem. Nonetheless, Radicals carry on, self-righteous in their convictions of moral superiority in an undemocratic society and confident in their capacity to withstand all forms of persecution.

Their tenacity paid off, and in 1973 when the military called new elections they were ready and waiting. But as in 1946 General Juan Perón got in their way again, this time by leading a campaign for his return that attracted half of the electorate to his stand-in candidate. Ricardo Balbín insisted on being the Radical nominee only to be embarrassed by attracting less of the vote than Illia had a decade before. An "old school" politician who, like Yrigoyen and Alvear before him, never recognized that his day had passed, Balbín alienated the younger members of his party, many of whom, like their predecessors in the 1930s, used the party's youth organization, the Juventud Radical, to lead an assault on his leadership. They complained of his ideological moderation and unwillingness to challenge the Peronists head on, a failure that made the Radicals look irrelevant to the country's politics and helpless in competition with Peronism. To make matters worse Balbín just patted them on the head and ignored their pleas with characteristic unconcern.

In their challenge to Balbín the Juventud were joined by a youthful grandfather named Raul Alfonsín, a lawyer and career politician who had never been admitted to the party's leadership because of a well-known independence of spirit that bred distrust among an old guard that demanded complete loyalty to the committee. In 1973 he formed the Movement of Renovation and Change in order to organize a campaign for the party's presidential nomination. It was a bold move, but Balbín survived it easily, leaving Alfonsín to settle for a seat in the Senate during the next three years. But it was the beginning of what would become a long and stubborn effort to become the party's leader, one that took longer than anyone expected and overcame great odds through skillful campaigning and substantial good fortune.[19]

Alfonsín went on the attack after Balbín's nomination, accusing him of having retarded the party's adjustment to a new age, one that demanded a bold new social democratic platform. When Isabel Perón moved to the right in 1975 in her battle with defiant labor unions,

Alfonsín urged his party to move to her left and make a serious effort to attract lower-class voters away from Peronism, which, he pointed out, was the only way it could become a majority party once again. But the more he and his colleagues tried to push Radicalism to the left, the more Balbín resisted them, leaving things much as they were when the military stepped in and closed all parties again in 1976. With the party back to reliance on the personal ties of its members for its sustenance, Alfonsín busied himself defending the human rights of victims of the military police state while at the same time laying the foundation for his next try for the party's presidential nomination should the opportunity ever arise again.

His first objective was to fashion an ideological stance that separated him from both Balbín and the Peronists. Innovation was his theme, though not at the cost of a complete break with the past. Thus, he criticized populist economics as obsolete and too costly to a country that could no longer afford high inflation and overbureaucratization. However, the free market principles of Martínez de Hoz and his colleagues were equally inappropriate, if only for their excessive simplicity and insensitivity to diversity within the country's economy. What was needed was something he called "integrated" economic development, a solution which offered a little something for everyone: improved wages for workers; real investment opportunities for the private sector; and reform of the public sector aimed at reducing waste and increasing its efficiency. Hardly radical ideas, even in Argentina, but as Alfonsín saw it, they offered a more realistic and, he hoped, more popular solution than those that had been tried previously.[20]

He also portrayed himself as the democrat that Argentina needed after nearly two decades of military and Peronist rule, criticizing them both as birds of the same autocratic feather. To spread his message he published the mandatory book of diagnoses and solutions, a 244-page paperback filled with high principles, economic prescriptions, and aspirations for the future titled *La cuestión argentina*. In it he offered a few new ideas, but at its core it was a very Radical statement, filled with the kind of moralism that had characterized party thinking since its founding nearly a century before. Like his predecessors he wanted everyone to know that

Radicalism is before anything a moral requisite. It was an ethic before an ideology. Better put, its ideas were developed from a moral conception that obligated it to fight to solve the problems of the dispossessed and raise highest the banner of human dignity and respect for essential rights. . . . Because it is an ethic, it cannot be put anywhere along a continuum from left to right. It does not represent any sector exclusively but can defend the concrete interest of any sector when it fits with the Radical morality. In other words Radicalism is neither left nor right nor just interested in the plight of the middle class as some would have you believe.[21]

Was this an example of dedication to the highest principles or just the propaganda of a politician pursuing a multiclass following? It was a little of both in Alfonsín's case, since he wanted to distinguish Radicals from everyone else, reminding a country that had grown weary of tyranny that Radicals were still the nation's most dedicated political liberals, and also to tell the working class that he, too, was different from the rest, ready to listen to their pleas in ways that more partisan Radicals never had.

But it was nothing but verbiage as long as Alfonsín was the renegade and not the leader of the Radical party. He had to gain the party's nomination before the next election, and to accomplish that, he had to get by his old nemesis, Ricardo Balbín. Without knowing when the election would be held, he quietly went to work laying the foundation of his campaign with the help of a small collection of people who were loyal to him and his advocacy of political renovation. Some were fellow dissidents within the Radical party, others young academics who thought they had found a progressive democrat who could defy the odds against his election. Together they worked on establishing Alfonsín's credibility within and outside the country, portraying him as a fresh alternative to his many older and discredited rivals.

His first break came when the seventy-seven-year-old Balbín died in September 1981, a year before Alfonsín announced his candidacy. Balbín's departure did not guarantee Alfonsín anything; there were still many others in the party who were determined to hold onto their positions by preventing his candidacy. But it did deny his opponents the leader they had relied on for the past twenty years, one who was tough and skilled at outmaneuvering his opponents. Moreover, it lifted the confidence of his supporters within the party, who were encouraged to know that the contest would be easier than anticipated.

The military also contributed to his good fortune. In an effort to weaken the control of Peronist bosses over the rank and file, the outgoing officers required that the delegates to presidential nominating conventions be selected in provincial primaries hastily called during the first half of 1983. This was exactly what Alfonsín needed, for it gave him the opportunity to use the grass-roots following that he had accumulated almost unnoticed during the previous three years to take on the candidate of the party establishment. Where his rival would depend on lifelong party members to secure endorsement, Alfonsín took advantage of the military's unsolicited assistance to recruit thousands of new members to the party.[22]

There was, of course, no certainty that elections would ever be held when he began his effort in the late 1970s. But such uncertainty has never stopped Argentine politicians, past or present, from pursuing public office. Their world is one neither of continuity nor of revolutionary change but of political cycles whose regularity they have come to take for granted. Obviously, it is also in the interest of party politicians to believe that the effects of military interventions will one day be reversed; that is what keeps them going in difficult times and prepares them for a counterattack when they are given a chance to launch it.

They sensed an opportunity for change when General Viola replaced Videla in March 1981. He inherited a deep recession and declining confidence in the military's management of the economy, especially among businessmen, who found themselves with huge debts and high interest rates and far too many bankruptcies. Jumping in, the Radicals and Peronists organized a multiparty coalition that petitioned Viola to schedule elections within two or three years. He refused, of course, but that did not discourage them. Still, it was not the protests of civilian politicians but defeat in the Malvinas War that ended the life of the military government. With its self-confidence temporarily shattered and recriminations within and among the three services tearing the new junta apart, the armed forces had to pull out and call elections. Another experiment in military authoritarianism had ended, only this time it came down with a bigger crash than ever before.

1983: A Very Special Election

The number of people who registered as Radicals when the books were opened again at the end of 1982 surprised even Alfonsín. The party was totally unprepared for its sudden popularity as were the Peronists, who looked on in amazement. What it meant could not be determined for another ten months, however, since both parties had to go through a succession of provincial primaries and conventions that would select candidates for nearly every office in the land, and then hold national elections in October. As the process went through each phase, Alfonsín implemented his opportunistic campaign strategy, starting with an attempt to attract previously apathetic middle- and upper-middle-class voters who feared the Peronists' return to the Casa Rosada. It was a long shot but it was the only one he had. Better yet, it worked. In one primary after another he was victorious, the momentum building until June 18, when he trounced rival Fernando de la Rua in the Buenos Aires provincial primary, always the stronghold of the party leadership. With a majority of the delegates securely under his control, he entered the convention in July already triumphant.

Success in the primaries taught Alfonsín what the Argentine middle class wanted in their politicians in the 1980s, most notably an ability to stand up to Peronists and the military whenever called upon to do so. Wrapping himself in the Radical banner was necessary for Alfonsín to keep the party's regulars behind him, but being a Radical did not help him with the rest of the electorate. Rather, for them he had to be the man whom they could put in charge of the country for five years. To accommodate them, he used television to attack the armed forces and their crimes and to denounce Peronists for their corruption and intolerance. Almost overnight this quiet, mild-mannered politician, known more for rumpled suits strewn with cigarette ashes than for anything resembling charisma, was transformed by his television appearances into a poised and deeply committed slayer of well-known dragons.[23] It was obviously what middle-class Argentines wanted to see. As one journalist remarked at the time:

> When I went in to see Alfonsín, he was holding his thirteenth grandchild in his arms. He was the same warm, decent man, the same convinced democrat, the same stickler for the law. But as Argentines discovered as they watched his campaign, something had happened to him. He had become the person who seemed able to save Argentina. The transformation he personifies is little short of miraculous.[24]

From the day of his nomination it became obvious that his chances depended as much on what the Peronists did as on his own efforts. The majority was theirs if they could keep it together, but this could no longer be taken for granted, given the loss of their supreme leader and their sad performance in the mid-1970s. They had always functioned better as a loosely organized mass movement whose labor leaders and white-collar politicians carried out Perón's directives than as a modern political party with sophisticated campaign organizations. Thus they were quite unprepared when primary elections were suddenly called. Previously, they had drawn their support from union members and the small-town poor, who had allowed Perón and CGT secretaries to choose candidates for them. Now, however, they were expected to register individual members and hold provincial primaries to elect delegates who would pick senatorial, congressional, and presidential candidates. It was not the Peronist way of doing things, and that is exactly why the armed forces did it.

Old habits die slowly, and the Peronists were not about to be democratized overnight, however. Well-known party bosses led most provincial delegations that went to the convention prepared to contest with one another over the nomination. In the past Perón would have made the critical choices, but now they had to manage without an authority to determine how their differences would be settled. There were "verticalists" who wanted exiled Isabel Perón to return home to pick a candidate for them, imitating her late husband as closely as possible, as well as "antiverticalists" who preferred to take their chances with back room bargaining over the nomination. Isabel may have favored the former, but she never said so, repeatedly refusing to exercise what authority she had. That is why when the national convention was held in early September it was wracked by confusion and quickly fell into a state of near chaos as rival factions challenged each other's credentials, postponing candidate selections for several days. Eventually the disputes were resolved and they turned to nominations, and before the week was out they had chosen ex-Senator Italo Luder to lead the ticket.

Luder was no Perón. A taciturn bourgeois lawyer, he made it to the top less on popularity than on his skill at sneaking up on his rivals within the party. Starting with a slight plurality among the delegates, he stayed aloof of the scuffling at the beginning, leaving the other candidates to knock each other off, which they proceeded to do. At the start, each of the two wings of the CGT favored a different candidate, the CGT-Azopardo backing Angel Robledo, while labor leader Lorenzo Miguel's CGT-Brasil went with Antonio Cafiero. But Azopardo dropped Robledo when it became obvious that he had little support among the rank and file, and Brasil leaders eventually shifted over to Luder after they became convinced that Cafiero could not get the nomination. To expedite the nomination Cafiero agreed to back Luder in exchange for the latter's supporting Cafiero for the governorship of Buenos Aires province, always a Peronist stronghold because most of its population came from the working-class suburbs that surrounded the nation's capital. That left the nomination to Luder, the patient compromise candidate who had quickly become everyone's second choice. It helped that Luder made it all seem quite reasonable, portraying himself as representative of a new, buttoned-down Peronist leadership that wanted to work with everyone to make the country a more democratic place. Bourgeois respectability, not blue-collar militancy, was the new look that he offered the movement, even if it was not quite ready for it.[25]

But no presidential candidate could unite the disparate and quarreling collection of politicians and labor leaders who called themselves Peronists in 1983. The best that Luder could hope for was their staying together long enough to mobilize mass support for the ticket. It would not be easy, however, since the rivalries that had torn apart the convention continued afterward. The biggest problem was posed by the antics of Buenos Aires provincial party leader Herminio Iglesias, a neofascist ward boss who refused to allow Cafiero the nomination for governor. Iglesias represented an old-fashioned Peronism and did not apologize for it, the kind that thrived on shouting insults at its opponents (he loved to call Alfonsín a bastard and a worm), and believed that democracy was whatever the *descamisados* and their orators said it was.[26] Luder could not shut him up and suffered for it throughout the campaign, his new image being tarnished every time Iglesias stood up and reminded everyone that Peronism had not matured after all. As election day approached Luder found himself boring crowds and Iglesias exciting them; at the last minute he panicked at the thought of losing and joined in the name calling, futilely trying to become a demagogue without the instinct for it. But that was all right with Alfonsín, for the more nasty Luder became, the more he played into the Radicals' hands, since fear of Peronism was the best thing they had going for them.[27]

Alfonsín could have treated the Peronists as respectable rivals in a democratic contest, trying to make the nation think it was choosing between two equally legitimate parties. Doing so might have strengthened democracy by making the contest resemble those of most other constitutional regimes, but it risked giving the respectability to the Peronists that they needed to win. That is why he chose to launch an attack on Peronism aimed at reminding non-Peronist voters what a menace Peronism really was. Unless conservatives and moderates from other parties voted for him to prevent the Peronists from doing what they did in 1973, the Radicals would remain a minority party. With that in mind he hit the Peronists hard, reminding the nation that his election was the only thing that stood in the way of their return.

The strategy was devious and brilliant. His attacks on the Peronists began on April 25, 1983, three months before he received the nomination, when he claimed that Peronist leaders had reached an agreement with military officers that promised absolution for all of the crimes they had committed in their antiterrorist campaign in exchange for the military's tolerating the formation of a Peronist government after the party won the election. Alfonsín never proved that such a plot had actually been hatched, but its plausibility allowed him to exploit it to the fullest.[28] The press was delighted to have the story, and they kept it alive until the election, just as he hoped they would, constantly reminding people that their armed forces were still plotting against them. It also gave Alfonsín the chance to portray himself as the human rights activist demanding justice while his Peronist opponents were doing what they could to obstruct its achievement. He was not, he claimed, trying to revive the old Peronist/anti-Peronist division in society, but merely living up to his pledge "always to say exactly what I think." Alfonsín the moralist thrived on defending political integrity against assaults on it, real or imagined, by unscrupulous Peronist bosses and their very unpopular military coconspirators. Of course, the Peronists denied the whole thing, but their doing so did little to change the minds of people who wanted to believe it.[29]

At the root of Alfonsín's handling of the Peronists was his determination to take advantage of their internal divisions not only to win the election but also to weaken their control over the working class permanently. In 1983 the Radicals still believed that Peronist strength in elections derived primarily from union control over the masses, a control that could be broken now that Perón was no longer there to keep it operating. By taking advantage of dissent and division within the movement using the power of government to draw workers away from Peronist union leaders, they intended to reorganize the electorate and expand the mass base of the Radical party simultaneously. Succeeding always seemed a little farfetched, even to most Radicals, but they had to try since even modest success was necessary to end Peronist domination in elections. So rather than write off the working class entirely, Alfonsín tried hard to appeal to workers who watched his campaign on television but avoided Peronist rallies, promising them real liberty and higher wages in return for their taking a chance on him. It was the line he and his wing of the party had been developing since they began their attack on Balbín in 1973, and now he was putting it to the test.[30]

What for the Radicals was a choice between good and evil never became so simple for most of the electorate. Confidence in the Radicals was not much greater than it was in the Peronists, especially among the middle and upper classes, for whom the election began as an unfortunate choice between suboptimal alternatives, neither of which promised the nation strong leadership. Frondizi and Illia were remembered less for their overthrow by the armed forces than for their weakness as leaders. No matter that they were not entirely at fault for their performance; many of the same forces were present in 1983, and it was not certain that a Radical could deal any better with a Peronist opposition, a disastrous economy, and the armed forces than his predecessors had. It was not uncommon to find executives from large corporations who even admitted a preference for Peronists over Radicals, not because of any affection for Peronism but because they had always found it so difficult to deal with the rigid legalism and intense partisanship practiced by

Radicals. In contrast the Peronists were always ready to "make deals." But, of course, executives had very few votes and, despite their wealth, little control over elections.

As election day approached most polls gave the Peronists a slight edge, in itself a surprise since until then their victory was believed inevitable. The key to their defeat would be Alfonsín's support among people who normally voted for one of the country's several minor parties on the left and right and his attracting some votes from people in the lower middle class who were not ready to be governed again by a Peronist president. October 30, 1983, when the votes were counted, the country was shocked, the Peronists embarrassed, and the Radicals elated to discover that 52 percent of an electorate had chosen Raul Alfonsín as their president. Commercials portraying Peronists as models of civic responsibility had obviously not been enough to deny the effect of the likes of Herminio Iglesias and his compatriots or to overcome memories of terrorism and economic chaos in 1976. The Peronists were not ready to govern the country in 1983 and many of them knew it. And until they were it would be the Radicals who did, thanks to the electorate's caution when it was given another opportunity to make democracy work.

As the vote was studied, it became clear how well Alfonsín had done in areas where he was not expected to triumph, like the suburbs around Buenos Aires, where the working class should have carried Luder to victory. Clearly he had attracted the vast majority of upper and middle classes to his side, but he had also penetrated working-class districts deeply enough to gain the votes of their more affluent residents. Nationally Luder won only seven of twenty-four provinces, nearly all of them the nation's poorest and most lightly populated: Tucuman, Jujuy, Chaco, Formosa, La Rioja, Santa Cruz, Santiago del Estero. A working-class vote for Alfonsín was not necessarily a vote against Peronism, however. Many of those who had abandoned Luder did not forsake their party, but split their tickets and sent Peronists to Congress, giving them a slight plurality in the Senate, 21 seats to the Radicals' 18, and second place in the Chamber of Deputies with 111 seats to the Radicals' 131-seat majority.

No one who wanted Argentina to learn to govern itself democratically could have hoped for a better result under the circumstances. Constitutional democracies are composed of majorities and minorities, elected officials who govern and loyal opponents who work with and against them according to rules respected by both. Argentines have never found it easy to practice politics in that manner, but they gave themselves a chance to try in 1983. To begin with they forced a new role on the Peronists. By taking their majority away from them in a free election Alfonsín denied them for the first time their credible claim of being the nation's only legitimate majority party. Since 1955 they had nurtured themselves by attacking the legitimacy of all Radical and military governments, but now the complaint had no basis in reality. No longer could they say that the Radicals "deserved" to be evicted because they had cheated the majority out of its right to rule the nation in a fraudulent election, as Frondizi and Illia had done; now the Radicals were the majority, giving the Peronists no real choice but to play the part of the loyal opposition if they wanted to attract a majority of the electorate back to their side. Equally important was the fact that the Peronists managed to hold on to substantial power in the legislature. They had not been excluded by their defeat but were able to block legislation and support or harass the president, putting a Peronist mark on his programs. Rather than alienating them from the process, the election had kept them within it, giving them an essential role to play and a chance to regain majority support as a reward for their success in the opposition. It was the strongest incentive yet to cooperation.

It was a powerful prescription for tutorials in democratic politics, though as always, one without any guarantee of success. But it did give democrats their best chance ever. It would be a very difficult test to pass, as everyone knew all too well. Political power is not easily confined to processes prescribed by law, nor is authority recognized because it is given to one person by a majority of the electorate. Moreover, the contest was not simply one involving Radicals, Peronists, and the politicians of minor parties. Equally critical to Alfonsín's survival was his treatment of a very sick economy and the way businessmen, farmers, laborers, and the armed forces responded to his cures.

Notes

1. Marcelo Luis Acuña, *De Frondizi a Alfonsín: La tradición política del radicalismo/1* (Buenos Aires: Centro Editor de America Latina, 1984), p. 24.

2. For details on what is obviously a more complicated period of political intrigue than presented here, see Roberto Etchepareborda, *Yrigoyen* (Buenos Aires: Centro Editor de America Latina, 1983), chs. 1–7.

3. These and other speculations about Saez Peña's motives are discussed in Acuña, *De Frondizi a Alfonsín*, p. 29.

4. Mark Falcoff, "Political Developments," in *Prologue to Peron: Argentina in Depression and War, 1930–1943*, ed. Mark Falcoff and Ronald Dokart (Berkeley: University of California Press, 1975), p. 42.

5. Etchepareborda, *Yrigoyen*, pp. 188–193.

6. Ibid.

7. From the periodical *La Fonda*, July 4, 1933, as quoted in Gerardo López Alonso, *Cincuenta años de historia argentina, 1930–1980* (Buenos Aires: Belgrano, 1982), p. 35.

8. Luis Gregorich, *La república perdida* (Buenos Aires: Sudamericana-Planeta, 1983), pp. 34–35.

9. Acuña, *De Frondizi a Alfonsín*, pp. 47–49.

10. Ibid., pp. 50–51.

11. For a detailed account of Radical preparations for their greatest electoral disappointment ever, see Francisco Hipólito Uzal, "La encrucijada radical de 1946," *Todo es historia*, no. 201 (January 1984): 8–40.

12. Miguel Angel Scenna, "El radicalismo: Noventa años de historia," *Todo es historia*, no. 170 (July 1981): 30–31. Also see Acuña, *De Frondizi a Alfonsín*, ch. 1.

13. On the *pacto* arranged between Frondizi and Perón, see Ramón Prieto, *El pacto: Ocho años de la política argentina* (Buenos Aires: En Marcha, 1963).

14. Gary W. Wynia, *Argentina in the Postwar Era* (Albuquerque: University of New Mexico Press, 1972), ch. 4. Also see Marcelo Cavarozzi, *Autoritarismo y democracia (1955–1983)* (Buenos Aires: Centro Editor de America Latina, 1983), pp. 13–35.

15. Guillermo O'Donnell, *El estado burocrático* (Buenos Aires: Belgrano, 1982), p. 76.

16. Ibid., pp. 65–84.

17. Ibid.

18. The story is told by Gerardo López Alonso in *Cincuenta años de historia argentina*, pp. 220–221.

19. Acuña, *De Frondizi a Alfonsín*, pp. 204–207.

20. Ibid., pp. 222–223.

21. Raul Alfonsín, *La cuestión argentina* (Buenos Aires: Propuesta Argentina, 1981), p. 191.

22. *Buenos Aires Herald*, July 24, 1983, p. 3.

23. An interesting little book was recently published on advertising by all candidates in the 1983 campaign by Alberto Borrini, titled *Como se hace un presidente* (Buenos Aires: El Cronista Comercial, 1984).

24. Robert Cox, "Argentina's Democratic Miracle," *The New Republic*, March 19, 1984, p. 22. Cox had watched Alfonsín's rise while he was editor of the daily *Buenos Aires Herald*, a post which he was forced to abandon in 1979 when the military threatened his life because he had refused to refrain from criticizing them.

25. *Buenos Aires Herald*, September 11, 1983, p. 3.

26. Ibid., October 16, 1983, p. 3.

27. Ibid., October 30, 1983, p. 3.

28. Alfonsín listed labor union leaders Lorenzo Miguel, Herminio Iglesias, Diego Ibanez, and Rogelio Papaleo as the Peronist culprits in the plot and generals Cristino Nicolaides, head of the army, Jorge Suárez Nelson, and Juan Carlos Trimarco as their collaborators at a news conference on May 2. See *Buenos Aires Herald*, May 8, 1983, p. 3.

29. In an interview Alfonsín stated: "I did not want to infest the campaign with the Peronist–anti-Peronist dichotomy, but work for the cause of national unity. I knew that if I revealed the plot they would accuse me of reviving the old antagonism that we need to overcome. . . . [But] . . . I was obligated to do it because my golden rule in politics is intellectual honesty, that is, to say exactly what I think." *SOMOS*, May 6, 1983, pp. 6–13.

30. Ibid., May 6, 1983, interview with Alfonsín and interview in *Sieta dias* 15, no. 830, p. 16.

6

An Economy at Bay

Raul Alfonsín inherited an economy in real trouble. The source of great pride before 1930, it had become the cause of much despair, steeped in recession, astronomical inflation, and record foreign debts, with real per capita income actually less than it was fifteen years before. That 30 million people who were nearly self-sufficient in petroleum, blessed with an abundance of food, and without a large rural proletariat should have fallen on such hard times is surprising but not impossible to explain.[1]

After World War II Argentina was supposed to "take off" into sustained growth and mass consumption, making it a regional power as affluent as the industrial nations of Western Europe. But its flight was a short one. Perón's subsidization of private industry proved costly and inefficient, nationalized enterprises and new social programs very expensive, and the confiscation of profits from grain exports damaging to farm production. And most of the investments made before and after 1955 were inefficient—the result of volatile and often inconsistent policies, import substitution, and high and variable inflation, forcing governments to impose severe austerity measures time and again that caused negative growth in 1952, 1959, and 1962–63. Some stability was achieved between 1964 and 1974 with the addition of heavier industry and an increase in crop production, encouraging people to hope that the era of "stop-go" cycles had ended, but such optimism proved unfounded. After a high of 8.5 percent in 1969, growth rates fell again, down to only 3.1 percent in 1972. And then in 1976 the economy went into a tailspin as inflation soared to 600 percent. The armed forces took over and tried to stabilize and "liberalize" the economy simultaneously, but in the end they too failed, especially in their attempts to trim the public sector deficits that had become a major source of the country's economic difficulties after 1973, financed as they were by an accumulating external debt and inflation-inducing monetary expansion. While countries like Brazil were doubling the dollar value of their exports between 1977 and 1981, the Argentine military could increase theirs by no more than 60 percent, a particular embarrassment since raising the level of exports had been one of their primary objectives.[2] By 1979 the Argentine share of the Latin American GNP, which had been 24 percent in 1950, had fallen to only 13.2 percent because countries like Brazil and Mexico had grown so much faster during the interim.[3] It only became worse when the country was hit by the world recession in 1981 and 1982 followed by the Malvinas War, which cut it off for a period from European financial markets (see Table 6.1).

6.1   National Product Annual Growth Rates, by Sector, 1979–84 (at 1970 prices)

Year	Per Capita GNP	Agriculture	Industry	Commerce
1979	5.0	3.5	10.2	11.0
1980	−0.8	−6.7	−3.8	5.6
1981	−7.9	2.4	−16.0	−6.8
1982	−6.9	6.4	−4.7	−18.3
1983	1.2	0.8	9.9	3.6
1984*	0.9	3.5	3.8	3.3

Source: Clarin, economic supp., November 4, 1984, p. 7.
*Estimates for 1984.

When democracy was tried again in 1983, the new government inherited 400 percent inflation, accelerating capital flight, and a foreign debt that had risen from $18.8 billion in 1978 to $48.4 billion in 1984, far more than the country could pay on schedule. It was the latest phase in an incredible history that had seen prices rise in great bursts, the annual rate of inflation peaking in 1976 at nearly 700 percent, then falling below 100 percent in 1980, only to rise to 1,000 in mid-1985.[4]

Argentines have adapted to inflation and stagnation by investing less in their economy. Financial wheeling and dealing, not long-term, productive investment, absorbed increasing amounts of national capital; so did investing abroad, so much so that officials estimated that 20 percent of the capital owned by Argentines was outside the country in 1985. It resembled a badly managed casino in which profit depended more on cunning and good fortune than on productivity as everyone hustled to anticipate price increases and currency devaluations.

Unless one experiences hyperinflation, it is hard to appreciate what it does to the saver and investor. The worst thing that one can do is nothing, holding onto pesos while inflation reduces their value by 15 to 20 percent monthly. Instead you spend them as fast as you can either for goods you can consume or for commodities that will retain value, like gold or dollars. Normal savings accounts are unprofitable since the interest paid usually lags behind inflation. For example, if you had deposited 100 pesos in an account in an Argentine bank at the beginning of 1984, their value would have increased to 257 pesos by October of that year because interest rates averaged 15.5 percent monthly during those nine months. Yet you were poorer than you had been in January since prices rose 20 percent a month during the same period, netting you 30 percent less in buying power. The only way that one can profit from such conditions is by moving money quickly from one commodity to another, trying to buy and sell at just the right moments. As one banker mused,

> A smart investor is constantly shifting his capital from place to place to ride the price increases. . . . He goes from the dollar to the stock market, the next day he sells the stocks and buys bricks, and the week after that he sells the bricks and lends in the intercompany loan market at 22 percent interest. Then he collects his loan in a month and goes back to the dollar. It all goes in a big circle, faster and faster. If you sleep ten hours, you lose.[5]

Everyone tries to cope, most often by delaying the payment of bills. But stores and industries anticipate such maneuvers and post prices high enough to compensate them for such delays, accelerating inflation as they do. People with money to invest and goods to sell often lose despite their best efforts in money markets, but they are not inflation's principal victims. It is the wage earner who suffers the most; without credit cards to delay payments or extra income to invest he can do little but watch his real income fall. He may fight for higher wages, but when inflation is as rampant as it was in Argentina in 1984 and 1985 even indexed wages could not really keep up. Worse still, the situation always becomes more painful before it gets better. Sooner or later authorities will decide to wage war against inflation, and when they do, real wages will fall. If their crusade works, nearly everyone will be better off eventually, but if it fails, as it often does, the wage earner will end up poorer than before. Labor leaders and the rank and file know this, and that is why they are so reluctant to cooperate with officials who promise them lower prices tomorrow in return for their accepting austerity today.

This is no way to run an economy, as every Argentine knows, but doing something about it is a monumental task. When Alfonsín looked about him in 1984 he saw much to worry about and a great deal that was beyond his power to cure. But there was no reason to give up on it, as he well knew, for alongside its many ills were some rather impressive achievements and great strengths on which to draw in order to pull the country through it all. Topping the list was a rural economy that had finally decided to become part of the modern world.

Beef and Grain

Being a commodity exporter remains an embarrassment to urbane Argentines, who think of the countryside as a vast space still populated by oligarchs and tenant farmers whom the country's modernization has left far behind. But were it not for farmers increasing their product substantially during the past two decades, the country would be in much worse shape than it is today.

North American farmers know what is happening on the *pampas* and are studying its effects with concern. What they see are the results of Argentina's second agricultural revolution. Cereal exports, which averaged around 12 million tons in the 1930s before falling to 5 million in the 1940s and 1950s, recovered and stabilized at around 8.5 million annually from 1962 to 1976. But then, almost unnoticed anywhere but in world commodity markets, Argentine grain production rose steadily to a 14 million ton average, reaching a peak in 1983 of 22 million tons, almost triple what it had been two decades before. At long last, it seemed, Argentine farmers were on their way to achieving what U.S. and Canadian farmers had accomplished forty years ago, namely putting technology to work to augment production significantly. Three advances accounted for most of the increase: the introduction of higher-yielding varieties, including hybrids; increased use of plant-protecting chemicals, such as fungicides, insecticides, and herbicides; and continued mechanization. They were also helped some by the U.S. government when it imposed an embargo on sales of grain to the Soviet Union in 1979, allowing Argentina to increase its share of the world grain and soybean market from 5.8 percent in 1979 to 11 percent in 1984, which, though substantially less than the U.S. share of 52 percent, marked an almost 100 percent increase.[6]

There was nothing easy or inevitable about the Argentine achievement. Sixty years ago its agricultural product grew at rates similar to those in the United States and Canada, but then it fell far behind, as farmers eschewed the technological innovations that transformed North American farming. Contentment with cheap and easy modes of production contributed to their inertia, but so did Juan Perón's redistribution of income from agriculture to industry. From then onward farmers were burdened by a host of policies that increased the costs of farm inputs and depressed domestic prices. Food prices were kept down to placate urban consumers, tariffs were placed on imported farm equipment to protect domestic industry, and commodity exports were taxed because they were a convenient source of revenue. Inevitably, import duties and export taxes produced major distortions in the ratio between the farmers' input costs and commodity prices, making innovation unprofitable even to the most ambitious farmers. Only when government policies were reformed and world prices rose high enough to make using higher-yielding varieties of grain profitable during the 1970s did production finally take off.[7]

Mechanization also became essential to growth after the depopulation of the countryside in the 1940s, when thousands went to the cities, where industry and government offered rural laborers and tenant farmers higher income. On the *pampas* alone the rural work force declined by 52 percent between 1947 and 1960. With less labor to draw upon, landowners initially fell back on cattle raising, leaving grain primarily to the tenants who remained.[8] Simultaneously, however, the land tenure structure began to change, the number of owner-operators increasing from 36 percent in 1947 to 74 percent by 1974, and the proportion of tenants and sharecroppers dropping by half, from 24 to 13 percent. Many things contributed to the shift in ownership, though much of the credit belongs to the freezing of land rents by populist governments after World War II, the longest episode lasting during the Peronist decade. Landowners occasionally found it more economical to sell pieces to tenants than pay rising taxes in a time of frozen rents.[9] None of this transformed the *pampas* into a province of egalitarian farmers since 5 percent of the landowners continued to hold nearly half of the land, but it did increase the number of middle-size farmers, who saw advantage in modernizing crop production rather than relying primarily on cattle raising.

Beef remains a major export, but it was surpassed by cereals in the 1970s and now brings only a third as much income to the country. The quality of Argentine beef is renowned, the Aberdeen Angus making up 80 percent of its stock, but that does not make selling it abroad any easier these days. The annual slaughter fell from 2 million to 1 million head during the 1940s, then rose to 3 million head in the 1960s, only to suffer the loss of its principal markets when Great Britain banned beef imports in 1967 and the European Common Market nations did likewise in the early 1970s in order to protect their own cattle industries. Argentine production fell back to 2 million in the mid-1970s, then rose again to 3 million at the end of the decade. However, Argentines consume between 80 and 90 percent of it, the rest going to a variety of markets in the Third World where they must compete with Brazilian as well as European exports. Consequently today they export 500,000 tons annually, about the same amount as they did in 1940.[10]

It is not hard to find *estancias* devoted entirely to cattle raising today, but the "typical" enterprise is a mixed operation. Some are quite large but many are "medium-size" farms (500–2,500 acres), their number having grown along with the increase in ownership and the consolidation of smaller units. It is usually owned and operated by a family or a manager working for a family living in a nearby town. They have some cattle, essential because they serve as "quasi-money" from which the owner can draw cash through sales whenever it is needed. Crop rotation is also common, with shifts from something like corn and flax one year to wheat the second and then all three the third. It is their reluctance to specialize in one crop that distinguishes most Argentine farmers from their U.S. and Canadian peers. Always preoccupied with unscheduled changes in government as well as fluctuations in world prices, the Argentine farmer is quite cautious and, therefore, always more interested in minimizing risk than in maximizing gain.

Argentine farmers complain a great deal about the disadvantages they suffer from the perpetuation of policies that keep prices of their inputs high and returns on their commodities lower than they prefer. Despite occasional government efforts to remove such obstacles, many remain. Worse still, in an economy like Argentina's the internal terms of trade for commodities continue to rise and fall wildly; for example, it took twice as much wheat to buy a harvester in 1980 as it had five years before, making it hard for farmers to plan long-term capital investments.[11] The country's need to pay its enormous foreign debt with dollars earned by commodity exports gives the rural sector some leverage over policy, but hardly enough to prevail against competing urban interests. Moreover, populists in the Peronist and Radical parties were unconvinced that the lowering of export taxes would increase production enough to induce increases in exports that would eventually raise revenues. Government revenue needs are too immediate to allow for the testing of such "supply-side" logic. In the meantime, the country has no choice but to hope that despite the handicaps they suffer its farmers will continue to supply the food they love to eat and the dollars they like to spend.

Marketing has also changed during the last half-century. Fifty years ago only a few firms dominated the grain market, the largest being the Bunge y Born Company, which handled nearly half, and the Louis Dreyfus Corporation, which marketed a third of the grain exported in 1930. They and a few other large grain traders continue to dominate trade in the private sector as they do worldwide. But the depression forced the government to become involved in trading in order to protect farmers, and then Perón created a public corporation through which most grain had to pass. Ever since, the government has gone in and out of the market depending on the economic philosophy of those in office, the Peronists increasing the state's share of trade to 52.9 percent in 1975, while their market-oriented military successors reduced it to only 5.6 percent in 1979.[12]

In contrast to the grain trade, foreigners have all but abandoned the meat-packing industry that was once their monopoly. British and U.S. firms began operating in Argentina in the 1880s. The British, worried about contamination from unhealthy imported livestock, required slaughter abroad before shipping. Foreign packers seized the opportunity, buying and expanding plants devoted previously to local production, three of them owned by North American corporations and two by British ones. Within only two decades they had cornered 90 percent of the beef export trade, the Armour and Wilson companies alone controlling 60 percent of it. They became notorious for rigging prices against cattlemen and playing them off against each other to weaken their opposition to such practices. It continued against little effective resistance until the 1930s, when the depression induced government intervention into the market and concessions to cattlemen who demanded the creation of a semipublic corporation that was guaranteed 11 percent of the British market by authorities. The meat packers' control over the market was never the same again, but in the end it was not Perón who sent them home—he never did nationalize them—but inevitable changes in the industry itself after 1950.[13]

When World War II broke out Argentines were consuming just a little more than half of the beef they produced, but Perón saw to it that the working class received more, and by 1955 there was only 14 percent of the annual slaughter left for export. Changes in technology struck the final blow. Ways were found to prepare meat in small cuts fit for shipping directly to markets, giving advantages to those who adopted the new technology. Conversion proved too costly for the antiquated foreign firms, so when several dozen local entrepreneurs built smaller and more efficient plants, they took over much of the market, forcing the foreigners to close down and go away.[14]

In the United States people occasionally wonder why the Argentines, even when governed by reactionary military regimes, sell so many commodities to the Soviets. The reason is quite obvious, at least to any Argentine: they have no other choice. As if pulled by an invisible hand, they have been forced to move slowly but steadily from west to east to find markets, from Great Britain before the war to Italy and Spain after it, and then, when their access to the continent was cut off by a decision of the Common Market in 1974, to Eastern Europe and the Soviet Union, the biggest step coming when the United States boycotted the Soviet market in 1979. Guided entirely by economic self-interest, Argentina's anticommunist military rulers stubbornly ignored U.S. requests that they participate in the boycott, preferring instead to capture a desperately needed new market. Consequently by 1981 almost 80 percent of the country's exported wheat was going to the Soviet Union, bringing the country $3 billion in return, and dividing the nation's total exports into almost three equal parts, one-third going to the Soviet Union, another to Europe, and the remaining third to the rest of the Americas, including the United States.[15] It is quite different when it comes to imports, however. Nearly 70 percent of what Argentina imports is raw products for industrial use and 17 percent capital goods, but only 2.4 percent of it came from the Soviet Union and Eastern Europe in 1984. The United States and Canada supplied 36 percent, Western Europe 29 percent, and the rest of Latin America 21 percent. The Soviets are insisting on more sales in Argentina, but so far little has changed.[16]

What the Argentines have learned from all of this is that they cannot, as they once did, rely only on other capitalist nations for trade. Nor can they count entirely on the socialist ones, for there is nothing to prevent the Soviets from buying large volumes from the Americans again. In other words, they know that their position in the world economy is quite vulnerable, making it essential that they remain flexible and aggressive within the world market. What they do with their grain, beef, and other exports in the future will have less to do with political ideology than with their need to keep commodities flowing fast enough to pay their enormous foreign debts.

What Became of the Industrial Revolution?

Agriculture earns desperately needed foreign exchange, but it is industry and commerce that generate the employment that keeps Argentines consuming. Unfortunately, industry has fallen on hard times lately, the sector's growth actually being negative three of the past five years (see Table 6.1). Industrialists do not invest as much as they once did simply because they and their potential stockholders are convinced that there are more profitable things to do with their money than back industry in an economy as depressed as Argentina's.

They started running into trouble in the mid-1970s when the Peronists governed. Production, hours worked, and employment fell, rose again after Videla took over, and then declined precipitously in 1979, languishing in recession for the next three years. Worst hit was the industrial work force, whose size fell by an incredible 30 percent between 1975 and 1982. Record numbers of medium and small firms went bankrupt, and several large ones merged with multinationals. Martínez de Hoz was not unhappy with all of this, of course, since he had wanted to shrink the industrial work force and improve productivity through plant modernization, but his cleansing of industry did not generate the new era of industrial growth that he had promised. Instead, authorities found themselves in the mid-1980s with an economy plagued by declining investment.

On the surface its industry does not look all that different from what one finds in the other industrializing Latin American countries. It developed gradually, rising to about 20 percent of the GDP by the time of the 1930 depression and then surpassing agriculture as a contributor to the national product in 1939. It continued to grow during and after the war, encouraged by government import substitution policies that protected national firms against competition from less expensive imports. The last big push came in the early 1960s, when multinational firms were invited to build plants in Argentina to produce basic goods like petrochemicals, vehicles, and machinery. Despite interruptions by occasional recessions, the industrial product grew by an annual average rate of 5.7 percent between 1950 and 1965, when it contributed nearly twice as much to the national product as did agriculture.[17]

As in most capitalist economies, a few large corporations dominate in most Argentine industries. Just 2 percent of the firms operating in Argentina employ 49 percent of the industrial work force and generate 65 percent of the industrial product. Their employees, nearly all of whom belong to labor organizations, earn, on the average, 50 percent more in wages than the employees of smaller firms.[18] Control over large industry is divided between foreign and nationally owned firms, the former dominating in the automotive, electronics, and chemical industries, with a share in petrochemicals, while national firms operate in the steel industry, building materials, packaged food, as well as chemicals and textiles. Of the largest 100 industrial enterprises ranked by sales in 1981, 41 were foreign owned.[19] Government enterprises are less well represented in manufacturing, being confined more to transportation and utilities, except for heavy participation in oil, steel, machinery, and weapons.[20]

Foreign investment has always played a prominent role in the country's industrialization, though initially a much greater one in the construction of the transportation and communications infrastructure and in banking than in industry. But investments in industry did accompany agricultural development at the turn of the century, and the flow remained steady until the depression struck in 1929, most of it English in origin, though Americans began competing with the British in the industrial sector after World War I. After a long pause brought on by Perón's hostility toward foreigners as well as uncertainty about where he was taking the country, foreigners came back in the early 1960s. This time most of them were North American multinationals invited by Radical president Arturo Frondizi to assist with the construction of more basic industries. By 1976 the U.S.-based firms owned 40 percent of what foreigners had invested in industry, most of it going to manufacturing, especially automobiles, rubber products, machinery, chemicals, and electronics. Switzerland was a surprising second with 12.2 percent concentrated in utilities, transportation equipment, chemicals, and food products. Great Britain was third with 7.7 percent, the Netherlands next with 6.2, and France and West Germany with 5.8 percent each. Japan, which is a heavy investor in Brazil, has shied away from less stable Argentina, supplying only 0.4 percent of the nation's foreign investment.[21]

What is most striking about foreign involvement is not the amount of it—though nationalists claim that there is far too much—but how much less Argentina has received than other industrializing nations in the region like Brazil and Mexico. The latter have attracted 35 and 30 percent, respectively, of all the foreign investment made in Latin America during the last two decades, while Argentina received only 3 percent of it. As a result, total foreign investment in Argentina by 1983 was just $5.8 billion, compared to $24.6 billion in Brazil and $13.6 billion in Mexico.[22] Quite obviously, its economic instability made it less inviting as did its government's frequent shifts in foreign investment policy, making entrance easy only to put extensive restrictions on it whenever it grew.

The most recent effort to extend hospitality to multinational firms was launched by Martínez de Hoz and the military in 1976. Commitments to invest nearly $3 billion were made, though some of them were canceled when recession hit in 1980; not surprisingly, 53 percent of it came from U.S.-based corporations, 12 percent from Italian ones, and 6.5 percent each from France and West Germany. This time it was spread over several sectors, with 19.7 percent going to mining, 17.8 percent to gas and petroleum production, 14 percent to automobiles, and 13.4 percent to banking. Investment in mining and fuel production was encouraged by the military, and banking also was promoted by a reduction of restrictions on foreign bankers; the financial sector remained largely in national hands, nevertheless, the government's banks holding 50 percent of all deposits, private national banks 35 percent, and foreigners 15 percent (the Bank of Boston ranked sixth and Citibank twelfth among the fifteen largest holders of deposits).[23]

The issue of foreign investment remains a very controversial one. Nationalism is strong and, as before, is often expressed as resentment of foreign capitalists and calls for their eviction. Some economists, however, claim that the country has no other reasonable alternative. The government is already overextended financially and is in no condition to create many more industrial enterprises on its own, and Argentine capitalists continue to fail to reinvest what the country needs. Moreover, if it is modern technology that industry needs in order to increase its productivity, multinationals can supply some of it. As much as they resent their country's dependence on foreign capital, Argentines are hard put to suggest effective alternatives to it. Even Peronists and Radicals admitted as much in their platforms in the 1983 election.

Big businesses are not the only kind that exist, of course. To a large degree the country remains a land of small enterprises. There are, for example, around 120,000 manufacturers, or 90 percent of the nation's total, which employ less than twenty-five persons. Small industries are common during the first stages of development, but in Argentina they have hung on in large numbers. There is a risk to it, naturally, since they are so vulnerable to inflation, credit squeezes, recessions, and other common features of the Argentine economy. But their total number stays about the same as people start over after bankruptcy or the sale of their firms, and new ones keep appearing.

Populists like the Peronists and Radicals have always defended small business, trying hard to protect it with high tariffs, subsidized interest rates, and stimulants to consumption. Economic liberals, in contrast, tried to withdraw protection in the late 1970s, driving some firms out of business deliberately. Nevertheless, Argentine entrepreneurs are a resilient lot, evidencing a spirit of enterprise begun by immigrants a century ago.

Nothing seems more essential in the days ahead than clear signals sent from government through its macroeconomic policies. They must be consistent and reliable. That was how they were advertised under the recent military regime, but they never came very close to the ideal. Eliminating price controls, increasing credit availability, and controlling unions were supposed to stimulate growth, but when accompanied by an inefficient financial sector that expanded without supervision and by enormous variations in relative prices, interest rates, and real effective exchange rates that reduced the time horizon and decision-making ability of industrialists, they had little effect.[24] Moreover, no matter who rules Argentina, be he Peronist, Radical, or someone else, he will have to find some way to promote the export of many more industrial products. With a domestic market too small to sustain sufficient growth, Argentines must manufacture for sale abroad, as difficult as it is against stiff competition from neighbors and the countries in the Far East. It does export 800 percent more now than it did twenty-five years ago, but total world exports have grown three times that during the same period. Only 22 percent of what it exports comes from industry, far too little if manufacturing is to grow again and employment return to previous levels. It will not be easy. Other nations are putting up trade barriers to protect their own industries, and consumption was reduced by recession in the early 1980s and is now recovering slowly. But if there is one thing that economists of both the Peronist and Radical parties can now agree upon, it is the need to sell what Argentina manufactures in as many parts of the world as possible.[25]

The State Entrepreneur

Few people have kind words for the government bureaucracy anymore. Even Radical and Peronist economists, once dedicated defenders of public enterprise, have resorted to blaming the nation's woes on government waste and inefficiency. Yet, neither has shown much capacity for taming the beast. Details of its actual size are never published, but we do know that there are seventeen major, nonfinancial government corporations, thirty military factories and mixed-equity enterprises, and around one hundred smaller ones like hotels, airlines, and television stations. Provincial and municipal governments own another eighty-nine enterprises.[26] An estimated 343,000 people are employed in the thirteen largest corporations (111,000 of them on the railways), or the equivalent of about 22 percent of the nation's industrial work force. Estimates of total public employees at all levels indicate that about 1.6 million persons are working in the public sector.[27]

In 1922 the Radicals created what has become the wealthiest of the public corporations, the petroleum-producing Yacimientos Petroleros Fiscales (YPF), which refines 70 percent of the crude that is processed within the country, the rest going to multinationals Esso and Shell, which refine 12 percent each. Most utilities are publicly owned as well, including nearly all gas, electricity, and telecommunications companies as well as the national railway and airline. The weight of the state is felt everywhere, most notably in its paying for half of all construction activity in the country and two-thirds of all investment in durable equipment purchased annually. It is all very expensive and the deficits of enterprises like the railways are notorious, causing the central government to spend about 5 percent of the domestic product to cover public enterprise losses.[28]

It is not hard to understand why Argentines complain so much about government enterprise, the quality of services, and persistent deficits: whether it deserves reprobation or not, the state is the perfect scapegoat. Nevertheless, it is a reality that few people are willing to change. As in all capitalist countries the nation's entrepreneurs curse it for its inefficiencies and high costs but rely heavily on its purchase of their products and services. Military officers claim to want inflation reduced, though never at the cost of cutting their portions of the budget or the financing of their enterprises. Thousands of public employees have made careers operating enterprises and delivering services and are organized to defend their power and privileges. And political parties, regardless of their platforms, are always torn between a fondness for the resources public office allows them to share with their constituents and their economists' advice to trim federal budgets. To an even greater degree than in other capitalist economies everyone relies too much on the Argentine state to make serious changes in it.

The Peronists are blamed for all of this coming about, but its growth began before Perón. Strong government was essential in Argentina just to put the nation back together after regional rivalries had torn it apart in the early nineteenth century. Originally authorities restricted themselves to clearing the way for the nation's private entrepreneurs, doing only what was necessary to assure the flow of grain and meat to European markets. Yet demands for greater state participation in the economy accompanied economic development, and by the turn of the century tenant farmers were demanding intervention into the land market on their behalf, cattlemen protection against meat packers, and labor unions state enforcement of collective bargaining.

The Radicals were the first to listen. Their reliance on thousands of grass-roots constituency organizations as well as their nationalism made them receptive to arguments for a more active government. They expanded public education, made the government responsible for the exploration and extraction of petroleum, and promulgated labor legislation sanctioning the eight-hour workday and the forty-eight-hour week. Hardly extreme measures by contemporary standards, but they marked a change for Argentina that brought with it new opportunities for patronage which in turn made citizens more dependent on the state for their well-being. Not only job seekers but also entrepreneurs in need of friends in high places began looking to government for assistance.

But, ironically, it was the oligarchy that really put the government into the marketplace when they dealt with the effects of the 1929 depression by regulating the beef and grain trade. Necessity dictated a more activist state. Later it took little imagination for Perón to use existing boards and commissions to buy and sell commodities whose profits he confiscated to finance the expansion of public enterprises. His nationalism, along with the enormous gold reserves that were accumulated during the war years when imports from Europe were halted, allowed his purchase of the nation's railways from the British and other utilities from foreign stockholders, and it permitted the construction of a merchant fleet, the expansion of government petroleum and coal companies, and the building of an iron and steel complex for the armed forces. Each measure generated hundreds of jobs, which Perón eagerly filled in order to absorb the labor surplus created by rural to urban migration during the war years. It also allowed him to play favorites, increasing the already partisan character of the Argentine state. Thanks to him and the Radicals before, it became the home of the middle and lower classes, giving them resources to compensate minimally for the disadvantages imposed on them by the oligarchy.

Not surprisingly, the Argentine government continually must increase its revenues to pay its bills. Total public expenditures equaled 34 percent of the GDP in 1970, rose to 39 percent in 1975, and then to an incredible 50 percent in 1983. Some of the growth was caused by military rearmaments, but by far the largest share was taken by the servicing of a rapidly growing debt, rising from 5.6 percent of the budget in 1974 to 37.1 percent in 1982 while consuming the equivalent of 15 percent of the gross domestic product. The central government was responsible for most of it, though state enterprises accounted for a third, and municipal and provincial governments nearly one-fourth. Deficits are common among state enterprises not only because of their well-known inefficiencies but also because authorities are reluctant to price public services high enough to cover their costs. Consequently, they leave themselves no choice but to borrow or raise revenues some other way.[29]

Deficits also result from the Argentines' refusal to pay their taxes. Tax evasion, in the words of a noted Argentine economist, "has become a sport for us, evidenced by the fact that at parties we praise the biggest evader as if he were a hero of some kind, ignoring how such behavior increases what the rest of us have to pay."[30] Today officials estimate that revenues equal to as much as 23 percent of the GDP are lost annually to tax evasion (about $4 billion in 1984).[31] Everyone does it, from the wage earner to the store owner to large corporations, though it is easier for the latter to get away with it than it is for the wage earners whom they employ. Lawyers, doctors, and dentists document very little of their income, and firms are notorious for underestimating their sales and foreign exchange dealings. As a result, income taxes generate no more than 6 percent of the government's income.[32]

Tax laws do exist but the system must rely very heavily on regressive sources of revenues to overcome the incapacity for efficient income tax collection. Most comes from excise taxes (principally on fuels), tariffs on imports, export taxes on agricultural commodities, a value-added sales tax, and social security taxes. The total intake fluctuates with the volume of exports and imports and the rate of inflation, ranging from highs of nearly 30 percent of the GDP to lows of 17 percent during the past decade, making tax revenues an unreliable source of finance. Equally indicative of its unreliability is the fact that total tax collections ranged from 75 percent of public expenditures in 1980 to just 46 percent two years later, largely due to the economy's lack of growth that year.[33] Such sudden changes in government income always occur when economies move from recession to growth and vice versa. But even if the Argentine economy begins growing again, it will have a long way to go before it has a tax system that is both equitable and effective. The problem is in part a technical one of law enforcement, but it is also very political since so many people are determined to use what influence they have to avoid paying for their share of public services. It does not help, of course, that the low quality of much of what they get for their money is not very conducive to their feeling any obligation to pay.

Poverty in Argentina?

As if inflation and recession were not already enough of a burden, Argentines have recently added poverty to their list of misfortunes. The poor have always been with them, but in smaller number than in neighboring countries, and many of them had migrated to Argentina from Paraguay and Chile. But when the economy went into a tailspin in the 1970s many more joined their ranks, nearly all of them Argentine to the core.

Authorities finally got around to taking a systematic look at the matter just a couple of years ago and assigned the staff of the national statistics institute to go over the 1980 census to see what they could find. They began by creating an index for measuring poverty made up of five indicators—children between six and twelve not in school; more than three persons to a room; precarious housing structures; unsafe water; living on a subsistence wage—and then used it to study their data. What they discovered was shocking, even to people who knew that poverty was on the rise. An estimated 22.3 percent of the nation's households were "poor," compared to only 8 percent in 1970. The proportion was much higher in rural areas—41.9 percent—than in cities with over 50,000 inhabitants—17.4 percent—as one might suspect, but that did not make the national total any more tolerable.[34] They also discovered that Argentines were less literate than they were supposed to be: nearly 27 percent were functional illiterates, among them almost a fourth of the people who lived in the Greater Buenos Aires area. In the northern provinces an estimated 54 percent of the population was functionally illiterate, a shocking figure for even the poorest parts of the country.[35]

The number and diversity of items used in the index undoubtedly exaggerated the severity of the problem somewhat; it is not uncommon for some people in remote towns to have bad water even though they earn more than the subsistence wage; moreover, even those below the subsistence wage usually find enough cheap food to keep from starving. But poverty is there and it is growing as the visitor to the northern provinces and to slums on the edges of the largest cities discovers. And despite recent government efforts to bring food to the most impoverished, prospects for poverty's reduction are not good given the austerity measures that authorities have been forced to impose on the public sector. Austerity increases unemployment and reduces real income for a time, making it probable that the number of poor will increase in the years ahead; and even should Argentina recover from its current plight in a decade or so, its poorest will be the last to benefit from the recovery.

Economic Interests, Politics, and Policy

The sources of some of Argentina's economic problems are deep and structural and without simple solutions, stemming from export and financial dependence, a bloated populist state, and heavily protected industries. A world capitalist economy that once sustained Argentina ceased doing so a long time ago. But something more than economic structure has inhibited progress toward the successful treatment of the nation's economic ills. People with concrete interests to protect also got in the way, some of them politicians and military officers, but others cattlemen, farmers, industrialists, foreign investors, and labor leaders, who are quite adept at defending their interests against policies that threaten them.

Argentines love to complain about villains. In fact, conspiracy theories abound, most arguing that *oligarquías* and *patrias financieras* (financial fatherlands) conspire to exploit everyone else. They are said to be very rich and often in collusion with foreigners, who delight in pillaging the national patrimony. Given the country's history of foreign penetration, the appeal of such notions is obvious. Businessmen do "wheel and deal," often at some cost to the nation, and they feed the corruption of officials, both civilian and military. Yet most of what authorities do to solve economic problems is not the result of perverse conspiracies but the consequence of endless struggle between government officials and well-known, organized and semi-organized private interests, just as it is in other capitalist countries. Landowners do not dictate the nation's course any longer, nor do industrialists or labor leaders, yet each is powerful enough to subvert most anything they wish if they are willing to accept the political costs for doing so.[36]

The wealthy are not hard to find, but that does not mean that they "run" the country. They only occasionally unite long enough to do battle with the proletariat; more often they function as a collection of separate economic interests who have much to contest for among themselves as well as to protect from other social classes. Diversification came with industrialization, and no amount of investment by cattlemen in industry or by industrialists in land has prevented substantial plurality among them.

Divisions also exist between people involved in one phase of production and those devoted to another. Take the rural sector, for example. Originally the richest cattlemen on the pampas were represented by the Argentine Rural Society (SRA), created in 1866. It was truly elitist at first, limiting membership to 2,500 cattlemen well into the 1930s. It was also powerful in politics, supplying half of all cabinet ministers who served between 1910 and 1943. But rich cattlemen were not the only ones in the countryside who spoke out in defense of the sector. In 1912 poorer tenant farmers organized the Agrarian Federation (FAA), a much larger organization than the Rural Society that contested with it over issues of land rents and tenant rights and championed the cause of progressive land redistribution. In 1932 both organizations were joined by another, the Confederation of Rural Associations of Buenos Aires and La Pampa (CARBAP), formed by cattle breeders who sought greater influence over policy affecting their relationship with cattle fatteners and meat packers. The three organizations and the people they represented were not implacable enemies, but they clashed often over policy, the first two on issues that separated the rich from the poor and the second two over narrow matters that separated breeders from fatteners. With the transformation of many tenants into middle-class farmers after World War II, class differences in the rural sector were reduced substantially, making sectoral unity on policy issues easier to achieve. Nevertheless, disagreements persist because of fundamental differences between the rich cattlemen who fatten herds on extensive holdings and invest much of their profits in industry and high finance and the fulltime farmers, whose profits depend almost entirely on what they earn from the land, much like their peers in North America. The latter feel discriminated against by populist governments who want to channel their surplus to consumers and industrialists and mistreated by military governments who do not compensate them sufficiently for their past losses despite promises to do so. They are not subsidized nearly as much as farmers in the United States and Western Europe are and resent it, claiming victimization by leaders devoted to pacifying urban society at their expense.[37]

Industrialists went into politics separately from cattlemen. A few hundred manufacturers formed the Industrial Union (UIA) in 1889 to advocate more favorable treatment of industry by governments that did not welcome it because of the threat it posed to British trading partners who supplied most of the country's consumer and capital goods. Even the Radicals were not enthusiastic about protecting domestic industry in the 1920s, though they did defend it from organized labor. During the 1930s the UIA received some of the subsidization it wanted, though less because of its political clout than because of the conservative government's decision to promote local enterprise with a Keynesian-style recovery program after the 1929 depression. Perón divided industrialists from one another, some preferring populist subsidization and others happier to go it alone. Among the former were many small, native-owned firms, several of them from cities in the interior of the country. During Perón's first presidency they formed an organization called the General Economic Confederation (CGE), which he invited to represent all industry in consultations with the government as industry's counterpart to labor's CGT. The military closed the CGE in 1955, but it was legalized again by Arturo Frondizi and allowed to represent the more nationalist wing of Argentine business, achieving its hiatus when its leader José Gelbard designed Perón's "social pact" in 1973 and served as Economy Minister in the Peronist government during its first eighteen months.[38]

Until the 1970s the UIA represented most of the country's largest firms, including multinational ones, leaving the vast majority of medium and small ones to the CGE. UIA and CGE leaders disagreed on many economic issues, the UIA being the more conservative of the two, especially on fiscal and monetary policy and relations with labor, and the CGE favoring a state paternalism characteristic of populist economics involving government subsidization of business and collusion between government, business, and labor in the design of policy. When he returned in 1973, Perón forced the two organizations to merge, ostensibly to help with his social pact, but it was little more than window dressing. In 1976 the military shut them both down in its efforts to restructure political participation, only to legalize the UIA again in 1983.

Industrialists would be the last to claim that they dictate economic policy. And they would be right. Many firms are powerful, and the mere fact of industrialization has made industry essential to the economy's development, bringing with it influence over policy. But industries do not benefit equally from all policies, and some even suffer from them, as happened often in the previous decade. It is also important to recall how dependent industry is on the government for its business. Though conservative industrialists can be heard complaining of the state's size and power, most industrialists rely on government purchases for a substantial portion of their incomes. Like industrialists everywhere, they are quite selective in what they want the government to do and not to do. They all want lower taxes, fewer regulations, and less government inefficiency, but as individuals they rely too heavily on the public sector to allow it to shrink very far. Businessmen love to complain of the government's favoring consumers and laborers, but let someone take away negative interest rates, import tariffs, and the government's purchase of goods, as Martínez de Hoz tried to do, and they are among the first to cry foul.

The relationship between the rural and industrial sectors is an important but hazy one. Some of the wealthy are involved in both and in finance as well. Their exact number has never been documented, but many connections are obvious. That does not mean, however, that today agriculture and industry are supervised by the same directorates; each sector is too large and too diverse to be linked so easily. Rather it means that some people are much more able than others to move resources from sector to sector to take advantage of the vicissitudes of the economy.

Where does this leave foreign capital? Its participation in national development is important and it too has a large stake in government policy. Ford, Renault, and Mercedes Benz rule the automotive industry; Firestone, Pirelli, and Goodrich supply tires; and Esso and Shell share petroleum retailing with the government's YPF. But the multinationals are not organized to dictate policy, aware as they are of the unpopularity of their appearing to manipulate authorities. Instead, they employ skilled Argentine executives who help them bargain with officials in unobtrusive ways. Nothing comes to them automatically anymore, but they are favored by the country's capital shortages and do exploit it. At the same time, economic instability makes operating in Argentina less attractive than in countries like Brazil and Mexico. In short, multinationals deal with authorities like everyone else does in Argentina, doing so as quietly as possible, seeking advantages where they can get them, sometimes in coincidence with national industry and at others in conflict with it.

Not to be overlooked is what some call the "state bourgeoisie." These are the people who staff government agencies and corporations, the military among them, and work to aggrandize their enterprises just as private capitalists do. They should be easier to control than private business but they seldom are. Their employees are well organized, either by the military or labor unions, and are well schooled in subverting presidential programs they oppose, able to draw support from clients on short notice. As in other Latin American countries where the state is equally large and heavily involved in the production of goods, they operate their largest enterprises in a subsidized, capitalist manner, much as many of the private firms do. If there is a structure to the economy, it is one that blends public and private enterprises in the exploitation of the nation's resources.

Finally there is organized labor, as influential in politics as any sector of the bourgeoisie. We learned in Chapter 3 that the Argentine labor movement is the most durable and independent of all that exist in Latin America. Those who lead the largest factions of the General Confederation of Labor represent the working class whether its members want representation or not, and in their own way they have become part of the nation's ruling "establishment," able to prevent any government from sustaining its programs for very long without their cooperation. It is this achievement and its exploitation by labor leaders that has earned them the envy and enmity of the country's economically impotent political left and the resentment of the middle and upper classes.

Such a diversity of interests is not unusual in capitalist economies, of course, so why is it important to understanding the trouble that Argentine authorities have in dealing with the country's economic woes? The answer rests not in their number or diversity, but in the way they have lined up into two opposing camps that have done so much to stop one another during the past quarter century. As in politics, each side takes its turn in government, only to relinquish the Ministry of Economy to the other before its job is done.

The National Debate

The same two issues have captured Argentine attention for the past forty years. One is the distribution of income and the other is economic growth. The annual reports of ministers and the financial sections of leading newspapers discuss little else.[39] It is the priority given to one or the other that sets Argentines apart from each other. On one side sit the "populists," a coalition joining organized labor, the state bourgeoisie, and the more nationalistic entrepreneurs of the CGE variety who put highest priority on income redistribution of a progressive variety. On the other is an "internationalist" coalition involving some combination of multinational firms, large local manufacturers, and the wealthier cattlemen, who are convinced that deliberate efforts to redistribute income "progressively" deter real growth and are the cause of the nation's primary development problems currently. The populists are more numerous, while internationalists hold immense economic power because of the nation's dependence on commodity exports and large manufacturers for its sustenance. But theirs is not just a simple class struggle between capitalists and proletarians. Capitalist mentalities dominate both coalitions, populists favoring some form of nationalistic, progressive redistribution of wealth and internationalists a more regressive one, at least for the short haul. In the former, for example, many industrialists and labor leaders share a devotion to high tariff protection and government subsidization of industry since both were nurtured on it by Perón. The national origins of a firm have less to do with its policy preferences than does the manner of its nurturing. That is why firms like the Ford Motor Company that grew up in Argentina under tariff protection will defend the status quo much more than foreign and national manufacturers who never depended on it. In other words, membership in either coalition is determined more by the particular economic self-interest of each manufacturer, farmer, labor leader, and government bureaucrat than it is by grand designs about how Argentina should be governed. Politics is a means to very concrete ends, the populists believing in the fruits of instant economic gratification and the internationalists confident that they have more to gain from domination over their competitors through the exercise of their advantages in freer markets, nationally and internationally.

How influential each coalition is at any particular moment depends a great deal on the country's economic condition at the time. It is during times of growth that the populists' wage increases, business subsidies, and public welfare programs are most affordable. But inevitably, populist measures lead to higher inflation, declines in private investment, and a bursting of the expansionary balloon. It is then that the internationalist coalition reasserts itself, telling authorities how to put everything back together again. Theirs is an income-regressive, investment strategy rather than a distributionist one, emphasizing the use of conservative fiscal and monetary policies to create conditions that make investment and production more profitable and long-term growth more sustainable. They are notorious for decrying the calamities caused by populism and demanding that the nation atone for its gluttonous ways by tightening its belt and disciplining its behavior.

But whatever their claims to truth and justice, neither coalition has solved Argentina's fundamental growth problem. Perón sought to redistribute income from the upper class to the working class, from agriculture to industry, and from foreign investors to the Argentine state in 1946. It lasted for five years, then droughts, the exhaustion of gold reserves, and balance-of-payments problems forced him to slow down and impose austerity measures to compensate for populist excesses. But faith in populism never died, and when they came back in 1973 the Peronists wanted to start all over again. Unfortunately high inflation prohibited their adopting all of the same expansionary measures this time, so they turned to the *pacto* for securing agreements between management and labor with a mixed package of wage restraint and fiscal and credit expansion. Yet, again inflation rose and within two years they were forced to impose another austerity program, provoking enough working-class opposition to undermine Isabel Perón's authority.

Is it impossible for populist economics to succeed in Argentina? The Peronists have done little to convince one otherwise: each time they tried they overheated the economy or were undermined by international adversities not of their making. Populism suffers from inherent weaknesses that will always undermine it unless fundamental changes in it are made. It redistributes some wealth, though never as much real income as it pretends, and it expands economic activity temporarily, but it never extracts enough resources to pay its own bills. Peronists seem content to take revenues that are readily available rather than make fundamental changes in income and property taxation. They rely far more on income from exports than they should. Inevitably they must borrow money or expand the monetary supply to pay their bills, measures which eventually accelerate inflation. Populist economics has relied on the government's skimming income off the top of the economy rather than really redistributing wealth and property from the rich to either the state or to the poor. It is a kind of "rip-off" strategy for progressive purposes that makes many people happy for a few years but is never enough to sustain its redistributions or to keep the populist coalition satisfied.

The internationalist strategy has not done much better, even though it is the more radical of the two. Populism created a state that exercised substantial influence over the economy and tried, when conditions permitted, to placate the lower class, elevate bureaucrats, and promote national industry. The advocates of the internationalist strategy, in contrast, sought to destroy the populist state, replacing it with a market economy in which everyone competed more and was subsidized less. Changing the status quo is a radical endeavor in Argentina, especially when it involves restoring the economy to many of its nineteenth-century ways. Like any "revolution" it can be carried out only through the exercise of immense authority against those who resist it. If Marxists require a Leninist state to crush counterrevolutionaries, Argentine internationalists must rely on the power of the armed forces to deal with their adversaries.

At first glance the military might seem to have what it takes to stamp out populism. But they repeatedly failed, as we learned in Chapter 4. Populists survive them every time because they know they have the power to do so, most of it coming from the labor movement and its ability to resist complete subjugation by austerity-minded internationalists. Argentine authorities simply cannot sustain the kind of repression against the masses that succeeded in Brazil, Chile, and Uruguay. Again and again military presidents learn to their regret that unless they find some way to incorporate labor into their design and implementation of policy, they cannot rebuild their country.

A State That Does Not Work

Argentina is in trouble not only because the people we label populists and internationalists differ over how their economy should operate. Its problem is as much institutional as ideological, stemming largely from its failure to develop the means for resolving the conflicts they create. The Argentine state is big and powerful, but it is more successful at preserving the interests of its bureaucratic machinery than it is in resolving the disputes of society's combative members.

Politics everywhere is the result of social relations reflecting a balance of forces in given situations. What individual agents do is determined by their own motives and relations with others as well as by the constraints imposed on them by structures that no one agent or set of agents can easily change. In societies possessing several competitive and well-organized interests, deliberate efforts are made to create structures that constrain the competition, bringing a form of order that is acceptable to the participants. Most common in modern capitalist societies is either a kind of pseudo-democracy known as pluralism or a more centrally coordinated form of politics commonly referred to as corporatism. Either one can do the job of organizing politics in a manner that supports the exercise of enough authority to keep the complex society operating, as the history of the pluralistic United States and neocorporatist democracies of Northern Europe demonstrate. Unfortunately, Argentina has found it impossible to live by the rules of either in recent times.[40]

Pluralist politics places the state at the service of the electorate while giving it enough autonomy to act as arbiter among competing interests. Government decisions may be influenced by some interests more than others, but none will actually control it completely, at least not for long periods. The "common good" is not defined centrally, but emerges from the resolution of disputes. The good of society is determined, in other words, by the accumulation of settlements among competitors. Pluralism never works as neatly in practice as it does in theory, but its approximation offers a convenient means of coexistence in the liberal democratic society.

When elections were held and a constitutional government was chosen in 1983, Argentina once again took on a pluralist veneer as interest groups rushed to Congress and the government's ministries to make their partisan cases before authorities. However, such appearances are deceiving, for no president, not even Raul Alfonsín in 1983, enjoyed enough authority to arbitrate disputes among interests whose leaders persistently refuse to be bound by settlements they dislike. Some presidents, of course, most notably those in uniform, show little interest in mediation, but even they find it hard to settle class and economic conflicts without repressing them, albeit temporarily. The result is a society that has little confidence in the ability of its would-be authorities to regulate much of anything that really matters.

But what about corporatism? If anything seemed necessary in a country as troubled by conflict as Argentina, it was the creation of a set of institutions that brought separate interests together where they could be closely supervised by the government "for the good of all." In this manner the state can exercise the authority needed to define and enforce a national agenda on the country. Disputes, if they arise at all, could be handled decisively and resistance quickly overcome by a powerful executive backed by all of the interests that have a stake in preventing any one of them from operating according to its own rules. That is exactly the kind of arrangement that Perón claimed he was creating when he flirted with corporatism during his first presidency and allowed his stand-in Hector Campora to supervise the *pacto social* in 1973. But Perón's corporatism turned out to be window dressing for his autocratic manipulation of everyone else.

Corporatism eludes Argentines for the same reason that pluralism does, namely, a public distrust of those who operate the nation's weak and partisan state apparatus. For corporatism to work the state must be accepted as independent of most interests and much stronger than all of them put together. But the Argentine state is neither, as we have seen repeatedly.

So what does this leave them with? A rather paradoxical condition, actually, in which a large and powerful state bureaucracy is headed by presidents whose authority over society lacks sufficient legitimacy for them to govern effectively. In other words, successive governments have increased the importance of public enterprise and government regulation without concomitantly institutionalizing a political process whose basic rules everyone comes to accept. This is why the state looks incredibly powerful but really is very weak. It is always quite powerful in its patronage, regulation, economic subsidization, and investments, creating for itself clienteles that are deeply involved in its activities regardless of who occupies the presidency. In fact, it is the reliance of these constituents on the government for subsidies that makes it so difficult for presidents to reduce its size. But political authority over society does not follow automatically from such state power. It is quite separable in Argentine minds, as their noncompliance with political authorities continues to show. While they work closely with the organs of the state, everyone continues to defy authorities when they can get away with it.

This arrangement is not without its benefits, though "consolations" might be a more appropriate term. For all of its waste and inefficiency, economic strangulation, and resistance to reform, the government does sustain a great portion of the society through bad times. That is one reason why Argentina does not self-destruct as a political society: too much of it has been bureaucratized (at a high price admittedly) to collapse under the pressure of a permanent political legitimacy crisis. It is not a very satisfactory arrangement, to be sure, but it does allow the nation to operate when so much of it is always breaking down.

It was into this that Raul Alfonsín confidently walked with the presidential sash around his neck in December 1983. As a life-long Radical, he retained a faith in government and a characteristic dedication to converting others to his civic religion. But as a politician unaccustomed to directing a country steeped in economic crisis, he would soon discover that he had much to learn about leading people who shared neither his trust of public authority nor his optimism about the nation's future.

Notes

1. *Clarín*, economic supp., October 28, 1984, p. 8.
2. Ibid., October 7, 1984, p. 9.

3. Brazil's share of the regional GNP rose from 21.7 to 34.1 percent during the same period. See Livio Guillermo Kuhl, *Una política industrial para la Argentina* (Buenos Aires: Club de Estudio, 1983), p. 566.

4. Guido Di Tella, "The Economic Policies of Argentina's Labour-Based Government, 1972–1976," Woodrow Wilson Center Latin American Program Working Paper, no. 47 (1981): 3–7.

5. Quoted in *The Washington Post National Weekly Edition,* October 8, 1984, p. 22.

6. *Wall Street Journal,* November 11, 1984, p. 1; and World Bank, *Economic Memorandum on Argentina,* June 1984, pp. 126–138.

7. World Bank, *Economic Memorandum on Argentina,* pp. 148–150. It has taken two to three times more wheat to buy the same amount of nitrogen in Argentina as it has in the United States during the past decade, for example.

8. This is the thesis of Jorge Federico Sabato, *La pampa prodiga: Claves de una frustración* (Buenos Aires: CIESA, 1980).

9. Osvaldo Barsky, Horacio Ciafardini, and Carlos Alberto Cristia, "Producción y tecnología en la región pampeana," *Primera historia integral* 28 (1980): 184.

10. Consejo Técnico de Inversiones, *Anuario-1983,* p. 334.

11. Jan Peter Wogart, "Combining Price Stabilization with Trade and Financial Liberalization Policies: The Argentine Experience, 1976–1981," *Journal of Inter-American and World Affairs* 25, no 4 (November 1983): 458.

12. Private shares in the marketing of wheat in 1979–80 were divided as follows: Bunge Born 10.5 percent, Andre 8.8, Cargill 14.1, Continental 8.0, Louis Dreyfus 3.0, others 13.4. Naciones Unidas, Estudios e informes de la Cepal, *Empresas transnacionales en la industría de alimientos: el caso argentino* (Santiago, 1983), pt. 2, p. 38.

13. Ibid., pp. 42–45.

14. Ibid.

15. Flacso Santiago, *America Latina–Union Sovietica* 1, no. 1 (November–December 1983): 8.

16. *Clarín,* economic supp., February 10, 1985, p. 10.

17. Argentina's industrial growth rate was slightly less than Brazil's (6.1 percent) and Mexico's (8.9) during the same period. See Adolfo Dorfman, *Cincuenta años de industrialización en la Argentina: 1930–1980* (Buenos Aires: Solar, 1983), p. 106, p. 576.

18. Consejo Técnico de Investigaciones, *La estructura de los mercados en Argentina–1979* (Buenos Aires: CTI, 1979), p. 17. Only 319 industrial firms employed more than 500 people, and another 1,986 employed between 100 and 500; added together they were 2 percent of the total firms and employed 49 percent of the industrial work force.

19. Jorge Schvarzer, "Cambios en el liderazgo industrial argentino en el periodo de Martínez de Hoz," *Desarrollo económico* 23, no. 91 (October–December 1983): 418–512. The largest foreign firms by sales rankings were: Esso (2); Ford (4); Massalin Particulares (5); Renault (6); Shell (7); IBM (13); Mercedes Benz (17); Volkswagen (22); Refineria de Maiz (25); Lever (27).

20. Dorfman, *Cincuenta años de industrialización en la Argentina,* pp. 390–392.

21. Kuhl, *Una política industrial para la Argentina,* pp. 508–527.

22. *Clarín,* economic supp., December 23, 1984, p. 5; and *Finance and Development* (March 1984): 33.

23. Latin American Linguistic Service, *Foreign Investment in Argentina: An Updated Handbook of Legislation and Statutes,* April 22, 1983, pp. 85–87; and *Mercado,* May 17, 1984, pp. 34–42. The largest public banks are the Banco Nacional de Desarrollo (1), Banco de la Nación (2), Banco de la Provincia de Buenos Aires (3), Banco Hipotecario Nacional (9), Banco de la Ciudad de Buenos Aires (10). Two American banks are in the top ten, both of them having been in Argentina for decades: Citibank (7), Banco de Boston (8).

24. World Bank, *Economic Memorandum on Argentina*, p. 162.

25. A detailed examination of Argentina's potential for industrial export development is made in Kuhl, *Una política industrial para la Argentina*.

26. Consejo Empresario Argentina, *Las empresas públicas en la economia argentina* (Buenos Aires: FIEL, 1976).

27. *Clarín*, economic supp., January 6, 1985, p. 9.

28. Kuhl, *Una política industrial para la Argentina*, pp. 194–205. Government industries in the top 100 industries in the country ranked by sales are: YPF—petroleum (1); Somisa—steel (8); Afne—shipyard (15); Fabricaciones Militares—weapons, machinery, chemicals (24); Siam—machinery (40); Petroquemica Mosconi—petrochemicals (48); Ing. La Esperanza—sugar (73); Giol—beverages (88). See Schvarzer, "Cambios en el liderazgo industrial argentino en el periodo de Martínez de Hoz," pp. 418–421.

29. World Bank, *Economic Memorandum on Argentina*, pp. 32–104. The World Bank study is the most complete to date on the financing of the Argentine public sector.

30. Juan Carlos de Pablo, *Mercado*, December 22, 1983, p. 53.

31. *Clarín*, July 26, 1984, p. 26.

32. World Bank, *Economic Memorandum on Argentina*, p. 99.

33. Ibid., pp. 96–121.

34. *Clarín*, international ed., November 19–25, 1984, p. 10; and *Clarín*, economic supp., January 13, 1985, pp. 6–10.

35. *Clarín*, international ed., September 3–9, 1984, p. 10; and *Latin America Weekly Report*, May 25, 1984, p. 8.

36. Alain Rouquie offers a summary of different perspectives on the Argentine power structure in his essay, "Hegemonía militar, estado, y dominación social," *Argentina, hoy* (Buenos Aires: Siglo Veintiuno, 1982), pp. 35–41.

37. See Gary W. Wynia, *Argentina in the Postwar Era* (Albuquerque, N.M.: University of New Mexico Press, 1978), pp. 23 ff.

38. Ibid., pp. 56 ff.

39. I am indebted to Professor Javier Villanueva and his students, who reached this conclusion about the persistence of the same two issues after examining ministerial documents from 1970 to 1982. He reports their findings in "Doce años de política económica en la Argentina—1970–1982," Unpublished paper, July 1983.

40. An enormous literature was written in the 1960s and 1970s about pluralism and corporatism in capitalist systems, pointing to the conditions that caused politics to move in either direction. A good place to start is with Andrew Shonfield, *Modern Capitalism: The Changing Balance of Public and Private Power* (New York: Oxford University Press, 1967); and Phillipe Schmitter, "Still the Century of Corporatism," *Review of Politics* 35 (1974): 85–131.

7

The Reeducation of
Raul Alfonsín

In most democracies the support of 52 percent of the electorate is enough to guarantee tenure. But not in Argentina, where each of the past four elected presidents was deposed by the military. As in the international sphere, where rules are seldom binding and national interests prevail, in Argentina there are few regulations that discipline the semisovereign competitors. Of course, none of this came as a surprise to Raul Alfonsín.

Getting Started

An elected president always starts with advantages as well as disadvantages, some earned and others caused by forces over which he has little or no control. In Alfonsín's case it was no different. His task may have seemed an impossible one, doomed to failure by political intolerance and economic infirmity, yet several things strengthened his leadership when he began. These included his personal popularity, the preoccupation of his Peronist opponents with conflicts within their movement, and the military's need to sort out its internal affairs after the war.

Alfonsín seemed to be "the right person for the time." He was new to national leadership, and few of his adversaries had scores to settle with him. And he conveyed a sincerity of purpose that was popular in a nation upset about the military's self-serving duplicity in government and war. Argentines were ready for a benign, industrious leader, and Alfonsín played the part well, devoted as he was to putting government back into the service of its citizens. No postwar president except Perón began his tenure enjoying as much popularity.

Alfonsín also benefited from winning an election that greatly simplified the structure of partisanship by concentrating nearly all of the legislative opposition in one party, as we learned in Chapter 5. Moreover, by relegating the Peronists to the opposition in honest elections whose rules they had accepted, the process had taken from them their favorite case for the illegitimacy of every government but their own. In 1963, when they were excluded from participation in the election of Radical Arturo Illia, they could justify their turning loose the CGT against his unfairly chosen government. But in 1984 even militant labor leaders realized that they had no choice but to allow Alfonsín a chance to prove his worth to them and the masses.

The creation of what was in effect a two-party system also simplified the legislative process for the new president. The other political parties did not wither and die, but they were pushed aside for the time being, left to regroup and prepare for congressional elections at the end of 1985. Conservatives of the free market variety had backed the Union of the Democratic Center (Unión de Centro Democrático), which was led by Alvaro Alsogaray, an economics minister twice before and an outspoken critic of populist economics. But the UCD won only two seats in the Chamber of Deputies. Ex-president Arturo Frondizi headed the Development and Integration Movement (Movimiento de Integración y Desarrollo), which he had founded after being deposed by the 1962 coup. However, the party's presidential candidate, Rogelio Frigerio, received fewer votes than his party had registered members and won only one seat in the Senate and none in the Chamber. To the left of the government ideologically stood the Christian Democratic party (Partido Democrata Cristiano), always a small one in Argentina, and the Intransigent party (Partido Intransigente), led by ex-Radical Oscar Alende, who spoke Marxist rhetoric but resembled a French or Spanish socialist more than he did Fidel Castro. Together, these two parties won four seats in the Chamber and none in the Senate. So, except for these few seats and a handful more occupied by small provincial parties, the legislature belonged to Radicals and Peronists.

Power struggles within the Peronist party also took some pressure off the new president, though he was hard put to take full advantage of them. Originally he had hoped to lay the foundation for a new Radical party capable of permanently pulling working-class voters away from the Peronists. His strategy had two parts, each directed at weakening the political control of CGT leaders over working-class voters. One was to "democratize" national union organizations by guaranteeing members proportional representation. As it was, the majority always took complete control, making it impossible for dissidents within the unions to police their leaders' political activities, including their spending of union funds. With the reform, members who were less inclined to Peronist politics or unhappy with bosses who monopolized power could at least expose any abuses to the membership. Thus, the Radicals hoped, some members might be led to protest by voting for another party. The union reform bill went to Congress just after the inauguration, with Alfonsín hoping to ram it through quickly. But the agile Peronists drew together in panic, and with the help of a couple of provincial parties, they turned their plurality in the Senate into a majority and blocked the bill's passage. No defeat could have disappointed the Radicals more.

The other part of the strategy involved denying the labor movement control over the *obras sociales* funds that were built from contributions by workers and employers ostensibly for the purpose of health care and other welfare projects. They formed a huge trough of savings, estimated at $2.5 billion, and it was no secret that the Peronists had paid their campaign bills and other expenses from them in the past. The armed forces had "intervened" the funds in 1976, putting them under the supervision of the federal bureaucracy, but when democracy was restored the Peronists demanded them back. Alfonsín refused, offering instead a joint, public-private, arrangement that would assure government supervision of their use. Keeping the funds out of political campaigns was essential to the Radicals' efforts to limit the power of Peronism at the polls, and Alfonsín made no secret of it. But an impasse developed, for after having lost his labor reform bill in the Senate he feared the same fate for the *obras sociales* reform, so the issue was left unresolved during his first two years.

But even had he secured the passage of both reforms, his attraction of working-class voters would not have come easily largely because of fundamental differences between the two parties. The Radicals were still a party led by middle-class merchants and professionals who believed that politics should be done carefully, deliberately, and democratically. The Peronists, in contrast, remained more concerned with substantive ends than with procedural means. They came from nearly all sectors in society, their leaders driven by a desire to use governmental power to deliver the goods to their kind of people, most of whom expected to be served by strong and belligerent politicians. They had little patience with the kind of deliberations that occupied so much of the Radicals' time. Nor did they find appeals to principle all that attractive. Incrementalism, the most characteristic mode of Radical behavior, requires more patience than the Peronist can tolerate. This is one reason why the two parties often appear to be talking right past each other. Another is the Radicals' self-righteousness in pretending that because their way of doing politics is morally superior to the Peronists', they do not have to defer to them, something Peronists find offensive.

Their antipathy for the Radicals did not prevent the Peronists from fighting among themselves, however. There had always been some tension between labor leaders and the white-collar party officials, the former being fearful that white-collar Peronists could not represent labor's interests. And those in the poorer provinces resented colleagues in Buenos Aires, the provincials being more concerned about the redistribution of resources from the urban center to the periphery than from management to labor. And as always, they also disagreed over matters of political strategy, some favoring cooperation with the government and others a more aggressive tack that insisted on the Radicals' adopting the Peronist economic platform. The disputes were kept under some control for a while, but the pressure built and about the time Alfonsín celebrated his first anniversary the Peronist party came apart.

It started at the party's annual convention in December 1984, when several delegates walked out of the Odeon Theater in the midst of the meeting and announced their intention to hold a convention of their own 765 miles to the north in Río Hondo. When the empty seats were counted it was clear that 413 of the 719 delegates had fled. Their motive was said to be principled, having to do with their demand for the election of party officers by the direct vote of all party members rather than by convention delegates as was currently the case, but equally important was their desire to rid the party of people like the infamous Herminio Iglesias, the Buenos Aires bully who had embarrassed white-collar leaders like Italo Luder with his histrionics from the platform in the 1983 campaign and who continued to do so by insulting the nation's president with shouts that he deserved to be killed. At Río Hondo white-collar Peronists and colleagues from the poorer provinces teamed up in an attempt to end the domination of Iglesias and entrenched labor leaders like Lorenzo Miguel, head of the CGT's political arm, who had relied on their control over carefully picked convention delegates to stay on top. The dissidents demanded an end to the old hierarchical party organization over which Juan and Isabel Perón had ruled and its replacement by a more democratic one better prepared to contest Radicals for popular support behind a social democratic platform. Initially they appeared to come out on top, securing rulings from federal courts that entitled them to represent the party, but their opponents were not about to roll over and play dead.[1]

It was a division that went deep into the CGT organization as well, separating unions that supported the Río Hondo dissidents from Lorenzo Miguel and the rest of the CGT. In March 1985 twelve unions with 561,000 members declared their loyalty to Miguel and the old guard, while sixteen others, with a total of 681,000 members, gave their blessing to the dissidents. Support within the CGT was essential to the success of the Río Hondo rebellion, for without it they were provincials and white-collar prima donnas alien to the labor movement.[2]

Lorenzo Miguel and his colleagues were also hurt by Isabel Perón's surprise resignation from the presidency of the party in a letter sent from her residence in Spain on February 4. It might seem of little importance given her deliberate absence from Argentina after she was released from house arrest and fled to her Spanish home in 1981. Alfonsín had invited her back on visits, welcoming her warmly during his inauguration, and in return she issued occasional manifestos calling on the party to work with him for democracy's sake, but that was all she did, persistently refusing to exercise real leadership over the party. People like Miguel had tried to exploit her presidency of the party, hoping to keep its hierarchy together, but she abandoned him and refused to endorse either of the party's quarreling factions when she did.[3]

The split threatened the Peronist party's command over nearly half of the electorate, and pressures grew for its hasty reunification before congressional elections in late 1985. In July, six months after they had split, leaders of the Odeon and Río Hondo factions finally agreed to convene a new party meeting, but it proved a disaster for the latter, since they arrived at the convention disorganized and unprepared to do battle with the old guard. Quickly seizing the initiative, the Odeon people took control of the party, and once in charge brazenly insisted on the reappointment of Isabel Perón as the titular party president, Senator Vicente Saadi as first vice president, union leader Jorge Triaca as second vice president, and Herminio Iglesias secretary general. It was in effect an unholy alliance among the CGT leaders, Buenos Aires provincial boss Iglesias, and agile politician Saadi, the ostensible leader of the party's left wing. Humbled and outraged by their instant defeat, the Río Hondo people walked out again, contenting themselves for the time being with working at the grass roots to build a stronger force to work for the party's democratization.

The Peronists' preoccupation with their own affairs distracted them for a time from doing battle with the Radicals, but Alfonsín's respite was only temporary. What the Peronist politicians could not achieve as a political force the CGT still could, despite divisions within its own ranks. Nothing brings union leaders back together faster than seeing their incomes assaulted by a government not of their own making, as Alfonsín and his austerity measures began to do in 1985. Union leaders like Saul Ubaldini were reluctant to collaborate with authorities in their anti-inflation drive, fearing rebellion by the rank and file if they did.

History had taught them that their control over member unions depended on their success in protecting wages, so they could not afford to stay with any program that failed to restore lost wages quickly. And therein rested the key to Alfonsín's success: no matter how much he bargained with the CGT leadership, it would do little good unless he could somehow convince organized laborers to go along with him. It seemed an impossible task, but he kept trying nevertheless.

Finally, Alfonsín was helped by the military's preoccupation with its internal problems in the wake of the war. They had fallen into disarray after their humiliating defeat and their weakness became his strength, giving him the chance to increase his authority as commander-in-chief. He set out to make it clear that he wanted a line of command that descended from the president through his civilian defense minister to the joint chiefs and then to the service chiefs. His purpose was to deprive the latter of what had become virtual military autonomy. When he made his intention known, the army was quick to test his resolve, its commander refusing to dismiss an officer who had defied presidential authority. Without hesitation the president dismissed the commander for insubordination, making it clear that he would not tolerate defiance. Moreover, during the next six months he sent into retirement all but three of the fifty-three generals who remained from the prewar administrations. It was a beginning, though he knew that it would not assure compliance from the armed forces since there was little in the removal of generals that ever deterred the involvement of future ones. Each new generation, believing itself innocent of its predecessors' blunders, is always ready to assert its authority when conditions dictate.[4]

Economic Illusions and Realities

Alfonsín's initial advantages helped sustain his presidency while he dealt with unprecedented economic infirmities. He inherited an economy that was in the fourth year of a deep recession and overwhelmed by an annual inflation rate that rose from 400 percent to more than 600 percent during his first six months. Moreover, the public sector deficit had risen to 20 percent of the gross domestic product, unemployment was at 10 percent, and dollar reserves in the Central Bank were nearly depleted. Worst of all, internationally Argentina faced a record foreign debt of $46 billion, whose servicing it could not pay. These were hardly the conditions under which one wanted to test the viability of democratic government.

Unfortunately, neither he nor his closest advisors were ready for the task that victory had given them. Not having expected to defeat the Peronists until the campaign's conclusion contributed to their lack of preparation, but so did the enormity of the problems they faced. Without a well-developed plan at their disposal, they approached the economy as if they believed that the president's popularity, along with some price controls and wage increases, would be enough to restore confidence in it. Such thinking is a common fault of Argentine politicians, none more so than Radicals, who always seem to assume that their honesty, integrity, and good populist intentions will cause everyone to relax economically. But creative management, not overconfidence, was what the economy needed, and Alfonsín's "trust me" approach failed to excite investors—gross investment reached a five-year low before his first year was over—or impress the working class. The government was also handicapped by the Radicals' conviction, one they shared with most members of society, that the oligarchy's greed, along with the stupidity and treachery of the armed forces, were responsible for the economy's malaise. Had José Martínez de Hoz and the insatiable financial elite not sold the country for their own profit, went the line, the current mess would have been avoided. It would be a year before they would admit to themselves that bankers and foreign investors had not created the mess, but only taken advantage of it. Its causes were more fundamental, starting with a failure to produce enough goods at competitive prices to earn the income required to sustain the standard of living to which its people have become accustomed. There was no quick fix that would overcome it all. Restoring confidence and investment in an economy as damaged and demoralized as the Argentine one was a monumental task beyond anyone's capacity to complete quickly.

Price controls, wage indexing, and personal appeals for public trust were a dismal failure, and inflation continued to rise and foreign debts mount during 1984. Industrialists complained that a dramatic rise in labor costs was destroying their profitability, making new investment impossible, and watched as the value of the peso fell rapidly after midyear as people rushed to acquire dollars to protect themselves from the effects of a hyperinflation that reached an annual rate of 800 percent in October. On top of this something had to be done about the country's foreign debt. It had risen from $12.5 billion at the end of 1978 to $46 billion when the Radicals took over, a nearly fourfold increase in five years, $31 billion of it belonging to the public sector and two-thirds held by over 300 foreign banks. The debt's size was bad enough, but its expansion, along with deterioration in the term structure of the debt and rising interest rates abroad, led to an alarming increase in the burden of debt service, from $4.9 billion in 1979 to $20.3 billion in 1982. As a result interest payments absorbed about 60 percent of the country's export earnings in 1982.[5]

As much as he disliked doing so, Alfonsín had no choice but to seek temporary help from the International Monetary Fund, an organization that nationalistic Radicals love to hate. On September 25, 1984 Minister of Economy Bernardo Grinspun stepped to the podium at the annual IMF meeting in Washington, D.C., and announced the dreaded agreement. In exchange for a standby loan of $1.5 billion, the Argentine government agreed to everything it had refused to do previously, including tightening monetary policy, limiting wage hikes, raising public service tariffs, and eliminating price controls, albeit over one year.[6] Two months later Central Bank president Enrique García Vázquez announced the refinancing of $25 billion of the debt.[7] This was done despite the fact that many bankers doubted that Argentina would be able to stay within the terms of its agreement with the IMF once unions protested their wage losses. Their skepticism proved justified, for by the time Alfonsín spoke to a joint session of the U.S. Congress on March 20 to plea for more U.S. toleration of debtor nations, it was apparent that Argentina had already violated the agreement.[8]

Alfonsín knew that he had failed economically and admitted as much as 1984 ended.[9] Then, while his people were seeking relief from a sweltering summer, he announced a new beginning, dismissing both Grinspun, his close friend and advisor, and Central Bank president García Vázquez, Grinspun's chief rival and critic in the economic cabinet.[10] Grinspun was replaced by Juan Sourrouille, an academic economist and author of a major study of economic policies in the 1960s, who was not a member of the Radical party. Where Grinspun was outspoken and argumentative, Sourrouille was the cool technocrat who spoke from behind dark glasses in a soft monotone, explaining the nation's plight like a seminar instructor intent on stating the truth.[11] He announced his own five-year recovery plan that set out to reorder priorities, starting with the promotion of agricultural exports and business investment, neither of which conformed to Alfonsín's original populist aspirations. It committed the government to making war on inflation by enforcing the unpopular austerities required in the September 1984 agreement with the IMF and private creditors and promoted the growth of export-related industries, much as Martínez de Hoz had tried to do, though without using such drastic methods to accomplish it. Tariffs would be reduced some and financing made available to exporters while taxes on commodity exports would be lowered. It mixed a little Milton Friedman with some John Maynard Keynes to come up with an innovative (critics would say contradictory) answer to Argentina's problem. Sourrouille was aware of the same realities that had convinced Martínez de Hoz that the country's future prosperity rested with the addition of industrial exports to its agricultural ones: Argentina had to grow outward to grow much at all, and to accomplish that the nationalism that had sustained the Radical party throughout its history had to be moderated.

Sourrouille was very frank about how slow the nation's economic recovery would be during the next five years, making it clear that the losses of the past decade could not be made up quickly. Between 1986 and 1989, if all went according to his design, the per capita national product would increase at an annual average rate of 2.5 percent, as would real per capita income, though both predictions were admittedly optimistic. The key to its success was an increase in annual investments from a –17.5 percent in 1984 to positive rates averaging 11.3 percent annually over the next five years, coupled with a 7 percent annual increase in exports. At the same time, a lid would be put on public sector outlays, reducing them from 44.5 percent of the national product in 1985 to 41.8 percent in 1989.[12]

It did not take much knowledge of economics to appreciate that Sourrouille was meeting the internationalists about half way. That was a long distance for someone like Alfonsín to go, given his belief in social reform and the need to supervise capitalists closely. But the choice was not really his to make anymore. Like social democrats abroad, most notably President Mitterand in France, Alfonsín had to "bite the bullet" and go to work on his unproductive economy. Europeans he respected had been telling him as much for almost a year, and he finally gave in.

If his people needed evidence of the seriousness of his intent, Alfonsín gave it at a massive rally in the Plaza de Mayo at the end of April, much as Perón had done under similar circumstances in 1952, telling the nation that it was in for very hard times and that everyone stood to lose something before they could gain anything again. In June everyone watched and waited to see if he really meant what he said, many hoping that, as before, he would "chicken out" under pressure from the CGT, whose leaders staged their own rally in May to express their opposition to further austerity.

The CGT demands were basically very simple. They wanted the government to break with the IMF and return to the "people," proving its devotion to them by decreeing huge wage increases and eliminating what was left of the "financial fatherland," by which was meant all of the wealthy people, native and foreign, who exploited the nation. The trouble was, of course, that the government could not possibly do such a thing without making the situation a great deal worse for everyone, including wage earners. The CGT belief that everything can be solved by a simple act of will is deeply rooted—the Radicals themselves were known to believe much the same thing before they came to office—and persuading them of the futility of such notions in 1985 seemed impossible.[13]

This duel between the Peronists and the president was a familiar sight. Governments and oppositions always try to demonstrate their respective power, but in most democracies their efforts are confined primarily to the legislative process, where votes are tallied and power measured. In Argentina Perón had added another arena to power politics when workers stormed the Plaza de Mayo on October 17, 1945, and secured his release from prison, and ever since mass gatherings have been crucial. Until 1983 it had been taken for granted that Peronists would always win the contests held in the plazas, but then Alfonsín came along and attracted hundreds of thousands to his campaign rallies, giving the Radicals a sense of power that they had not known since Yrigoyen. After he was inaugurated and the challenge of the CGT began, journalists spent much of their time counting heads to determine which of the two political masses was the largest, giving politics the appearance of a popularity contest measured by the number of people who showed up at demonstrations. When he spoke to an estimated 200,000 enthusiasts in the Plaza de Mayo in late April his popularity was judged to be as great as ever and his power still intact. Then the Peronists announced their intention to fill the same plaza and the lines were drawn. As one journalist noted:

> If the labour unions fail dismally—and until a few days ago failure seemed certain—to get near this figure [200,000], the Radicals will be able to heave a sigh of relief and carry on as before. Should the CGT rally prove really big, however, they will be in deeper trouble than at any time since winning power.[14]

Of course the Peronists did attract about the same number, and no sighs of relief were heard.

Nevertheless, Alfonsín did not give in this time. Instead, he announced drastic measures that were intended to catch everyone by surprise and force a drastic change in economic assumptions and expectations, breaking the familiar vicious cycle of promise, doubt, and economic subversion for personal gain.

In April he was informed by Sourrouille that procrastination since September 1984 had put Argentina $1 billion in arrears in the payment of its foreign debt, and the amount was continuing to rise at a rate of $150 million a month, threatening to force a downgrading of the country's credit rating internationally, which would deny it the new funds that it needed. His only recourse was to return to the IMF to ask for another $1.2 billion in standby loans and to the U.S. government for help in arranging a $450 million "bridge" loan from sympathetic countries. Economist Mario Brodersohn went to Washington and a new package was signed on June 11. But before he left Buenos Aires, Sourrouille and his team had worked out their own grand solution, one that was more drastic and comprehensive than anything tried before.[15]

In a national broadcast on Friday, June 14, the Argentine people learned what their government was up to. As the president made clear: "I come to you to present the battle plan so that together we will be able to definitely cancel the chapter of national decay. . . . We do not have any option, we have to reconstruct Argentina."[16] What this meant concretely was the cessation of the Central Bank's printing money to pay the public debt (it was paying about 25 percent of it then) and the raising of tariffs on government services to make up the difference. Equally important was the announcement of a new currency, called the austral, whose value was established by dropping three zeros from the peso and making it worth $1.28 U.S. currency, and whose worth the government promised to protect. Moreover, prices and salaries were frozen for an indefinite period, and authorities promised to reduce the federal deficit from 10 to 5 percent of the GDP.[17]

It was a strange sight, for shock treatments had never been a Radical pastime. They had always preferred to see themselves as the party of patronage and service, having built their constituency by elevating the middle class, with subsidies to small business, jobs in government, and education for all. Demanding sacrifices was alien to them, but now Alfonsín was announcing that they had no choice but to pay for society's past sins. Needless to say, the program was quite unpopular within the Radical party, with politicians fearing that it would lead to their defeat in the November congressional elections. But they were not running the country, Alfonsín and Sourrouille were, and the program was to proceed whether party stalwarts liked it or not.

Especially disturbing to Radicals was Alfonsín's reliance for advice on technocrats who had little or no ties to Radicalism and expounded an economics they had learned at places such as Harvard and Minnesota, where they, like Martínez de Hoz's advisors, had received their doctorates.[18] Alfonsín also sought help from Europeans. He listened carefully to French and Spanish economists who had engineered austerity programs for their socialist governments and to a team of Germans from Kiel University, invited to give their assessments early in the year. What the Germans concluded was typical of the messages that reached the Casa Rosada. As they saw it, the country's inflation was primarily the result of a huge public sector deficit, which had steadily risen to nearly 15 percent of the national product the year before as a result of salary increases, subsidies to industry and banking, and military spending. They recommended its swift reduction by keeping wages below the rate of inflation, making state corporations operate for profit, and reducing subsidies and transfer payments. A new currency was also suggested, as was the elimination of multiple exchange rates. Overwhelmed by the consensus of expert opinion, Alfonsín did as his tutors recommended.

Even more amazing than the president's decision to go ahead with the plan was the public's response. When Alfonsín made his announcement on June 14, he immediately closed all banks and waited for the inevitable outcry. But to his surprise it never came. Instead, an uncharacteristic calm fell over the nation, followed by praise from nearly every sector for the president's courage and common sense. Argentines, it seemed, were relieved that something had been done to stop the economic insanity into which they had plunged. In a few days trading on the stock market picked up, the dollar stabilized, and, most impressive, prices rose only 3 percent in August and 2 percent in September (compared to 30 percent in June). And, as inflation came down, Alfonsín's popularity ascended to levels it had not seen since his election eighteen months before.

Despite renewed popularity, Alfonsín could not be comfortable until his party had passed the test of congressional elections in November 1985 when half of the Chamber of Deputies' 254 seats were contested. The 19 million voters who participated in the nation's first midterm election in 20 years found over a dozen parties awaiting them on the ballot. During the campaign, the Radicals had asked them to reconfirm their support for democracy by voting for the president's party, while the Peronists were devoting most of their energies to contesting with each other, even running two slates of candidates from rival factions in Buenos Aires province. Minor parties, meanwhile, denounced the president for becoming "a lackey of International Monetary Fund imperialists," hoping to use the hardship caused by his Austral Plan to attract some of those who had voted for Alfonsín back to their parties.

The Radicals were victorious nevertheless, though just barely. Rather than sweeping the contest as they had hoped, they added just one seat to their 129 member Chamber majority, with 44 percent of the vote nationally, 9 percent less than Alfonsín had received in 1983. The Peronists, meanwhile, did poorly, losing seven of their seats while capturing only 35.5 percent of the vote, their lowest total ever. Moreover, within the Peronist party, reformers led by Antonio Cafiero did substantially better than candidates backed by the CGT old guard. If any doubts remained about Peronism entering a new era, they were put to rest on November 4 with the poor showing of party bosses. It was obvious that a reorganization and reorientation of the party was essential if it were to stand a chance of regaining majority support. It was equally obvious, however, that electoral considerations would not guarantee changes in so entrenched a power structure anytime soon.

The 1985 election settled nothing definitively; few elections do. It only tampered with the political status quo, reminding the president that his leadership was appreciated more than his party's politics in Congress were, telling the Peronists that their strength was weakening and would continue to do so if they persisted in fighting acrimoniously for power within the movement, and encouraging leaders of small parties—like the leftist Intransigent party that picked up a few seats the Peronists lost—to believe that Argentina's democracy was not yet entirely a two-party one. There was no electoral panacea for the country's inability to create and sustain legitimate governments; democracy offered some hope, but to succeed it had to survive new variations of the old partisan contests that had always torn it apart.

The Austral Plan was a major achievement whether or not its initial success endured. Government studies had shown that it was overspending financed by the treasury's printing presses that had sustained public expectations of continued inflation. No one believed that a president, least of all a democractically elected one, would have the courage to just shut down the presses and suffer the consequences of reduced spending. But when Alfonsín finally did, most people were actually relieved, at least for the time being. Until then everyone had been afraid to pull up and stop running at full speed, even though they were exhausted by it all; someone else had to stop the race, and that is what Sourrouille and his foreign and domestic collaborators got Alfonsín to do.

There was no guarantee that the plan would prevail in the end. Much depended on how long faith in it would last. This was something the government could affect with its later decisions but never entirely determine. Deciding when to end price and wage controls and how long to adhere to austere budgets would be critical. The plan would be hard on everyone for some time, but there was much that Argentines had going for them if they could just get their fears under control. The country was, after all, nearly self-sufficient in petroleum, enjoyed large agricultural surpluses, and had a diverse industrial base. Raising industrial exports was not impossible. Export of manufactures totaled $2.9 billion in 1982, but if each subsector merely exported at its previous peak, the total would rise to $4.9 billion in constant dollars. Many enterprises had achieved a level of technology and scale of production that made them capable of competing in world markets, and the potential for growth was especially good in food processing, metalworking, and oil- and gas-based manufactures. To promote such exports more realistic exchange rates were essential, and that is what Alfonsín was trying to secure.[19] Moreover, grain production, already growing at a good pace, could be accelerated by 50 percent if more fertilizer were used. No one could guarantee Argentina markets for its exports, but having commodities and manufactured goods to sell was a cause for hope.[20]

The Price of Justice

Alfonsín promised to restore justice in Argentina, but he knew this would take more than the appointment of a new judiciary. To his supporters, justice meant first and foremost the trial and conviction of the military officers who had supervised the killing of 9,000 people during the war against terrorism. A defender of human rights during the dark days of military repression, Alfonsín was expected to act swiftly in prosecuting hundreds of officers. Yet he knew the risk of moving too swiftly, aware as he was that a direct assault on the armed forces would provoke military retaliation. Accordingly, he went at it incrementally, step by step, taking the nation through a long exercise in self-discovery before singling out any officers for prosecution.

A twelve-member civilian presidential commission investigated the entire episode, trying to determine once and for all the fate of those who had disappeared. Chaired by novelist Ernesto Sábato, the commission took testimony from 5,792 witnesses over a nine-month period before submitting its 350-page report and 50,000 pages of evidence to the president in September 1984. Its findings, which confirmed what the country's eight human rights groups had been saying for years, documented the disappearance of 8,800 people and the torture of many of them in the nation's 280 secret prisons. It also named 1,200 police and military personnel who had participated directly in the secret operations, most of them still in uniform and some routinely promoted by the president and the legislature just before the report was issued.

Within the military Alfonsín authorized the formation of a council of twenty retired officers charged with investigating and court-marshaling personnel who had exceeded their authority during the armed forces' rule. Council members interviewed officers for almost five months in 1984, while people anxiously awaited their findings. Had they found some people guilty, pressure on the president for civil action might have been somewhat reduced. But, true to form, they balked, announcing in September that they found no one guilty. As they saw it, the armed forces had fought a war to save the country, doing what was essential to win it, and that was no crime.[21] Thus, Alfonsín was left with no choice but to start civil prosecutions, albeit slowly, beginning with the service commanders who were members of the juntas that had governed between 1976 and 1983. The process took some time to get started, but in March 1985 a federal prosecutor announced that Presidents Videla, Viola, and Galtieri and the other six members of their juntas would be tried on 711 accounts, ranging from torture to murder, starting in May. In their defense, attorneys argued that they had begun the war under the orders of Juan and Isabel Perón and had merely continued the assignment after replacing the Peronists. Civilians, not military officers, were responsible for what they had done. The weakness of such a defense soon became apparent, however, as military witnesses admitted to having been part of a deliberate "holy war" against godless communism and dozens of victims testified to their ruthless treatment. The evidence was overwhelming, but when the judges announced their verdict in December 1985, they satisfied no one entirely. Five of the nine junta members were convicted, General Videla and his colleague Admiral Massera receiving life sentences, and four were acquitted, among them the entire Galtieri junta. Alfonsín accepted the results calmly, hoping that the military would learn to live with them and that critics would cease demanding more trials. For him, the unprecedented conviction of military officers for political crimes by a civilian court was a major achievement, and though hardly sufficient punishment for the crimes that were committed, it would help wrench the nation from preoccupation with its gruesome past.[22]

Actually, Alfonsín had little choice in the matter. If he had been president of a normal democracy, criminals would have been convicted and jailed and the armed forces reorganized under civilian scrutiny. But Argentina's democracy was still tentative, as vulnerable as ever to interventions by disgruntled soldiers. The president could not simply purge the armed forces of the thousand or more soldiers who had commanded what the Sábato commission called the "most savage tragedy in our history." To do so would provoke a new wave of military terrorism aimed at undermining the government's authority and prompting another coup. It was naive to expect that the armed forces would accept justice without fighting back, as Alfonsín knew too well. Yet as long as he did little or nothing to bring them to justice, many well-trained and unscrupulous torturers and murderers, equipped with vast amounts of

weapons, would remain at large, beyond the control of constitutional
authorities. His only practical choice, it seemed, was to leave most of the
criminals alone for the moment, hoping that time and dedication to
democratic processes by everyone else would reduce the usefulness of
such characters to the society.[23]

Caution Abroad

Alfonsín surprised the nation and many within his own party when he
appointed young technocrat Dante Caputo as his minister of foreign
relations. Traditionally, this post was filled by a party elder or distinguished statesman. But Alfonsín wanted to inject some carefully
considered pragmatism into a foreign policy that had fallen into dis-
repute after the Malvinas War, and Caputo became his means for doing
so. Radicals had always been nationalists, often doctrinaire ones, and
while in principle Alfonsín was no different, he knew that Argentina
could afford much less nationalism in the wake of war and punishing
foreign debts. So he set out to prove that he could be as reasonable as
anyone else if dealt with fairly by allies and adversaries.

He started with the dispute with Chile over three little islands in
the Beagle Channel, a disagreement that had nearly brought the two
countries to war in 1978. At issue were not just three islands but
fundamental principles of foreign relations. Argentines were not accustomed to yielding territory that they believed was theirs nor to giving
the appearance of compromising with an adversary weaker than themselves. World War II had freed them from British domination, and Perón
had tried to increase the country's "independence" in every way possible. Independence means many different things, but to Argentine populists it meant defiance of other nations, especially the industrial ones in
Europe and North America. It also meant a commitment to territoriality
and the notion that national power was derived in part from land and its
defense.

Before Alfonsín became president, critics of such notions had been
arguing for the abandonment of these old obsessions, claiming that they
were counterproductive because they mistook territorial independence
for real power. What Argentines needed to recognize, they argued, was
that more could be gained by involvement in an interdependent world
than by trying to achieve independence from it. A nation acquires and
exercises power today not by standing apart from the rest of the world
but by using all of its resources and ingenuity to maximize gains in
competition with others. Bargaining was the appropriate method, not
the either/or ultimatums that had dragged the country into war with

Great Britain. In 1984 Argentina did not need the Beagle Channel Islands as much as it needed peace with Chile to free it for more important matters, the argument went.[24]

As he did in so much of his policy, Alfonsín mixed some of these new ideas with popular old ones, abandoning the principle of territoriality in the case of the Beagle dispute while insisting on it for the Malvinas. As to the former, he concluded that the dispute with Chile impaired his control over a military that insisted on standing ready for war with its neighbor and it distracted energies from the more important and difficult Malvinas issue. Accordingly, he took advantage of the results of five years of mediation by the Vatican to create an agreement almost overnight. Vatican officials made public the draft of the treaty in October 1984, giving the islands to Chile while allowing Argentina to keep the eastern access to the Straits of Magellan. Chile was allowed some access to the Atlantic but denied juridical claims over it, and both countries were asked to agree to abstain from warfare in the area and to serve on a binational commission devoted to achieving the economic integration of the region.

Ratification came easily in dictator Pinochet's Chile but its prospects were not good in Argentina, where nationalists mounted a campaign against Chilean possession of the islands. Alfonsín's suggestion that Argentina accept the treaty seemed to give his opponents the issue that they had been looking for to assault his popularity before the end of his first year. But just as the debate got underway, he surprised them, announcing a plebiscite intended to allow the public to express its opinion on the subject without binding senators, who would take up ratification after the first of the year. It was a gamble that paid off handsomely, for on November 25 nearly 73 percent of the eligible voters turned out and 77 percent of them approved ratification.[25] It was an adroit move not only for putting critics on the defensive but also for giving senators the courage they needed to ratify it. It was close enough as it was, ratified after intense debate by a vote of twenty-three to twenty-two with one abstention on March 14, 1985.

Similar progress was not made with the Malvinas/Falklands issue, however. Technically the two nations remained at war in 1985 since Argentina has not declared the conflict over. Nevertheless contacts with the British were made and discussions were held briefly in Switzerland in July 1984, but Foreign Minister Caputo left when the British refused to discuss the sovereignty issue unless Argentina first declared an end to the war. It seemed there was no chance of compromise no matter what the Argentines did since the Thatcher government apparently had already decided Argentina's starting the war sacrificed its right to govern the islands. Though some members of the opposition in Parliament would express an interest in talking with Alfonsín about some kind of "lease-back" arrangement in which Argentina would be given sovereignty over the islands on the condition that they lease them to the Falklands Company or to the British government, Thatcher would have none of it. Meanwhile her government would pay 300 million pounds a year to fortify the islands, an expense that began losing popularity in Great Britain in 1985. But until Thatcher were replaced, little progress was expected in Argentina or in Britain.[26]

A Nuclear Power?

There has always been something ominous about Argentina and nuclear power, at least to foreigners who envision Perón assisted by Nazi scientists plotting an assault on the rest of the world. Actually, reality departs a great deal from such nightmares. Perón never accomplished much with his nuclear policies and Argentina has yet to develop a nuclear weapon. Nevertheless, the country has come a long way, gradually but steadily developing its own indigenous research capacity and, with the help of foreign technology, its own nuclear power industry. Alfonsín inherited it all, convinced that Argentina had as much right as anyone to advance its peaceful uses of nuclear energy while assuring any who cared to listen that weapon development was not on his agenda.

Preoccupation with Argentina's intentions results in large part from the refusal of its governments to sign existing nonproliferation treaties. For example, they have yet to ratify the 1967 Inter-American Treaty of Tlatelolco aimed at prohibiting nuclear weapons in Latin America or the more international Nuclear Non-Proliferation Treaty opened in 1968. In their defense they have always argued that the treaties are discriminatory since they ask nations like Argentina not to build weapons but allow those who already have them to continue their production. If weapons development is to be prevented, the Argentines argue, then every nation must agree to stop building bombs and delivery systems.

In the meantime Alfonsín finds himself with an impressive nuclear enterprise, much of which has been under military supervision. It began in 1950, when a few exiled German scientists helped Perón get some research started, but today Argentines, educated in nuclear physics and engineering at home and abroad, run it. At the top is the presidentially appointed Nuclear Commission, whose president has been an admiral through most of its history. Under its tutelage the country began processing native uranium in 1953 and built its first reactor in 1958, adding three more research reactors by 1967. In 1968 it started work on its first nuclear power plant, Atucha I, located just upriver from Buenos Aires, using West German technology, completing the heavy-water/natural uranium 320-megawatt facility in 1974. A second power plant with twice Atucha's capacity was completed with Italian and Canadian technology at Embalse, Córdoba, in 1983, and a third one, Atucha II, is slated for operation in the early 1990s, though current economic problems are bound to slow its completion. Most impressive, however, is the variety of facilities that operate in the country, among them two uranium mining sites, four mills, an industrial-scale heavy-water plant, a plutonium plant, and eight reactors used primarily for research.[27]

Nothing indicated how far Argentina had come better than the announcement just before Alfonsín's inauguration that it had completed construction of an uranium enrichment plant (one that uses the gaseous diffusion method). Work on it had been kept secret and nuclear authorities around the world were caught totally by surprise. The new plant, located in the south at Pilcaniyeu, could, in principle at least, provide the capability to enrich uranium to weapons-grade levels, though Argentines denied that such an objective was ever their intention. Instead, it was explained, it had been built to compensate for the U.S. government's cutoff of enriched uranium for the country's nuclear reactors in 1978; Argentina also needed to assure itself a supply for use in radioisotopes in medicine and agriculture, as well as for fuel in the reactors that it had begun selling to other Latin American nations for their research programs. Undoubtedly authorities also wanted to keep up with the Brazilians, who had signed agreements in 1975 with the West Germans for the construction of reprocessing and enrichment plants. The rivalry between the two countries is important, yet it does not appear to be escalating toward weapons development, and to emphasize that point they have recently signed agreements intended to foster greater cooperation, including Argentina's leasing of uranium concentrate, the exchange of technical information, and reciprocal training programs.[28]

Alfonsín was concerned to assure civilian control over nuclear policy as part of his effort to put the military beneath him in the constitutional hierarchy. He started at the top by replacing long-time Nuclear Commission president Admiral Carlos Castro Cordero. Under Cordero the industry had become one of the best-financed activities of the federal government, concluding with the building of one of the most modern headquarters and research facilities outside the United States and Soviet Union. Civilian engineer Alberto Constantini was made the president in what looked to be a major shake-up, but on closer examination it was apparent that little had actually changed within the organization except for cuts in its budget as part of the austerity program; moreover, a special commission appointed by the president to review nuclear policy recommended the continuation of existing policies. This leaves Argentina with an emerging capacity to develop nuclear weapons but a declared intention not to do so. A recent study of nuclear policy concluded:

> There is little question that Argentina today has the general scientific and industrial infrastructure necessary for the development of nuclear weapons. Indeed, Argentine officials have said as much since the mid-1970s, when the nation's nuclear specialists first separated small amounts of plutonium. At present, however, the nation lacks facilities—enrichment and reprocessing plants—for the production of the nuclear weapons materials in significant quantities, although both types of plants are under development.[29]

In sum, Alfonsín, though not intending to develop his own weapons, is Argentine enough to want to retain as much independence for his country on the nuclear issue as he can. To some extent it is a matter of national pride: what Argentina has achieved technologically is impressive, and in a day when it has few signs of national accomplishment in which to take pride, the nuclear program stands out for adulation. But it is also a part of a larger ploy which he and Caputo hope will project Argentina into world diplomacy. They want a role to play and pushing for nuclear arms reductions by the nuclear powers is one such role. No one expects that they can by themselves make a real difference, but by having something to sacrifice if others do likewise it at least has a position from which to claim the attention it wants on nuclear issues. It is a small prize in today's world, but for the time being it is the best that Alfonsín can hope for.

The Challenge

Alfonsín began as a popular president, making it easy for wishful thinkers to view him as the founding father of a new Argentina. But the country was not really his to transform. Habits are well entrenched throughout society, old institutions strong, and the power structure intact. Changing them was more than any single person could be expected to do, no matter how large his mandate.

What served him best during his first two years was not his popularity but his commitment to operating like a practical politician, unspectacular and not exceptionally idealistic, but willing to work with everyone to move the country along. As a Radical he loved working hard at making the most mundane democratic procedures work, perhaps to a fault, convinced that it would be self-defeating as well as dishonorable to do otherwise. But he was also a political pragmatist who learned that he could work no miracles for his country, or even accomplish many of his objectives quickly. He had to deal with all of the political forces in society, from the armed forces to the Peronist unions. He wanted to convince them that they had nowhere to turn but to the authorities created by the constitution to govern society. To do otherwise was to invite alienation and the rejection of the political process as well as its executive officer. None of this was a new discovery, but Alfonsín was one of the first presidents in some time to be empirical enough in his approach to politics to operate by careful trial and error in his treatment of both allies and opponents.

But there was much more than its president that made Argentina different in 1984. Underneath the veneer of competitive politics was a not very well hidden new affection for democracy, most notably among the urban middle class, which was enjoying its liberties. Buying every kind of book and magazine, listening to debates of all issues on the radio and viewing them on television, and watching Ford Falcons drive by without being frightened by their occupants was a new and highly valued experience for most people. What made it so special to many of them, most notably those under the age of thirty-five, was getting a taste of freedom after having spent all of their adult lives under military and Peronist governments. It was truly different and they liked it. Of course, no amount of affection for democracy would prevent military officers from using their weapons to restore authoritarian government to the country. But as even the most reactionary of those in uniform knew in 1985, after Alfonsín it would be harder than ever to convince people that they were threatened more by civilian abuse of liberty than they were by the authoritarians' elimination of it.

Notes

1. *Buenos Aires Herald,* January 27, 1985, p. 3; and *New York Times,* February 13, 1985, p. 3.
2. *Buenos Aires Herald,* March 3, 1985, p. 2.
3. *Clarín,* international ed., February 18–24, 1985, p. 1.
4. *Buenos Aires Herald,* July 26, 1984, p. 3, and March 10, 1985, p. 3.
5. An excellent survey of the country's economic condition in early 1984, and the one from which this data is taken, is World Bank, *Economic Memorandum on Argentina,* June 22, 1984.

6. *New York Times*, September 12, 1984, p. 41. (The largest American creditors were Manufacturers Hanover, Citicorp, and Chase Manhattan.)

7. *Washington Post*, October 13, 1984, p. D1.

8. *New York Times*, March 21, 1985, p. 5.

9. In a lengthy year-end interview Alfonsín pointed to his failure to get any control over inflation as his biggest disappointment and made it clear that he knew that he would lose what respect his people had shown for him if he let it continue for another year. What he would do about it was not apparent at first, then came the announcement of a new "plan" followed by Sourrouille's appointment and finally Alfonsín's "bitter medicine" address four months later in May. *Clarín*, international ed., December 10–16, 1984, p. 3.

10. Radicals never abandon their friends entirely, and a month later Alfonsín gave Grinspun Sourrouille's old job as head of the planning agency.

11. R. D. Mallon and J. V. Sourrouille, *Economic Policymaking in a Conflict Society: The Argentine Case* (Cambridge: Harvard University Press, 1975).

12. *Clarín*, international ed., January 7–13, 1985, p. 6.

13. *Buenos Aires Herald*, May 19, 1985, p. 3.

14. James Neilson is editor and writes a weekly column on politics and labor in the English-language daily *Buenos Aires Herald*. This quote is taken from the one he wrote on May 18, 1985, p. 3.

15. *New York Times*, June 12, 1985, pp. 1, 34–35.

16. *New York Times*, June 15, 1985, p. 1.

17. Changing the currency was not a Radical innovation, actually; the military had knocked four zeros off the old peso in mid-1983. This time, however, the government intended to make a special effort to help the austral keep its value while letting the peso wilt. Also part of the program were a 33 percent increase in the rates of public services, transfer of paying debt obligations to the state firms who owed them, a 2.5 percent tax increase, and reduction in public employment through attrition. They set as their goals the reduction of the treasury deficit by the equivalent of 2 percent of the GDP, and the reduction of the overall deficit to 6.2 percent of the GDP in 1985 and 2.6 percent by the end of the first quarter of 1986. Meanwhile, inflation was to be brought down to only 150 percent by the end of the first quarter in 1986. See *Clarín*, international ed., June 10–16, 1985, pp. 1–5.

18. Sourrouille's principal assistants who held doctorates were: Mario Brodersohn, from Harvard: José Luís Machinea, University of Minnesota; and Adolfo Canitrot, Stanford.

19. World Bank, *Economic Memorandum on Argentina*, pp. 196–204.

20. Ibid., pp. 156–157. World Bank economists argue that price distortions caused by import and export taxes are what discourage the use of fertilizers and seeds of the "green revolution" variety and that corrections in these price distortions could bring about rapid and significant increases in production. To achieve that end they recommend the replacement of export taxes and tariffs on imported farm inputs with a land tax of the potential production variety, more research and extension services, and the development of a domestic fertilizer industry that takes advantage of natural gas resources.

21. *Somos*, July 20, 1984, pp. 9–16.

22. *Minneapolis Tribune*, March 21, 1985, p. 21A. Other members of the juntas who were put on trial with the three presidents were former navy chiefs Emilio Massera, Armando Lambruschini, and Jorge Anaya and former air force commanders Orlando Agosti, Omar Graffigna, and Basilio Lami Dozo.

23. *Buenos Aires Herald*, September 23, 1984, p. 3.

24. One of the most outspoken critics of the obsession with "independence" objectives

was historian Carlos Escude. See his *La Argentina: Paría internacional?* (Buenos Aires: Belgrano, 1984).

25. *Clarín,* international ed., November 19–25, 1984, p. 1.

26. *The Economist,* May 4, 1985, p. 18.

27. Leonard S. Spector, *Nuclear Proliferation Today* (New York: Vintage, 1984), pp. 199–209.

28. Ibid., pp. 213–224.

29. Ibid., p. 228.

8

Conclusions

Democracy will triumph and the Constitution will never again be subverted, the nation's wealth will never again be squandered, and the Argentine family will never again be assaulted by poverty and despotism. The regime of shame and decadence is already ending and the Argentine people will recover all its power. (Radical party leader Fernando de la Rua, March 1983)

The military are not the only people with a fascist background . . . there are many civilians who are as fascist as they are, or even more so. (Retired General Manuel Laprida, September 1984)

The biggest danger facing Argentine democracy does not come from the action of antidemocratic groups but from the apparent inability of the system to resolve the problems affecting the daily lives of the country's inhabitants. (Conservative legislator Alvaro Alsogaray, October 1984)

The crisis is so deep that the government is unable to give straight away a positive response to every sector and, as a result, the struggle going on erodes and weakens the efficiency of democratic institutions. (Radical Interior Minister Antonio Troccoli, April 1985)[1]

No one who visits Argentina today leaves the country believing that its case is hopeless. To be sure, its past is filled with much doom and gloom, casting doubt on the nation's capacity for ongoing economic and political recovery. Yet, Argentines continue to exhibit an incredible resilience in the midst of crisis and an impressive dexterity in coping with adversity. Even if they do not have as many natural resources as they claim or are not as talented as they like to believe, they do have more natural wealth and human talent than almost any nation in the southern hemisphere and that alone justifies optimism.

What the previous seven chapters reveal is not an atrophied society nearing its demise but a vigorous one composed of a contentious people, some of whom are too imperious and truculent for the nation's own good. We have seen them at work time and again: military officers, labor leaders, industrialists, farmers, party politicians, and the like, all of them trying to prevail. What they lack is not energy or intelligence but an ability and a willingness to regulate their combative urges in the political arena. In theory it should not be all that difficult. Reason alone should lead people to appreciate the need to accommodate themselves to others for mutual gain. But Argentines are maximizers not optimizers, committed by habit to gaining everything they can when what they want becomes available and to protecting themselves tenaciously when it is not.

One explanation for their contumacious ways suggests that their choice of behavior was never really theirs to make. Like so many Third World nations, Argentina is a victim of forces beyond its control, which are manifested most profoundly in a world economic structure that determines how it exploits its resources and expends its labor. Domestic politics is little more than a means for securing society's conformity with the dictates of this larger structure. This interpretation of the country's plight is appealing because of its surface plausibility and simplicity. The oligarchy's return in 1930 was influenced by the country's being forced to adjust to the adversity of an unexpected world depression, and the contemporary financial crisis dictates the path that the government must follow. It is also appealing because it leaves most Argentines blameless for the nation's condition. However, the structuralist explanation relies far too much on a single source of political conduct to explain it adequately, and it ignores the fact that countries that face similar economic constraints do not always share Argentina's political vices. To explain Argentine behavior something more is quite obviously required.

One possibility occasionally suggested by Argentines themselves points to Hispanic heritage and the legacy of its absolutistic political culture. Authoritarianism was learned early and then passed on from generation to generation, never fully disguised by the liberal veneer that was imposed on the system in the mid-nineteenth century. The addition of Spanish and Italian immigrants, who came from similar cultures, only served to reinforce the basic tendencies.

While this cultural explanation is not irrelevant, it, too, is insufficient. A heritage has to be sustained against efforts to overcome it, and whether or not it survives depends on the ability of reactionaries to stand guard, which is precisely what the oligarchy did far into this century. They taught the nation the advantages of monopolistic politics for those who were on top, a lesson that was never forgotten, as Perón and two generations of military officers demonstrated subsequently.

The fact that so many tried to run the country in an authoritarian manner without succeeding produced a kind of revolving-door politics that made democracy impossible, as Frenchman Alain Rouquie pointed out at the conclusion of his monumental study of the Argentine military:

All of the social forces and interest groups defend their rights and privileges without paying attention to the formal rules of democratic politics even though doing so never satisfies their needs. It is as if the group's triumph over its rivals was vital to its survival, or at least sufficient to cause it to ignore the rules that society needs to secure the co-existence of its members. Loyalty to group, of an almost tribal character, gives rise to an "everyone for himself" attitude evident in political parties as well as economic interest groups. The military wants to save the military, labor unions the CGT . . . and every opposition party is intent on getting revenge no matter how much their doing so undermines the community.[2]

What this mentality created was a most uncivil political life, which invited military interventions to restore order only to perpetuate disorder. But that is not all. Political scientist Marcelo Cavarozzi insists that it also bred a modern authoritarian political culture that reinforced intolerance of dissidence and criticism throughout the political system, an intolerance that makes the creation of liberal democracy, with its demand for toleration, almost impossible. Writing in 1983 he warned:

The recent failure of authoritarianism should not blind us to the fact that its values endure because of our experience with it. . . . The intensity of this systematic attempt to conquer Argentine society using authoritarian means has reinforced atomistic behavior and weakened associative practices. The social disorganizing that resulted can only make it more difficult to operate democratically in Argentina, something that in fact may now be beyond our capacity.[3]

Although there exist no comprehensive contemporary surveys of Argentine attitudes to test such claims, inhospitality to democratic government is evident nonetheless. The record makes it clear that while Argentina has not become the home of millions of wayward fascists, as sensationalists contend, many of its people accept authoritarian government as a necessary part of their lives, viewing its frequent return as inevitable. In 1966 and again in 1976, majorities not only failed to protest military intervention but justified it to themselves as essential for dealing with the country's more important economic and security needs.

But to portray Argentines as selfish, rigid, and self-destructive authoritarians does them a disservice by ignoring a more conventional set of motives that also influence their behavior. Like everyone else, they learn early in life how to satisfy their needs and wants, acquiring basic ideas about the purpose of politics and economics as they do. Of the abundant knowledge they acquire nothing becomes more fixed in their minds than the dangers posed to them by the nation's economy and the way authorities try to manipulate it.

They started their education a century ago, in a time of growth and optimism. Then, when hard times set in, Juan Perón came along and promised to lift the nation up again. But his ambitious, simple-minded exercise failed to deliver on its promise. British and American investors had profited from their dealings in the country, but their eviction did not leave a huge trough of capital for Argentines to invest. Quite the contrary; by going it alone as he did, Perón restored pride without igniting much growth. At a time when most other export economies were booming, Argentina's languished, never exploiting its natural advantages efficiently enough to sustain its modernization and growth.

So what did Argentines learn from all of this? They discovered that Perón's failures had left them in a hole from which there was no easy escape. What they were given by authorities after Perón's flight were not plans for immediate prosperity but frequent demands for sacrifices to make up for past errors and misfortunes. Austerity, more than growth, became the principal objective of government, as authorities dealt with high inflation and balance-of-payments deficits. That is how it was with Perón in 1952, Frondizi in 1959, Onganía in 1966, Perón again in 1973, Videla in 1976, and Alfonsín in 1985. Unfortunately, Argentines do not enjoy making sacrifices any more than anyone else does. Even worse, experience has taught them that even when they do make sacrifices, little good ever comes of it.

Under such conditions, conduct is governed by the need to survive the adversities brought on by the authorities' repeated attempts to enforce economic austerity of one kind or another. What people learn is not compromise and cooperation but how to look out for their own interests by escaping policies that were intended to take something from them. It does not matter that their defiance undermines the very policies that were designed to benefit everyone over the long haul; people are convinced that if they do not act on the assumption of failure, others will, making them the losers in the competition.

They are quite rational and calculating about it all. People who read about the government's wage increases and its fiscal deficits also know what both will do to the cost of living, and they keep tabs on payments deficits and dollar reserves to determine how long it will be before authorities reverse their exchange policies. In short, they make their calculations about the performance of austerity measures and act accordingly, doing what they can to prevent losses to themselves.

The kind of self-defense practiced by Argentines also grows from a pessimism about their society's immediate future and a lack of confidence in authorities that is not hard to understand. It is reinforced by a proud individualism that draws its gratification and confirmation from defiance of those who seek to discipline society. Argentines have developed powerful defenses against authority, but in doing so they have damaged severely what there is of a national community, leaving society with an insecurity that invites desperate attempts to reconstruct a community overnight.

Breaking out of such socially destructive practices may be impossible given their deep-rootedness. And the options for breaking out are certainly not very abundant. One, obviously, is revolution, the kind that destroys existing structures and forces a redefinition of interests. Its cleansing effects will always hold some appeal to those frustrated with the status quo, especially to ideologues on the left and dissidents within the labor movement. But its likelihood in Argentina is slim given the interests that all classes have vested in capitalism, not to mention the military's demonstrated capacity to defeat revolutionaries in combat. This leaves less dramatic ways of changing individual and sectoral behavior for society's benefit.

If a democrat were to offer a list of recommended reforms of behavior, aimed at increasing civility and improving democracy's chances, there would be nothing spectacular in it, but that would not diminish its value. It might begin by suggesting that the nation's wealthiest citizens admit to themselves the futility of regarding politicians as parasites and labor leaders as alien intruders. Nor does it help to insist that the armed forces govern the unruly nation. If the upper classes learned anything from two disastrous attempts at military rule, it should have been the futility of treating Argentines as if they were juveniles to be kept in check until they had learned to respect and obey their "superiors."

For their part, military officers need to relinquish their insistence on instant gratification whenever they want something from the rest of society. When they seek to influence politics, they might try behaving more like politicians than tank commanders, accepting constitutional authorities as legitimate and then exercising limited influence over them. Treatment of their paranoia about unceasing conspiracies against them is also essential. Most of their critics are well intentioned, determined simply to police the military whenever it fails to police itself. Rather than go after them as if they were hatching plots to destroy the nation, officers need to recognize that their critics' aversion to left-wing revolution is often as great as theirs. If they do not learn to distinguish these realities from their own fictions, democracy's chances of surviving in Argentina will not improve.

Foreigners who do business in Argentina are not exempt either. They could begin by changing their expectations a little. Argentines will never make life easy for them; they are too proud to stop harassing them, even when it would benefit them to do so. Nor will an economy as vulnerable as Argentina's ever operate smoothly for very long. Perpetual insecurity and overreaction to economic adversity will remain a way of life as long as the European Common Market and North American governments exclude so many Argentine products from their markets and the nation's creditors refuse to live with the consequences of their own mistakes.

Political parties could adjust some, too. Radicals, if they are to govern everyone, cannot sustain themselves on the narrow partisanship that bolstered their spirits when they were in the opposition. Peronists have no choice but to be "respectable" if they want to occupy the Casa Rosada again. Equally important is the behavior of the smaller parties, which often find it so hard to admit Peronist and Radical dominance. Little is gained by their using the media to defame elected incumbents and gleefully weaken their authority. Electoral politics is not a roulette wheel which, if spun enough times, will inevitably come up once in every party's favor. Contributing to the downfall of incumbents may add more turns to the wheel, but when it does, minor parties are seldom the beneficiaries of the additional chances so earned.

Last but not least is organized labor. What makes Argentina different from other countries with free labor movements is the persistent waging of symbolic and substantive wars between labor and government. Not only do labor leaders believe their political combat is popular among the rank and file, but they are addicted to achieving personal fame by pounding on public institutions regardless of how ineffective such battering really is. It is time they gave up dreams of regaining as much power and prominence as Perón gave them in the 1940s. The Peronist state cannot be replicated in its original form, and even though Peronist leaders know it, they pretend otherwise. Protest politics are easy to undertake in Argentina but, unless channeled into constructive reform, promise to divide society perpetually. That is why some Peronist leaders tried to chart a new course for the party in 1984, only to be devoured by a labor establishment addicted to the demagoguery of days past. That does not mean that change will not come within the movement; it will, but it would help if it came sooner rather than later.

Argentines are not naive; they know that there is much work to do if they are to recover their wealth and dignity as a people. They may appear incredibly rhetorical, sentimental, and aggressive, especially in their politics. But they can be as serious, precise, and careful as they need be, evidencing a capacity to do what they must to progress in the years ahead. No matter how bountiful a country's natural resources or how spectacular its human qualities, it will be condemned to decay unless its assets are put to productive use by means of substantial physical and mental labor. It was with this in mind that Alfonsín told his people in the midst of the 1985 economic crisis that "we have two roads ahead of us for solving our socioeconomic problems: nostalgic whimpering or working. . . . We can take turns blaming one another, or get down to working half as hard as our grandparents did."[4]

The grandparents of most Argentines were immigrants, and it is from memories of their labors that Alfonsín hoped their descendants would draw the inspiration they needed to build a new and more civil nation in the twenty-first century. Perhaps that is too much to ask, but you cannot blame him for trying.

Notes

1. All of these quotes are taken from the weekly "Quotes" section of the *Buenos Aires Herald,* the first on March 27, 1983; the second September 30, 1984; the third October 7, 1984; the fourth April 7, 1985.

2. Alain Rouquie, *Poder militar y sociedad política en la Argentina, Vol. II: 1943–1973* (Buenos Aires: EMECE, 1978), p. 380.

3. Marcelo Cavarozzi, *Autoritarismo y democracia (1955–1983)* (Buenos Aires: Centro Editor de America Latina, 1983), p. 70.

4. *Buenos Aires Herald,* May 26, 1985, pp. 2, 16.

Index